The **Soldier's** Guidebook

The Soldier's Guidebook

Col. Raymond K. Bluhm, Jr., USA (Ret.)
and
Col. James B. Motley, USA (Ret.)

BRASSEY'S
WASHINGTON • LONDON

Library of Congress Cataloging-in-Publication Data
Bluhm, Raymond, K.
The soldier's guidebook/Raymond K. Bluhm, Jr. and James B. Motley.
p. cm.
Includes bibliographical references and index.
ISBN 0-02-881035-X
1. United States. Army—Handbooks, manuals, etc. I. Motley, James B. II. title.
U113.B58 1995
355'.00973—dc20 95-4004
CIP

DESIGNED BY ROBERT FREESE

Except where noted, all photos courtesy U.S. Army

Printed in the United States of America

10 9 8 7 6 5 4 3 2

Contents

Foreword

Many of those who read this volume are considering joining the Army; others are fairly new to our profession; and some are seasoned veterans. Regardless of which category you fit into, *The Soldier's Guidebook* was developed to provide you with valuable insights into Army life.

Since colonial times, Americans such as you have served in the U.S. Army and faced danger, hardship, and sacrifice in defense of your homeland and U.S. security. Today, sophisticated technologies and weapon systems continue to change the nature of ground warfare, while soldiers must be prepared to conduct operations anywhere at short notice. Compounding these challenges are fiscal realities that mean a reduced military budget and a smaller Army. The result will be an even greater emphasis on high-quality soldiers.

The Army is a large, complex organization. Soldiers often feel it will be a long time before they can truly have a sense of the unique culture of the Army, and they are often confused by seemingly strange everyday practices. Thus, a book that explains "how the Army works" can reduce the complications and challenges already posed to a soldier who is mastering difficult skills. That is why the Association of the U.S. Army (AUSA) believes it can help the Army and its new members by supporting the development of this handy guidebook. It is intended to answer a number of general questions about the U.S. Army and what life in the Army is like.

Speaking for members of the association of the U.S. Army, I invite high-quality men and women to join our Army, welcome new recruits, and congratulate the experienced professionals who have worked to build our Army into the quality organization it is today. Rest assured that there are tens of thousands of members of the AUSA who stand behind and support you, and who understand how important you are to the safe future of America.

Jack N. Merritt
General, U.S. Army (Ret.)
President, Association of the U.S. Army

Preface

The Soldier's Guidebook is a basic reference on the Army. It is primarily intended for young men and women who are considering joining the Army for the first time, and new soldiers just beginning their Army experience. It is also a valuable reference for career soldiers.

There are many different and specialized sources of information on the Army. This guidebook brings together into one book much of that key information. You should use the table of contents and the index to find material to answer your immediate questions. Later, when you have more time, browse through the *Guidebook* to learn more about the Army and its traditions. The more you know and understand the Army the better soldier you will be. During your time in the Army, you may have many occasions to refer to *The Soldier's Guidebook* as you learn your profession. Use it well in your professional development.

This first edition condenses information from U.S. Army field manuals, training circulars, regulations, pamphlets, and other public sources. It is written for men and women who are looking to the future and making plans for it. The Army can give these individuals a good start on their future and can be an important part of their plans.

The Soldier's Guidebook focuses on the active, or Regular Army, but also addresses many aspects of the other two components that make up the Total Army—the Army National Guard and the Army Reserve. While the emphasis is on providing practical information for the new soldier, there is also important information for a soldier to use throughout a full career.

This edition provides the answers to many questions on such subjects as the soldier's life, skills, assignments, promotions, weapons and equipment, pay, education, Army history and organization, and a peek at the future of the Army. It will serve as a valuable tool for all members of the Total Army and provide assistance to Army recruiters and career counselors.

Preface

The 1990s are a period of great change and uncertainty for all the military services of the United States. The world is very different than it was only a few years ago and it presents a variety of challenges to the Army. To properly meet those challenges, the Army is undergoing major restructuring and a reexamination of its strategic missions. The Army is searching for the best way to accomplish these missions. At the same time new and exciting technology is being developed that will have a major impact on the Army of the future. This is not a new situation for the Army, however. Its history is filled with change and the need to meet new challenges—and as in the past the men and women of the Army are equal to the task. As the largest of the military services and the most visible of U.S. overseas commitments, the soldiers of the U.S. Army will continue to be the backbone of America's defense, and the key to victory on the battlefield.

Every effort has been made to insure *The Soldier's Guidebook* contains the correct and latest information available at the time of writing. The authors take full responsibility for any errors. Users of this guidebook are encouraged to recommend changes that will improve the clarity and utility of future editions. Changes and comments should be forwarded to the publisher.

An AUSA Book

The Association of the United States Army (AUSA) was founded in 1950 as a not-for-profit organization dedicated to education concerning the role of the U.S. Army, to providing material for military professional development, and to the promotion of proper recognition and appreciation of the profession of arms. Its constituencies include those who serve in the Army today, including Army National Guard, Army Reserve, and Army civilians, the retirees and veterans who have served in the past, and all their families. A large number of public-minded citizens and business leaders are also an important constituency. The association seeks to educate the public, elected and appointed officials, and leaders of the defense industry on crucial issues involving the adequacy of our national defense, particularly those issues affecting land warfare.

In 1988 the AUSA established within its existing organization a new entity known as the Institute of Land Warfare. Its purpose is to extend the educational work of the AUSA by sponsoring scholarly publications, to include books, monographs, and essays on key defense issues, as well as workshops and symposia. Among the volumes chosen for designation as "An AUSA Institute of Land Warfare Book" are both new texts and reprints of titles of enduring value that are no longer in print. Topics include history, policy issues, strategy, and tactics. Publication as an AUSA book does not necessarily indicate that the Association of the United States Army and the publisher agree with everything in the book, but does suggest that the AUSA and the publisher believe it will stimulate the thinking of AUSA members and others concerned about important issues.

I. You and the Army:
What to Expect

1. Introduction to the Army

"America calls, and the Army answers—'Count on us!' "
Gen. G. R. Sullivan, Chief of Staff, 1993

So, you are thinking about joining the Army! Or perhaps you have just enlisted. In either case your decision is one of the biggest and most important a young man or woman can make. By deciding to enlist, you are volunteering to enter the finest army in the world. You will be joining the thousands of other young Americans who are accepting the responsibilities of citizenship to their country. You will be the latest of the many proud generations of American soldiers stretching back over two hundred years who answered the call for service to the nation. Whether you remain for a full career or not, you are taking the first step toward one of the most exciting and educational experiences of your life.

What Is the Army?

The Army is the senior and the largest military service established by the Constitution to protect the United States. It is composed of the most highly trained people, military and civilian, and the most technologically advanced equipment in the world today. Although it is raised and maintained by Congress, the Army's commander in chief is the President. Today all soldiers are volunteers who swear an oath to defend the Constitution and to obey the lawful orders of their superiors.

Soldiers are different from civilians. By design and necessity the Army is very different from the civilian world. Organized into various types of units, soldiers are commanded and supervised by officers, with commissioned authority from Congress, and by noncommissioned officers (NCOs). In addition to civil law, soldiers are also subject to a specific set of laws established by Congress called the Uniform Code of Military

Fig. 1.1. Seal of the U.S. Army

Justice. On duty, soldiers wear different clothes, obey different rules, follow different traditions, speak a different slang, have different responsibilities, and move more frequently than their civilian friends.

The Army today is not the Army of only a few years ago, and it continues to change. The Army is more family-oriented with fewer overseas assignments, and it is smaller. At the end of 1993 active-duty strength was about 575,000 and it is expected to be even lower by 1996, perhaps as low as 500,000. Most active-duty soldiers are in the Regular Army, which means they are full-time professional soldiers. They are augmented by soldiers from two other components, the Army Reserve and the Army National Guard. The term "Total Army" was used to describe the three components together in the 1970s and '80s. In 1994 the term became "America's Army." Whatever they are called, these three components together form an integrated, cohesive team that is the heart of the nation's defense.

Missions of the Army

The existence of the Army is based on the need recognized in the Constitution of the United States to ". . . insure domestic tranquillity, [and] provide for the common defense. . . ." The most basic mission of the Army is to defend the rights, privileges, and system of government guaranteed to the American people by the Constitution. The Army does this by protecting the internal and external security of the United States and by deterring war. When deterrence fails, the Army must quickly and decisively defeat any enemy, anytime, anywhere. The Army usually does this as a part of a joint team with the other U.S. military services. While all military forces have the power to deny the use of an area or to destroy it, only the Army has the power to exercise direct, continuing, and comprehensive control over land, its resources, and its people. At times the Army may also operate in conjunction with foreign allies or international organizations. It is the job of every soldier to be ready and able to support the Army in the accomplishment of all its missions listed below.

- Maintain combat-ready forces at home and overseas
- Be prepared to deploy Army forces of all types
- Be ready to reinforce U.S. forces in peace or war
- Protect American citizens and be prepared to evacuate them from danger
- Support the nation's war on drugs
- Provide assistance to friendly nations
- Provide assistance to U.S. authorities

History of the Army

The Army is older than the United States. Much of what you will see in the Army today is a result of the Army's experience over the past 220 years. A short history of the Army will help you understand the reasons that soldiers are so proud of their units and the Army. It will also help you understand many aspects of the Army as an organization, its activities, and its responsibilities as the primary guardian of the American people. Traditions are simply history remembered, and the Army has many traditions. Its history is really the history of the United States—a history of excitement, sacrifice, dedication, and adventure. It is the ongoing story of men and women of all races working together, and yes, facing danger together as a team—a team you will be proud to join.

The Revolution (1775–1783)

The birthday of the United States Army is June 14, 1775. On that date the Continental Congress voted to enlist ten companies of riflemen directly into Continental service. Prior to this, each of the colonies had its own part-time militia for defense.

Fig. 1.2. Artilleryman and infantrymen, 1781

Recognizing the need for a more permanent and professional force, or "Regulars," directly under its control, Congress established the first Continental troops. A militia colonel, George Washington, was appointed a three-star general and named commander in chief of all American forces. Congress also selected general officers, set up military administrative offices, decided pay and rations (food), and adopted the first code of military justice, called the Articles of War.

Although the number of Continental units increased during the Revolution, and plans were made to create more, enlistments were never enough. Washington had to depend on the colony militias to maintain sufficient strength in the field. The Continental units were composed mostly of infantry and artillery, with some light cavalry, engineers, and support troops.

Despite the many problems it faced, the Army won a number of significant victories. Learning its drills under the stern direction of Baron Frederick von Steuben, the Continental Army was able to stand face to face against the most veteran

British troops. While minor fighting continued until 1783, the war really culminated when, with the assistance of the French, the Army forced the surrender of British General Cornwallis at Yorktown in October 1781. The American Army had been formed in battle, severely tested in six years of war, and emerged victorious. The Treaty of Paris formally ended the war in September 1783.

Between the Wars (1783–1812)

Four days after the peace treaty was signed, Congress directed Washington to discharge the bulk of the Continental Army. Efforts were unsuccessful to maintain a larger permanent Army for frontier and other duties. Because of costs and the fear of a "large" permanent Army, it was reduced to about six hundred men stationed at various locations to guard Army property and supplies. On 2 June 1784 Congress further reduced the Army to a strength of only eighty artillerymen plus a few officers. This is the smallest the Army has ever been. This lone artillery unit has an active duty descendent today in 1st Battalion, 5th Field Artillery (Alexander Hamilton Battery), the oldest unit in the Regular Army.

However, there was concern about the security of the Northwest Territories. The next day Congress authorized a regiment of militia volunteers called the 1st American Regiment. This regiment, containing both infantry and, finally, artillery, evolved into a regular unit. Its modern descendant, the 3d Infantry Regiment (The Old Guard), is the oldest active infantry regiment.

When the Constitution was approved in 1789, the new Congress adopted the tiny Army that had been authorized under the old Articles of Confederation. The President was designated as commander in chief, but Congress kept the power to determine the size and funds of the Army. The states also retained their own militias. This firmly established the dual system of a professional Regular Army and a non-federal citizen-soldier National Guard force.

The 2d American Regiment was approved in 1791. Because of the many reorganizations of units over the years, the number of a regiment has little relation to its age. The modern descendent of this unit is the 1st Infantry Regiment. Other efforts to strengthen the Army failed until two disastrous defeats by the Indians caused Congress to increase the Army and fund new equipment. President Washington placed General Anthony Wayne in charge of the new forces that were organized into "legions" containing cavalry, infantry, and artillery. Wayne trained his legions to a fine edge and, reinforced by militia, they won a decisive victory against the Indians at Fallen Timbers in 1794.

The small Army of the early 1800s played a major role in opening the West. The United States Military Academy was established at West Point in 1802 as the first American engineering school, and many of its graduates led soldiers working to improve the nation's expanding transportation system. In 1804 Capt. Merriwether Lewis, Lt. William Clark, and twenty-seven soldiers formed a "Corps of Discovery" that explored the newly purchased Louisiana Territory. Captain Zebulon Pike led soldiers on two other western expeditions. The last, in 1807, took him into the Spanish Southwest. Other soldiers performed escort and guard duty in the West securing the increasing number of frontier settlements.

Opening the West and the War with England (1812–1846)

The first months of the War of 1812 were disastrous for U.S. land forces. The Regular Army had only seven thousand men, scattered in small groups around the country, and the quality of both the Regulars and the militia was poor. After a number of defeats, the first real U.S. victory was finally won by a mixed force of Regular infantry and Kentucky militia at the Thames River, Canada, in mid-1813. This success reversed the earlier British victories and restored frontier security in the Northwest.

Increases to the Army were approved in early 1814, and a tough period of training was begun. It paid off in July when American Regular infantry successfully fought toe to toe with British Regulars at Chippewa and Lundy's Lane in Canada. Watching the U.S. troops at Chippewa advance unflinchingly through heavy fire, the British commander, who had presumed he faced militia, exclaimed, "Those are Regulars, by God!" Overall, the land war was a draw, but the final major battle at the barricades outside New Orleans was a decisive American victory. For its actions there the 7th U.S. Infantry won the nickname "The Cottonbalers."

The difficult experience of raising and training an army during wartime convinced many of the need for a larger permanent Army. West Point was expanded and more of the graduates entered the Army, improving overall quality and professionalism. Schools for training artillery and infantry soldiers were also set up. A special corps of military mapmakers called Topographical Engineers aided in building the nation's transportation system and making surveys of the new western

Fig. 1.3. General and staff officers, riflemen, 1814

lands. Army engineers also did major work in clearing the rivers and improving harbors.

In the West numerous Army expeditions led by Lt. John C. Frémont and other officers blazed new trails to the California and Oregon territories. As settlers pushed farther west, new forts were built. The long series of conflicts with the Indians continued, including the difficult six-year Second Seminole War in the swamps of Florida. To answer the mobility challenge of the horse-mounted plains Indians, the Army recreated its own mounted units of riflemen and dragoons. The nation's movement westward also brought the Army into a war with Mexico.

Mexico, Texas, and California (1846–1860)

The U.S. Army that went to war against the Mexican Army in 1846 was small, inexperienced in large-unit tactics, but tough.

Fig. 1.4. Dragoon and infantrymen, Mexico, 1847

Its Regular soldiers had spent hard years fighting Indians and adverse weather on the plains, and it was well served by having a high percentage of excellent officers from West Point. Reinforced by militia and volunteers, Army columns under generals Winfield Scott, John Wool, and Zachary Taylor moved south into Mexico. At the same time, Col. Steven Kearny led a force west to Santa Fe and then on to help Frémont capture California. After eighteen months of hard-fought battles, including its first major amphibious landing at Vera Cruz, the American Army scaled the walls of the Chapultepec Castle and captured Mexico City. Today a number of Army units still commemorate their distinguished service in the war with historic nicknames such as "Brave Rifles" (3d Armored Cavalry) or by symbols on their unit insignia.

The Army learned a lot from its experience against Mexico. For the first time it used formal divisions to organize itself, had light artillery, experimented with rockets, and used an effective intelligence system. A set of drill manuals was used to provide training to the militia and for a year after the Mexican surrender the Army performed its first occupation duties in a foreign nation. The war with Mexico was the training ground for men like Grant, Sherman, Lee, Jackson, and many others who later served with distinction on both sides in the Civil War.

The war also expanded the responsibilities of the Army in the West as settlers moved into the former Mexican territories. Among its first tasks was to continue the exploration of the new lands and seek routes for the railroads to cross the continent. In addition, the pioneer trails were being subjected to Indian attacks. New forts had to be built and the trails secured. Despite the new missions, however, the Army was again reduced.

The Civil War (1860–1865)

In 1860 the small, scattered Regular Army of about sixteen thousand men was torn apart by sectional loyalties. Men who had served together for years split to different sides. About one third of the Regular officers resigned from the Army to join the Confederacy, and a number of enlisted soldiers joined them. Following the attack on Fort Sumter, the U.S. installations located throughout the South were seized by local rebel forces. Unable to withdraw all the Regulars from their security duties at the frontier posts and needing a large number of forces quickly, President Lincoln requested militia forces from the states. He also established temporary volunteer units, but Congress only slightly increased the size of the Regular Army. It was with this mix of forces that the Union fought the war. The South took similar steps, also depending primarily on militia and volunteer soldiers for its army.

The two armies had their first major clash at Bull Run in July 1861, and then fought time after bloody time for the next four years. It was America's first modern war with railroads, telegraph, rifled muskets and artillery, repeating rifles, hot-air balloons, the beginnings of a national weather service, and a draft to support a huge army of over one million men. Different organizational configurations were tried, and for the first time black Americans were enlisted into their own volunteer units. In fact, by the end of the war both sides had formed Negro units. Also for the first time in history, the Army had a four-star general when Ulysses S. Grant was placed in command of all Union armies.

The Union Army struggled at first to find the right combination of leaders and tactics, but by the end of the summer of 1863 it had found itself—and a group of winning commanders.

Fig. 1.5. Engineer officer, horse artillery, and infantrymen, 1863

Even the famed Confederate cavalry was matched by the Union's horsemen. By the end of the war the victorious Union Army was the strongest, most experienced, and best equipped force in the world. It carried dozens of battle and campaign honors with names like Shiloh, Antietam, Vicksburg, Gettysburg, Wilderness, Franklin, and Chattanooga on its flags. Proud of their units, Union soldiers began wearing distinctive badges for their division and corps. Heroic performance also won units honored titles like "Rock of Chickamauga" (19th Infantry) and "Right of the Line" (14th Infantry), but the cost of the war to both the Union and Confederate armies had been staggering.

Reconstruction and the West (1865–1898)

After the war the militia and volunteers were quickly released. A reorganized but reduced and scattered Regular Army again faced a variety of difficult tasks. There were twelve years of occupation and peace-enforcement duty in the South. A threat of conflict with French forces in Mexico arose along with a requirement to restore order in northern areas suffering from civil disturbances and labor disputes. From 1867 to 1868 the Army had responsibility for supervising the new Alaskan Territory. For many years the Army remained deeply involved in the far north, sending exploration expeditions and developing plans for Arctic settlement. In 1871 Army troops helped Chicago recover from its disastrous fire.

Peace brought a renewed surge of settlers into the West and a fresh outbreak of Indian problems that continued for thirty years. Troops of Indian Scouts from friendly tribes were used by the Army, and four black regiments were also added: the 24th and 25th Infantry, and the 9th and 10th Cavalry. Although subject to prejudice, the "Buffalo Soldiers" of these units established a strong tradition of exceptional Army service that continues today. Other units, such as the 4th, 5th, and 7th Cavalry, and 3d, 5th, 6th, and 18th Infantry also won honors in the over 940 engagements of the Indian campaigns that finally ended in 1891.

The Army was also involved in more peaceful activities. Army engineers constructed a number of public buildings in Washington, D.C., including the Library of Congress, Old Executive Building, and the Washington Monument. In the area of medical science, the Army's medical department began two initiatives that developed into world-class collections: a medical library and the medical museum that is now the National Institute of Pathology. The number of Army officers sent as military instructors to the military training programs at land-grant colleges was increased, strengthening what would eventually develop into the Reserve Officer Training Corps (ROTC). This program would play a critical role in providing large numbers of officers in times of crisis such as World War I and World War II. Today ROTC provides the majority of Army officers.

Despite reduced funds and a growing sense of isolation from the mainstream of American life, the Army continued to seek to improve. The Western experience showed the need to better prepare new soldiers, so the Army developed training programs in the recruit depots. A system of advanced schools for the officers began to develop and observers were sent overseas to learn from foreign armies. A good repeating rifle using smokeless powder was adopted in 1893, and some regiments trained together as units for the first time in years. The Army also experimented with improved artillery. Although a difficult period, the Army built the base to meet its worldwide duties in the next century.

Entrance onto the World Stage (1898–1917)

It was a small but frontier-hardened Army that entered the Spanish-American War. The Regular Army was enlarged and augmented by volunteer units, such as the 1st U.S. Volunteer Cavalry (The Rough Riders). In spite of poor preparations and lack of supplies, the Army deployed forces to Cuba and the Philippines in three months. In Cuba, a series of fights near Santiago at San Juan Hill, Kettle Hill, and El Caney ended with a Spanish surrender. In a short time U.S. forces occupied Cuba and Puerto Rico.

Casualties from enemy fire were suffered, but more deadly than Spanish bullets were tropical diseases. Yellow fever, malaria, and other illnesses struck the American forces hard. Maj. Walter Reed and others in the Medical Corps began the search for the cause of yellow fever. They initiated a famous research program that the Army continues today to study tropical diseases and find ways to protect U.S. troops. Gen. Leonard Wood turned Cuba over to its elected government in 1902, but Army troops had to return several times over the next fifteen years to help restore order.

The war against the Spanish in the Philippines ended quickly with the capture of Manila, but bitter fighting soon ensued against native insurgents. The most difficult was a five-year struggle against Moro tribes on the smaller islands. Using the example of the Indian Scouts, the Army formed units of Philippine Scouts. The Army also adopted the hard-hitting M1911 .45-caliber pistol as a close-in weapon to stop fanatical sword-wielding Moro warriors. Gradually the respect and loyalty of the Philippine people were won; independence was granted to the islands in 1946.

Increased involvement of the United States in world affairs meant expanded commitments for the Army. In 1900 Army units were sent to China as part of an international relief force to help put down the Boxer Rebellion. This was the first time since the Revolution that the United States joined with foreign nations in a military operation. Units sent included the 14th and 9th Infantry and 6th Cavalry regiments. The 14th scaled the walls of Peking and Battery F, 5th Artillery, blasted open the gates to the Inner City. After its experiences, the 9th Infantry adopted the nickname "The Manchus." Members of both the 9th and 14th today wear a Chinese dragon on their unit insignia. American soldiers remained in China until 1938, and came to be called "Old China Hands."

A major accomplishment of the Army at this time was the construction of the Panama Canal. Under the leadership of Army engineer Col. George W. Goethals, the Corps of Engi-

Fig. 1.6. Medical Department officer and enlisted personnel, artilleryman, Cuba, 1898

neers began work on the Canal in 1907. Not only were there staggering engineering, labor, and housing problems, but also the old enemy of tropical diseases had to be defeated. In 1914 the canal was successfully opened. It was one of the engineering marvels of the world. Greatly reducing the travel distance between the Pacific and Atlantic, the canal became a major strategic possession of the United States. The responsibility for its security was given to the Army, a mission it will keep until the Canal Zone is turned over to the Panamanian government in 1999.

Political unrest and a series of revolutions in Mexico resulted in the Army involvement there once again. A large Army force was gathered along the Mexican border in 1911, and in 1914 American soldiers and Marines landed at Vera Cruz and occupied the city for seven months. Raids by Mexican groups across the border into the United States gradually escalated and American citizens in Mexico were singled out for murder and mistreatment by Mexican revolutionaries under Pancho Villa. Finally, after a group led by Villa attacked the town of Columbus, New Mexico, in 1916, a large Army force under General John J. Pershing was sent south across the border in pursuit. Other Army forces moved to reinforce the border areas. Although several small fights occurred, Villa was never captured. The raids, however, did cease and the troops were recalled in January 1917 as the crisis in Europe escalated.

The expedition into Mexico was not a wasted effort. The Army made significant efforts to learn from its Mexican experiences and modernize. The mobilization of the Army and National Guard gave valuable experience in moving and training large numbers of troops, experience that would be needed for Europe within a few months. It was a difficult campaign over desert and mountainous terrain. The Army used telephones and the airplanes of the Signal Corps' new aviation service in real operations for the first time. Motor vehicles began to replace horse-drawn wagons. Perhaps the last mounted charge by a U.S. Cavalry unit was made by the 11th Cavalry against a band of Villa's men. Although few cavalrymen would admit it, the day of the horse soldier was over. The new machine guns were used on a larger scale for the first time and the highly accurate M1903 Springfield rifle was the standard infantry weapon.

During the crisis with Mexico, Congress voted to enlarge the Army, passed laws to mobilize National Guard units under the federal government, and initiated a plan for ex-Regular soldiers to serve in Army Reserve units, thus not totally losing the benefit of their experience. These actions laid the foundation for the Guard and Reserve system used today. They also helped prepare the country for the approaching war in Europe. Within a few months of his return from Mexico, General Pershing was leading many of the same U.S. soldiers who had served with him in Mexico off of their troop ships and onto the battlefields of France and Belgium.

World War I and After (1917–1920)

On April 6, 1917, the United States declared war on Germany. By June, the first soldiers of the American Expeditionary Force (AEF) were in France. These were the first of over two million men and women who were to serve in Europe.

The Army's basic organization was the regiment. Two regiments of infantry formed a brigade, and two brigades with artillery, engineers, transportation, and supporting troops made a division. The Army's 2d Division included a brigade of Ma-

Fig. 1.7. Artillery officer, machine gun sergeant, and field telephone crew, France, 1918

rines, and for a while the division was commanded by Marine General John Lejeune. Ultimately sixty-one divisions would be organized, with forty-two sent to Europe.

To provide the necessary manpower, Congress instituted a draft and called National Guard units and Reservists to federal service. Continued concern about the security of the Mexican border kept the four existing Regular black regiments at their posts there. Four other separate infantry regiments and one division of African-American soldiers were formed. Arriving in France at a time of crisis in the French Army, these regiments were assigned to the French where they served with great distinction, winning high awards for heroism. For the first time women also served overseas in several types of units, including work as telephone operators and nurses near the front lines.

Where he could, General Pershing strongly resisted efforts by the British and French to integrate small American units into the European forces. The rush to send troops overseas did not allow much time for training in the states. Pershing saw a grave need for more intensive training of both men and units before committing them to battle. He developed a program in which U.S. units were assigned for short periods to Allied sectors along the front to gradually build American experience and knowledge. In one small action, three American companies assigned to train with the Australian Army joined them in an attack on German lines at Hamal, Belgium. The courage and enthusiasm of the American infantrymen won the respect and praise of the veteran Aussies.

Throughout the winter the Americans trained, then began taking over their own sectors of the front. The rookie U.S. units were harshly tested by the Germans in nighttime trench raids. In May and again in July 1918 the Germans launched major offensives to cross the Marne River in sectors held by the 3d Infantry Division. Despite severe losses, the division held the line, earning the nickname "The Marne Division." Other U.S. divisions fought with distinction at Belleau Wood and Soissons. The 26th Infantry Regiment won the title "Lions of Cantigny" for their service during the first American offensive as American soldiers experienced the full brunt of trench warfare. Night raids, gas attacks, machine guns, flamethrowers, heavy artillery bombardments, snipers, tanks, barbed wire, and mud became their life.

Army divisions marked their unit property with various symbols to distinguish it from the property of other units. When the 81st Division arrived in France, the AEF inspectors discovered the men had made cloth replicas of the division's wildcat symbol and sewn the insignia to the upper sleeves of their uniforms. While division and corps insignia had been worn in the Civil and Spanish-American wars, they were no longer authorized. However, when AEF officials ordered the insignia removed the men appealed to General Pershing. He recognized the positive morale factor of the insignia and authorized its use. Other units soon had their own shoulder-sleeve insignias designed and approved, beginning a strong and colorful Army tradition of shoulder-sleeve insignia that continues today.

With the help of the Americans, the Allies stopped the last major German offensive in mid-summer of 1918. Then the Allied counteroffensive began. After first assisting in two successful Allied attacks, the Americans finally got their own chance. Pershing's First Army hit the Germans at Saint-Mihiel, where Lt. Col. George S. Patton, Jr., led the U.S. tanks. The Germans fell back, and the Americans, after pausing to reorganize, hit them again, breaking through three defensive lines in the Argonne Forest. By November the Germans were in retreat and ready for peace. The "war to end all wars" ended on November 11, 1918, and most of the National Guard units and draftee-filled units quickly returned home. The reduced Regular Army, however, had other duties.

Divisions of the newly activated Third U.S. Army were sent into Germany along the Rhine River near Coblenz as an occupation force and one regiment spent four months in Austria. In addition several Army units remained in North Russia and Siberia where they had been sent in early 1918 to guard supplies and defend a railroad from Bolshevik forces. Among these units was the 31st Infantry. It earned the nickname "The Polar Bears" for its exploits in Siberia. Members of the regiment wear a small polar bear as a unit insignia. The last American units were finally withdrawn from Europe and Russia in 1923.

Between the World Wars (1920–1941)

Rapid demobilization and a strong pacifist sentiment in the United States after the war left the Army small and poorly funded. Congress did make a fundamental reorganization, officially establishing the "Army of the United States" to describe the expanded army of World War I that had been composed of the Regular Army, federalized National Guard, and Reserves. Congress designated it the basic land force of the country.

The Army made internal changes as well. Based on war experience, the regiment was found to be too inflexible and the division was made the primary field unit. Regiments remained, but their importance as a tactical unit declined. Staff procedures and organization were modernized, and a separate Air Service, Chemical Warfare Service, and Finance Department were created. A system of over thirty Army schools plus three senior staff colleges providing training for enlisted soldiers and officers was set up. The quality of the Reserves was improved by bringing the ROTC program and the Citizen's Military Training Camps (CMTC) under closer Army control.

The Depression and labor disputes in the early 1930s caused the Army to be used on several occasions to reestablish domestic order. This type of duty was never pleasant for the Army, but insuring domestic peace when necessary is a constitutional and lawful Army mission. The most distasteful episode was the requirement to break up demonstrations by veterans demanding a bonus for their service in World War I. As one of the few organizations prepared and equipped to react quickly, the Army was also used to provide civilian relief

Fig. 1.8. General officer, sergeant, and enlisted personnel, mechanized cavalry, Fort Knox, Kentucky, 1938

during floods, blizzards, and hurricanes. The engineers continued their traditional job of harbor and river improvement, and for a short period the Army acted as the nation's air mail service.

While keeping its eye on developments in China and Europe in the 1930s, the Army made efforts to improve and expand the new Army Air Corps. The famous M-1 Garand rifle was adopted as was a new artillery howitzer and better tanks. A more flexible division structure was organized. Officers destined for fame in World War II such as Eisenhower, Collins, Patton, Bradley, Stilwell, and others continued to study the skills of their profession at schools and small Army posts around the world. While their staffs developed war plans for a variety of possible conflicts, senior Army leaders like generals MacArthur and Marshall continued their struggles to get money for modern equipment and more men.

The aggressive actions by Japan, Germany, and Italy in the late 1930s finally caused increased Congressional concern about the readiness of the U.S. Army. Funding was increased, and in September 1940 the first peacetime draft law was passed and the Army was directed to mobilize. In early 1941 the National Guard and Reserves were called up. When the attack on Pearl Harbor took place, the Army was far from ready, but it was also far advanced from its condition of only a few years before.

World War II (1941–1945)

December 7, 1941, changed everything. The early losses in Hawaii, and the surrender of the U.S. and Filipino forces under General Wainwright in the Philippines after a desperate six-month defense were bitter setbacks for the Army. The courage and determination of the American soldier and his Filipino allies was never tested harder than it was on the Bataan Death March. The Japanese also attacked the Aleutians and captured two of the islands. Army units spread from Alaska to the Panama Canal were reinforced as much as possible. Germany and Italy declared war, and for the first time in its history, the Army faced enemies on two fronts.

The Army's response to the Japanese attacks came in April 1942 with the daring attack of Air Corps bombers on Tokyo. This was followed by the dispatch of troops to Australia and key islands in the southwest Pacific. In October the first of two Army divisions reinforced the Marines on Guadalcanal while units of another division moved against Japanese forces on New Guinea. In the China-Burma-India theater, Gen. Joseph Stilwell sought to organize and support Chinese troops, while in England U.S. planning began with the British for operations against the Germans and Italians.

Remembering the untrained units of 1917, the Army developed an extensive system of basic training that taught soldiers their basic skills, then advanced them level by level to more complex tasks and finished with maneuvers for entire divisions. The Army's ability to process and train large numbers of soldiers grew tremendously. By the end of 1942 the Army had 5.4 million men, and at the end of the war almost 9 million soldiers were in 89 divisions and other units.

Women also served again, first as volunteers, and then as Regulars in the Women's Army Corps (WAC). The Army remained officially segregated, so black soldiers were kept together in their own units usually under white officers. While the majority were assigned to support units, many had the opportunity to be in a combat unit. Two infantry divisions of African-American soldiers were formed, and the 2d Cavalry Division, composed mainly of black units, was also in existence for a short time. A number of segregated artillery, tank, and tank destroyer battalions earned proud combat records, along with their hard-driving fellow blacks in the famous "Red Ball Express," which rushed badly needed supplies to the front lines in Europe. Other black Americans joined the Army's segregated Air Corps fighter squadron, winning the respect of friend and foe alike.

The Army made its first move against Hitler in November 1942 with landings in North Africa. U.S. Rangers and airborne troops were used for the first time. When the German-Italian army attacked the U.S. II Corps at Kasserine Pass, Tunisia, the inexperienced American units suffered heavy losses. A joint U.S.-British offensive pushed the German-Italian forces back, however, and by May 1943 had trapped them against the sea. That same month the 7th Division landed in the Aleutians and destroyed the Japanese garrison. This ended the only occupation of U.S. soil by foreign forces since the war of 1812.

Following the victory in Africa, Sicily was invaded and captured in a matter of weeks. Then Army units landed in Italy and began a long hard fought campaign north up the length of the country. Battles at places with names like Salerno, Anzio, Monte Cassino, and the Volturno and Rapido rivers cost the lives of thousands of American soldiers. One unit, the 442d Regimental Combat Team, particularly stood out for its continual heroic acts. Made up of Japanese-Americans, the 442d's motto "Go for Broke" perfectly described the all-out attacks that made it a highly decorated unit. Meanwhile, other Army forces gathered in England and trained for the main assault against Europe. The Army Air Corps also increased its daylight bombing raids against Germany.

Army units in the Pacific under General Douglas MacArthur began a series of landings in the Solomon Islands as first steps to eliminate the major Japanese base on Rabaul. Through 1943 and into 1944 soldiers followed up with landings throughout the Pacific, including New Guinea, Bougainville, New Britain, the Admiralty Islands, Makin, Kwajalein, Saipan, Guam, and many others. These opened the way back to the Philippines and ultimately to the Japanese home islands themselves.

D-Day, June 6, 1944, is a date that will forever be remembered in the Army. On that day the largest Army assault force ever gathered stormed by sea and air into Normandy, France, and began the liberation of Europe. Extremely tough fighting through fortified hedgerows gradually expanded the Allied

Fig. 1.9. Infantrymen during amphibious landing, Pacific theater of operations, 1944

toehold. Using the new Sherman tank, General Omar Bradley's First Army broke out at St. Lô. General Patton's Third Army joined the fight, and together with Army forces from a second landing on the south coast of France, they pushed to the German border.

In October, General MacArthur kept his promise to return to the Philippines. When four U.S. Army divisions landed on the Philippine island of Leyte, the commander of the 34th Infantry led his men off the beach in the face of heavy enemy fire with the cry "Follow me," an embodiment of the famous motto of all American infantrymen. Heavy combat continued in the Philippine jungles and mountains, finally bringing relief to the American-led Philippine guerrilla bands that had been harassing the Japanese for two years. In January, amphibious landings put army units on the main island of Luzon. Their move on Manila was swift, with the 1st Cavalry Division (The First Team) first into the city. After a month of bitter house-to-house fighting, Manila was taken and the prison camps there were soon liberated. The paratroopers of the 503d Parachute Infantry jumped onto the rocky island fortress of Corregidor, raised the Stars and Stripes, and earned the motto of "The Rock."

A last desperate offensive by the Germans in December 1944 hit the American divisions holding the front in the rough, forested area of Belgium and Luxembourg called the Ardennes. Surprised and outnumbered, Army units were overrun and initially forced back. The 101st Airborne Division refused to surrender and fought surrounded in the town of Bastogne for several weeks while other units fought delaying actions and Patton's tanks raced to help.

By January the heroic actions of many units finally stopped the Germans, and the tide reversed. A terrible battle in the depths of the Huertgen Forest on the German border had resulted in the breaking of the German defensive position called the Siegfried Line. American units seized a bridge over the Rhine River at Remagen and fought across Germany and into Austria. On April 25 a linkup was made with Russian forces at the Elbe River in eastern Germany.

In the Pacific the last Philippine operations got under way and U.S. forces moved into position for the invasion of Japan itself. The island of Okinawa was needed as a base, so in April 1945 a joint Army-Marine assault force landed to capture the island. The three-month battle was one of the most costly of the Pacific campaign, but by the end of June it was over. U.S. forces including army units transferred from Europe gathered for operations Olympic and Coronet, the invasion of Japan. However, on August 6, 1945, a B-29 of the U.S. Army Air Force dropped the first operational atomic bomb on Japan. General MacArthur, with General Wainwright at his side, took the Japanese surrender on the deck of the U.S.S. *Missouri*. The war had ended, but the nuclear age had begun.

The Cold War and Korea (1946–1953)

Within a year following World War II the mightiest army in the world was demobilized. National Guard units went home, and the Army of the United States became again a relatively small Regular force. The end of the war also once again brought occupation duties. Army Civil Affairs units provided government for the American Sector of Germany, Berlin, part of Austria, and all of Japan. In addition, the Philippines and dozens of small islands captured in the Pacific required proper administration. The Army filled the gap until civilian governments could be set up. Occupation of Germany lasted almost ten years.

As the U.S.-Soviet wartime friendship shown on the Elbe River died, U.S. soldiers found themselves conducting armed patrols along the Iron Curtain that divided Europe into two hostile camps. This "cold war" continued for almost fifty years, during which a number of soldiers lost their lives in small "incidents." Nuclear weapons for ground forces were introduced into the Army, and the Air Force broke away to become an independent military service. All military services were ordered to desegregate their units in 1947, but the order was widely ignored. Money for equipment and training was cut, and many units on soft occupation duty let their combat readiness slip.

An attempted takeover by Communist forces in Greece and threats against Turkey brought the Army into the role of providing military advice, support, and assistance to friendly nations. American soldiers were assigned around the world to help improve foreign forces, South Korean and South Vietnamese among them. Expanding on its old role of coastal defense, the Army also assumed the mission of ground-based air defense of the United States. Soon many major American cities were the sites of Army antiaircraft missile bases.

The Cold War suddenly became hot in June 1950 when the Soviet-trained North Korean People's Army (NKPA) launched a surprise attack against South Korea. Unprepared U.S. Army units armed with weapons from World War II rushed into battle from occupation duty in Japan, and a new mobilization began under the flag of the United Nations.

Task Force Smith, armed with light weapons, was the first Army unit to meet the North Koreans. The NKPA rolled over it and continued south. The Americans and South Koreans fought a delaying retreat into a defensive position around the port of Pusan. Reinforced, they held the line against determined enemy attacks through the summer. In an effort to improve the Army's fighting strength, desegregation of all units was enforced—with excellent results. The Army introduced a new tank, better antitank weapons, and improved equipment. A number of combined-arms regimental combat teams were formed.

In September 1950 a surprise American landing at Inchon in the rear of the North Koreans reversed the situation. Striking north, the United Nations forces pursued the fleeing NKPA to the Chinese border. The 1st Cavalry Division captured the North Korean capital, and 7th Infantry Division (Bayonet Division) patrols stood on the banks of the Yalu River, the border

Fig. 1.10. Infantrymen, Korea, 1950

with China. In November, the Communists gave another surprise—the Chinese Army struck across the border, overwhelming a number of units. In bitter cold surviving soldiers of the 31st and 32d Infantry fought their way south with Marine comrades out of the trap at the Chosin Reservoir and reformed their lines.

Under a new UN Commander, General Matthew Ridgway, revitalized and reequiped UN forces halted the Chinese advance. The major Chinese offensive smashed itself against the 23d Infantry—supported by French troops and artillery—at the village of Chipyong-ni. The Chinese were pushed back north. The battle lines swayed back and forth for months over places called Iron Triangle, Pork Chop Hill, and Heartbreak Ridge. A truce was finally reached in July 1953 and a Demilitarized Zone set up to keep the two sides apart. Over the years the truce has been broken numerous times by the Communists and American soldiers have been killed in North Korean ambushes. The 2d Infantry Division (Indianhead) remains on guard in South Korea today as a symbol of the American commitment.

From Korea to Vietnam (1954–1965)

After Korea the Army went through a series of reorganizations and testing of organizational concepts in the search to find the right combination of men and weapons for the nuclear battlefield while still maintaining the flexibility to meet other types of missions. In some respects two armies evolved. One was the armor-heavy mechanized force that faced the Soviet Army and its Warsaw Pact allies in Europe. The other was a lighter-equipped army that experimented with new concepts of airmobility, counterinsurgency, guerrilla warfare, and a concept called "nation building" for developing third world countries.

The Army remained committed around the world. In addition to the units in Europe and Korea, the 82d Airborne Division (All American) was sent to the Dominican Republic in 1965 to restore internal peace. Other units remained on guard in Alaska, Hawaii, and Panama. New weapons like the M-14 rifle, M-60 machine gun, and M-79 grenade launcher were introduced, along with more modern radios and improved food rations. Army medical service had become the finest in the world, and continued to improve its competence. Women were only accepted into certain limited-duty positions, but racial segregation in the Army was a thing of the past. Officers and NCOs of all races commanded soldiers of all races.

The division remained the main tactical unit since it effectively combined the arms of infantry, artillery, and armor with other supporting elements. The regiment as a single unit; however, was eliminated in all but a few cases. It was too big and inflexible with only one type of arm—infantry or armor. For a while the Army used "battle groups," but that was only temporary. More flexibility was gained by making the battalion the basic tactical building block for field operations, and then combining different types of battalions into brigades. A brigade could then be tailored to meet many missions. Battalions retained their regimental names, but with few exceptions the regimental headquarters were eliminated. Divisions were given three brigade headquarters to command the combat battalions and a support command for support units.

The Vietnam War (1965–1972)

Fear about the spread of communism in Asia brought the Army into its longest and most trying conflict. The first American Army advisers arrived in Vietnam in 1950. When the

Fig. 1.11. Infantry under sniper fire, Vietnam, 1965

French began leaving after 1954, the United States became the principal supporter of the new South Vietnamese government. It faced a complex situation, with an internal insurgency led and strongly supported by the North Vietnamese. By the early 1960s the Army found itself providing an increasing number of advisers to help the South Vietnamese army. The size and scope of the American commitment gradually increased as political instability in the South and an increasingly effective enemy caused a rapidly deteriorating situation. Finally, in 1965, regular U.S. Army units had to be sent; thus began one of the most painful sagas in the history of the Army.

The Army had to fight a difficult dual-natured conflict. Large regular units of the North Vietnamese Army (NVA) up to regimental size roamed the countryside while fierce bands of local communist guerrillas called Vietcong (VC) hid in the civilian population while they established a shadow government. A number of tactics were tried, but nothing was a cure-all. Army advisers and Special Forces teams worked with the Army of South Vietnam (ARVN) while American field units provided a shield. Battles with names like Ia Drang Valley, Khe Sanh, Iron Triangle, Bo Lo Woods, Hamburger Hill, and the A Shau Valley filled American television screens.

The 1st Cavalry Division, organized as the first airmobile division in history, used the latest in Army helicopters and aviation to be the most mobile division in the world. It pioneered new ideas in the use of air assault and air support. The 101st Airborne Division (Screaming Eagles) followed suit. More conventional units like the 1st, 25th, and 4th Divisions also used the air. Helicopters added a new dimension to combat. They became the trucks, scouts, aerial artillery, command posts, and light tanks of the Army. Soldiers received specialized jungle uniforms and equipment. The Army's system of soldier training was again proven effective, and new subjects particular to the war were added to the instruction.

In the swamps and river deltas of South Vietnam the 9th Division (Old Reliables) developed a mobile riverine concept, placing itself entirely on armored boats. The VC and NVA were pursued into their most secure bases in Vietnam, Cambodia, and Laos and destroyed. Working with allies from South Korea, Thailand, and Australia, the Army made slow but positive gains against the enemy. However, supplies and reinforcements from North Vietnam continued to flow south to communist forces as fighting took place in all areas of the country.

As casualties increased, American public support for South Vietnam diminished. At the same time America went through wrenching social turmoil. The civil rights movement and a strong coalition of antiwar and antidraft activists took their grievances into the streets. Regular and National Guard troops were required to restore order. To lessen the impact of the war on America, a political decision was made to limit mobilization of National Guardsmen and Reservists. Draftees and soldiers pulled from the Europe-based divisions were used to fill the units in Vietnam. Reflecting the problems of American society and the stress of the war, Army units suffered from morale and discipline problems. Despite the difficulties, however, South Vietnam made progress.

Sensing their advantage was deteriorating, the North Vietnamese leaders directed a surprise offensive for the 1967–68 Tet holiday season. The attackers captured portions of some cities, but the anticipated popular uprising did not occur. Suffering terrible losses, the surviving VC and NVA withdrew to their base areas. The North suffered a military defeat, but it won a political and psychological victory. The shock of seeing a supposedly defeated foe strike with such vigor turned American public opinion against the war. Unfortunately, this hostility was often taken out on the men and women serving their country honorably in the Army.

The war continued four more years, but in March 1973, steadily increasing domestic opposition brought the last American ground unit home. Military advisers stayed longer to try to help the South, but it was no use. Without American aid the South Vietnamese could not hold out against the increased

Northern pressure. A final NVA attack by eighteen divisions led by tanks crushed the Southern forces in 1975. America's longest war was over. While the cost in total U.S. casualities was not heavy considering the length and ferocity of the war, the cost to the spirit and morale of the Army was severe.

Post-Vietnam and Hot Spots (1973–1990)

Departure from Vietnam brought reduced Army budgets and manpower levels. The Army looked inward, reevaluated, and set about rebuilding itself. A major change came when the draft ended and the shift made to an all-volunteer army. It was a return to the professional Regular force the Army had not seen since 1940. Procedures for quick removal of troublesome soldiers and tightened entry standards brought high-quality soldiers into the Army. Opportunities for women also improved. Female cadets were accepted into West Point and female pilots took their places in Army cockpits. New and better concepts of training were introduced, more responsibility given to the NCOs, and a series of formal schools for their professional development set up. To economize training funds, experiments began with computer simulations and new high-tech devices like lasers.

Army doctrine refocused on Europe and the units there were brought to full strength again and modernized. Almost half of the Army's strength stood guard in Europe, braced for a Warsaw Pact attack. Army patrols from the famous old dragoon and cavalry regiments, the 2d and 11th Armored Cavalry, patrolled the borders of East Germany and Czechoslovakia, watching and listening with electronic ears for the first sign of an attack. In Berlin, the Army's Berlin Brigade kept watch over the wall that divided the city. Evaluation of the Soviet threat caused great concern. If attacked, the Army would have to fight outnumbered and outgunned. Analysis showed a need for improved electronic warfare, nuclear-chemical-biological (NBC) defense, as well as better tanks and antiarmor weapons. At the same time international terrorism was on the increase. Many argued for more money to be spent on preparation for low-intensity conflicts, a possibility that seemed more likely than nuclear war or even a conventional Soviet attack.

The feared weakness in unconventional operations was confirmed in 1979 when a joint U.S. force led by the Army had to abort its mission to rescue American hostages held in Iran. Improvements in special operations training and units began immediately. The Ranger Regiment was formed. Special Forces units increased and many improvements in equipment were made. Four years later the investment began to pay off when

Fig. 1.12. Patrolling the East German border, 1970s

Army special operations units, the Rangers, and two brigades of the 82d Airborne Division were deployed to the island of Grenada. The Army forces successfully stopped a pro-communist takeover and rescued a group of American students. In other activities Army Special Forces teams continued their work with Latin American and other allies around the world.

The 1980s brought many changes to Army weapons and equipment. The Huey transport and Cobra gunship helicopters of Vietnam were replaced by the sleek and fast Blackhawk and Apache. A new family of armored vehicles was introduced. These included a new heavy tank, the M1A1 Abrams, and its companion armored infantry and cavalry scout vehicles, the M-2 and M-3 Bradley. These fast, powerful vehicles carried thermal and infrared sights, computer-assisted guns, and a satellite-based electronic locator system called GPS. They were designed to stand up against the best the Soviets had. To match Soviet artillery, a new multiple-launched rocket system, the MLRS, which fired rockets carrying many small deadly warheads was also obtained. The faithful jeep was replaced by the HMMWV (Hummer). Among the new items for the individual soldier was a new-design helmet, a camouflage "battle dress uniform," a new bayonet, improved NBC mask and protective suit, plus other items of wear. The old M-1911 .45 pistol was replaced, the M-16 rifle improved, and a new automatic weapon (SAW) given to each rifle squad.

Reconfigured 1st Cavalry and 9th Infantry Divisions tested new types of mobility and combinations of weapons. In the mid-1980s, the 10th Mountain and the 6th Infantry, well-decorated World War II divisions, were reactivated as fast-reaction light divisions. Their purpose was to give the Army the capability to rapidly reinforce any part of the world using fast aircraft rather than slower ships. This brought the number of active divisions up to eighteen, more than the Army could adequately man. Many of the active divisions were therefore reduced to two brigades. A National Guard brigade, called a "round-out" brigade, was selected to provide the third brigade for each division. Future events in the Middle East would show this was not a totally workable arrangement.

The Army was called on again in December 1989 for low-intensity action. The Panamanian dictator Manuel Noriega was known to be helping transport shipments of illegal drugs and relations had deteriorated to the point that Americans were publicly mistreated on the streets of Panama City. It became necessary to correct the situation. Striking swiftly, Army units successfully completed their mission to disperse the Panamanian military and soon had Noriega in custody. Improved equipment and communications as well as top-quality soldiers and training brought a quick victory.

The end of 1989 also brought one of the most historic moments in recent times—the destruction of the Berlin wall. As Army soldiers watched, the fabric of East Germany came apart and the wall fell under the hammers of thousands of Germans from both sides. In a matter of months the whole balance of power in Europe changed. The Warsaw Pact countries declared their independence and the Soviet Union itself started to crumble. With this threat apparently gone, the Army began to return most of its soldiers home after almost half a century in Europe. At the same time the Army was ordered to reduce its size and close selected posts in the States. Just as the Army began the drawdown, a new crisis arose.

Desert Storm and Peacekeeping (1991–1994)

The real test of the Army's recovery from its post-Vietnam troubles came in August 1990, only eight months after Grenada, when the Iraqi Army invaded Kuwait. Operations Desert Shield and Desert Storm were unique in several ways. The Army was in the midst of a major reduction of size and at the same time it was withdrawing most of its forces from Europe.

When the alert came, the Army quickly shifted its plans. Units bound from Europe to the states were diverted to the Middle East, and the release of soldiers was stopped. Mobilized stateside units quickly moved toward ports and airfields. The Army organized and pulled together a force of almost ten divisions from Europe and the United States. The suddenness of the crisis did not permit the National Guard round-out brigades to be brought to full readiness, and they were unable to join their Regular divisions.

In record time Army units deployed to Saudi Arabia and moved into position. The first to arrive was the 82d Airborne, the Army's fast-reaction force. Other heavy mechanized and armor units including the 1st (Big Red One), and 24th (Victory) Infantry, and 1st Cavalry divisions soon followed. Initially positioned to deter further Iraqi advances, the U.S. forces under Army General Norman Schwarzkopf used deception to reposition themselves for offensive action. On G-Day, February 24, 1991, they struck across the border into Iraq. The Army units, organized into two corps, drove north toward the Euphrates River, then turned east, destroying the enemy as they went. The 101st Airborne (Air Assault) leaped forward in a series of air assaults along the left flank. It was a textbook example of a truly professional army bringing together its doctrine, training, equipment, and soldiers into total effort. Within one hundred hours the U.S. forces and their allies had the remaining Iraqi units pinned against the coast. The war was over.

The end of Operation Desert Storm was not the end of Army involvement with Iraq. The 1990s began an era of emphasis on peacekeeping operations. In the north of Iraq U.S. Army troops were tasked for Operation Provide Comfort, providing a protective shield for Kurdish tribes threatened with extinction by the Iraqis. Army forces also began a major effort to assist the Kuwaitis in restoring their country.

In other parts of the world American soldiers were called upon to assist a number of UN peacekeeping activities. A hospital unit was deployed to Bosnia and an infantry company joined British troops on the border between Macedonia and Bosnia. An Army battalion also continued to be deployed to the Sinai Desert as a part of the UN Truce Observer Forces.

A dramatic and large commitment of Army troops occurred in the war and famine-racked country of Somalia. Initially sent in as a part of the UN effort to distribute food and medical supplies to the starving Somali people, the soldiers soon found themselves in the middle of the civil war between the tribal clans. In October 1993 a task force of Rangers and Special Forces was cut off and pinned down in the back streets of the

Fig. 1.13. M1A1 Abrams tanks pass destroyed Iraqi armor, Desert Storm, 1991

city of Mogadishu. Under siege for hours in their makeshift positions, the Rangers suffered heavy casualties, but refused to abandon their dead and wounded. They fought outnumbered until reached by a relief force of the 14th Infantry (Golden Dragons). Nowhere was the complexity of the challenge to the modern American soldier better illustrated than in the mixture of humanitarian aid and deadly combat experienced in Somalia. Thousands of Somalis lived because of the generosity and service of the American soldiers there, yet many also died in attacks on those same servicemen. The U.S. and European allies withdrew their military forces from Somalia by the early spring of 1994.

The Army no sooner left Somalia when it was again called in for a complex nation-saving mission in Haiti. Initially prepared to force entry, paratroopers and Rangers were already en route when a high-level American negotiating team reached a peaceful agreement with the Haitian government. U.S. troops poured into Haiti and quickly got to work stabilizing the situation and performing many of the civic action and civil-military assistance operations that have been required from them in the past. Haiti was not a new mission for the U.S. Army.

Today and Beyond

In 1994 the Army continued to reduce its forces following a plan that will bring it to the ordered level by the end of 1995. Many Army posts closed and the number of soldiers in Europe continued to drop. The Army will end with a force of only ten divisions, although concerns have been voiced that perhaps the cuts are too deep. As a result of the Desert Storm experience, Army plans called for a return to active divisions of three full brigades. National Guard brigades will act as fourth "round up" units. Although funds were reduced, the Army continued its research and development of new equipment and improvement of the old. Army commitments worldwide continued. By the end of 1994 there were twenty thousand soldiers working in sixty different countries. These were in addition to soldiers in Europe and South Korea.

If history is any indication, in the not-too-distant future events will again cause a need for a larger Army. In the meantime the Army continues to welcome high-quality men and women who want to be the finest soldiers in the world. If you think the past was exciting, wait until you see the future!

2. The First Step

The Army Recruiter

At this stage of your life, it's natural that you should be looking to the future and making plans for it. The Army can play an important part in those plans by giving you the start that you need for a successful future. In addition to helping you get things in focus, the Army can provide you with excellent training and education for what you want to do in the Army and later in civilian life.

It all starts with the Army recruiter. This person is a trained, knowledgeable representative of the U.S. Army. He or she was selected from thousands of volunteers and put through a tough school before being assigned to work with young people like you. The Army recruiter is interested in learning how well you measure up to Army standards and in helping you to understand what the Army is all about and what it can offer you.

Army Aptitude Tests

The Armed Services Vocational Aptitude Battery (ASVAB) test is offered through the Department of Defense Student Testing Program to interested high schools and postsecondary institutions. The Army uses the ASVAB test results to match the right person to the right skill. If you have questions about the ASVAB test, see your local Army recruiter. The recruiter will explain the test and the training opportunities you are best qualified for based on your ASVAB scores.

If your ASVAB test scores qualify, you may also take the Defense Language Aptitude Battery (DLAB) test. This test indicates the ability of a person to learn a new language and is used to screen candidates for specialized language training.

The Army has more than 250 specialties from which to choose, many in the forefront of high technology. If you qual-

Fig. 2.1. Meeting the recruiter

Fig. 2.2. Learning about the Army

ify, the Army can guarantee skill training for you in fields like avionics, electronics, microwave communications, computer technology, and television and radio broadcasting, to name just a few.

Skill transferability between what you learn in military service and civilian employment is high. This means the leadership, self-discipline, and skill training you receive in the Army can be used as a springboard to success in a civilian career.

Your Initial Interview

Your initial interview with the Army recruiter is usually at a time and place you both have agreed on. It may be at the recruiting office, your home, at work, or even at school. Regardless of where you meet, the recruiter will welcome the idea of including the people who are important to you—such as your parents, spouse, or friends—to sit in on the initial interview.

It is important to remember that this is not a sign of any type of commitment by either you or the recruiter. This interview is simply your opportunity to ask any questions that you may have about the Army. To make sure you don't forget any of the questions you want to ask the Army recruiter, it's a good idea to write them down ahead of time. The recruiter will have a variety of means for providing you with information about the Army opportunities available to you. He or she may use films, brochures, pamphlets, and of course examples from his or her own years of Army experience.

At the same time you're learning about the Army, the recruiter will be learning more about you. He or she will want to know about your goals, interests, and hobbies. After all, the recruiter's job is to provide qualified, motivated applicants for service in the Army and, in turn, to give you a realistic picture of how the Army can meet your goals.

The initial interview may be followed by other meetings. At some point in the discussions the recruiter will ask you a series of preliminary questions about your education, health, and any involvement with the police. It is important that you answer all the questions truthfully. Should you attempt to conceal anything, it could prove embarrassing to you later or even result in your discharge from the Army.

You will be required to show the following documents to the recruiter:

- Birth certificate
- High school diploma

Fig. 2.3. The initial interview

- College transcript, showing credits earned while attending college
- Social Security card
- Letter from your doctor, if you have (or had) any special medical condition

Assuming that the recruiter's evaluation of you is favorable and you want to pursue the idea of joining the Army, you are ready for your next step.

The Recruiting Station

Once you have decided it's time to learn more about how and where you fit into today's Army, your recruiter will make arrangements for you to take the ASVAB (if you haven't done so previously) and a physical examination (at no expense to you). In some areas, the aptitude test may be given at a location near the Recruiting Station called a Mobile Examining Team (MET) site. If you take your aptitude test at an MET site, preliminary results may be available immediately and fully verified scores returned to your recruiter in a few days. You and your recruiter will discuss these scores before scheduling your physical examination.

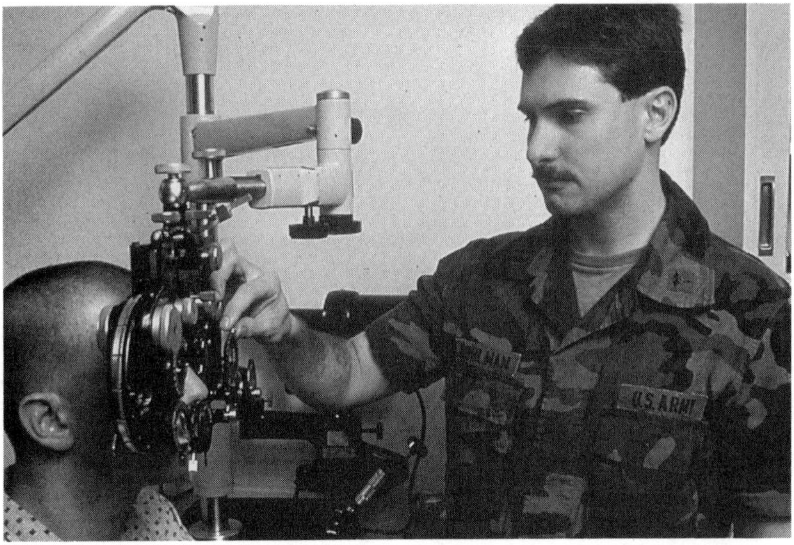

Fig. 2.4. Medical examination during initial processing

This physical examination can only be done at the Military Enlistment Processing Station nearest your home. If required, meals and overnight lodging will be provided for you at a facility near the processing station. Your day will start early, normally 7:00 A.M. You will be briefed on what to expect about your processing and provided the opportunity to ask questions. After this briefing, you will start your processing, which is divided into three general areas: mental qualification tests (unless you were previously tested at an MET site), medical examination, and administrative processing.

The mental qualification evaluation is usually the first part in your processing day. The test requires about 2½ hours to complete. It is extremely important that you do your very best. It is recommended you get a good night's sleep prior to taking the tests. The results of these examinations will have considerable bearing on your selection of options before you enter the Army.

Your medical examination will be performed by medical doctors and trained technicians. Bring with you any pertinent medical documents that you have not already given to your recruiter. These papers will help the doctor in evaluating your physical condition.

Women will be examined separately and in privacy, with a female escort present. Their physical examination (to include a pelvic examination) will take about 2 hours.

Fig. 2.5. Swearing-in ceremony

After the exam is completed, you will have a conference with the doctor. If any medical problems have been discovered, they will be discussed with you at the conference.

Your administrative processing will come later, after you have had the opportunity to talk with your Army guidance counselor about the results of all the tests and physical exam.

Matching Your Qualifications with the Army's Needs

The Army guidance counselor will take your mental test scores, physical evaluation, and all the things the Army has learned about you and feed this information into a computer through a REQUEST Terminal. It will analyze your data and compare them with the Army's eligibility requirements. Based on the results of the comparison, the recruiter will be provided with potential skill options for you that fit both your qualifications and the Army's needs.

This system is designed to see that you get off on the right foot in the Army by matching your interests and abilities with the best training program for you. If you decide to enlist for the option the guidance counselor proposes, your reservation for that training is immediately confirmed on the REQUEST

Terminal. You are now on your way to becoming a member of the U.S. Army.

The Enlistment Agreement

Based on your tests and your selection of training options, an enlistment agreement is prepared. This written document (actually a series of forms) spells out all of the conditions of your enlistment. It is a contract between you and the Army. In it, you will find training guarantees for the period of service for which you enlisted. Also your enlistment agreement will include a long list of technical points you will be asked to review thoroughly with your guidance counselor. You should take your time and examine the agreement closely because only those things listed in it are guaranteed by the Army. If you are in doubt about anything, ask for an explanation—before you sign your enlistment agreement! After you sign, you will be given specific instructions on reporting for training.

3. Meeting the Challenge

Where Will You Train?

Nothing surpasses the excitement of that first day when you leave for Basic Combat Training (BCT). You will leave from the processing station, where you will be given a last-minute physical spot check to make sure you are still healthy. If there has been a lapse in time since your last visit, you will also go through some interviews to see if there have been any changes in your eligibility. After your records and orders are complete, you will leave by bus or plane for an Army Reception Battalion at one of the Army's installations.

The Army conducts its BCT and Advanced Individual Training (AIT) at Army posts specifically designed to conduct these types of training. In some cases both BCT and AIT are conducted at the same post. Soldiers enlisting in the combat arms (see Chapter 18) may remain at the same post and with the same unit for both BCT and AIT. This is called One Station/Unit Training (OSUT). Other soldiers will have their training at two different Army installations. A list of the locations for each type of training is shown below. Figure 3.1 is a map showing the locations of the major Army installations, including the training locations.

BCT/AIT Installations (* = OSUT)

Fort Benning, GA*
Fort Sill, OK*
Fort Knox, KY*
Fort Leonard Wood, MO*
Fort Jackson, SC
Fort McClellan, AL*

AIT Installations

Aberdeen Proving Ground, MD
Fort Bliss, TX
Fitzsimmons Army Medical Center, CO
Fort Devens, MA

Fort Eustis, VA
Fort Gordon, GA
Fort Huachuca, AZ
Fort Lee, VA
Fort Monmouth, NJ
Fort Rucker, AL
Fort Sam Houston, TX
Madigan Army Medical Center, WA
Presidio of Monterey, CA
Redstone Arsenal, AL
Walter Reed Army Medical Center, DC
William Beaumont Army Medical Center, TX
Naval Amphibious Base, Little Creek, VA

As the name implies, the Army Reception Battalion is where new soldiers are received into the training center where they will undergo BCT.

Reception Battalion Processing

Before starting BCT, each new enlistee undergoes Reception Battalion processing. Normally, you will stay at the Reception Battalion for about 3 days before picking up your new Army gear and being assigned to a training company. This processing helps prepare new soldiers for training and later military life. Reception Battalion processing includes the following:

- Uniform issue and fitting
- Personnel records processing
- Identification (ID) card issue
- Immunizations (shots)
- Orientation regarding postal service, medical facilities, legal assistance, post exchange facilities, pay and allowances, visitors, and so on
- Eye and dental exams
- Haircuts

There will also be some classes in barracks life, physical training (exercise), drill (marching), and other subjects that will introduce you to Army living. You will learn a lot at the Reception Battalion, but you are going to learn a great deal more during BCT.

Basic Combat Training (BCT)

Basic combat training consists of a variety of activities including physical fitness training, basic soldier training, and orien-

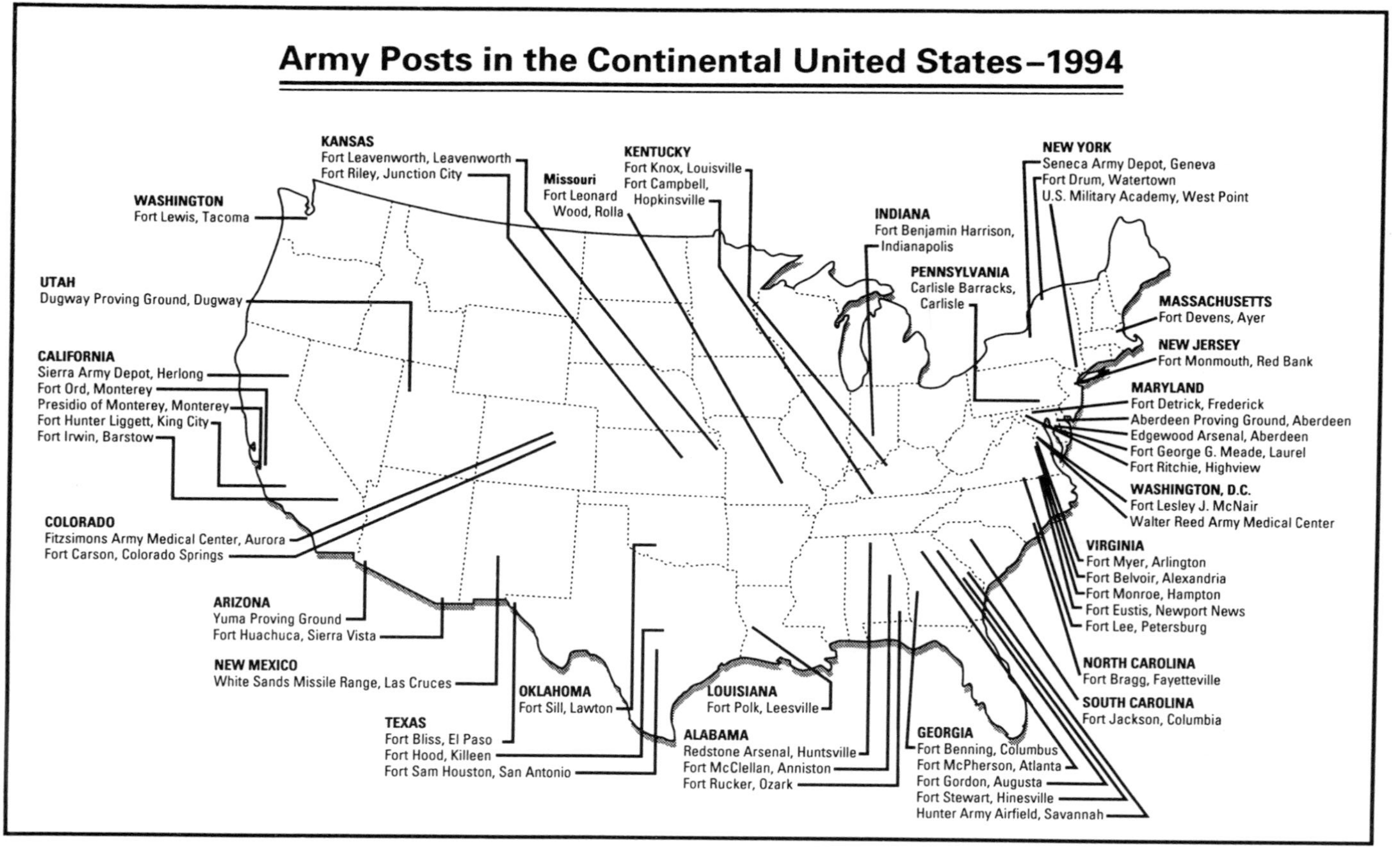
Army Posts in the Continental United States–1994
KANSAS
Fort Leavenworth, Leavenworth
Fort Riley, Junction City
WASHINGTON
Fort Lewis, Tacoma
Missouri
Fort Leonard Wood, Rolla
KENTUCKY
Fort Knox, Louisville
Fort Campbell, Hopkinsville
NEW YORK
Seneca Army Depot, Geneva
Fort Drum, Watertown
U.S. Military Academy, West Point
INDIANA
Fort Benjamin Harrison, Indianapolis
PENNSYLVANIA
Carlisle Barracks, Carlisle
UTAH
Dugway Proving Ground, Dugway
MASSACHUSETTS
Fort Devens, Ayer
NEW JERSEY
Fort Monmouth, Red Bank
CALIFORNIA
Sierra Army Depot, Herlong
Fort Ord, Monterey
Presidio of Monterey, Monterey
Fort Hunter Liggett, King City
Fort Irwin, Barstow
MARYLAND
Fort Detrick, Frederick
Aberdeen Proving Ground, Aberdeen
Edgewood Arsenal, Aberdeen
Fort George G. Meade, Laurel
Fort Ritchie, Highview
WASHINGTON, D.C.
Fort Lesley J. McNair
Walter Reed Army Medical Center
COLORADO
Fitzsimons Army Medical Center, Aurora
Fort Carson, Colorado Springs
VIRGINIA
Fort Myer, Arlington
Fort Belvoir, Alexandria
Fort Monroe, Hampton
Fort Eustis, Newport News
Fort Lee, Petersburg
ARIZONA
Yuma Proving Ground
Fort Huachuca, Sierra Vista
NEW MEXICO
White Sands Missile Range, Las Cruces
NORTH CAROLINA
Fort Bragg, Fayetteville
OKLAHOMA
Fort Sill, Lawton
LOUISIANA
Fort Polk, Leesville
SOUTH CAROLINA
Fort Jackson, Columbia
TEXAS
Fort Bliss, El Paso
Fort Hood, Killeen
Fort Sam Houston, San Antonio
ALABAMA
Redstone Arsenal, Huntsville
Fort McClellan, Anniston
Fort Rucker, Ozark
GEORGIA
Fort Benning, Columbus
Fort McPherson, Atlanta
Fort Gordon, Augusta
Fort Stewart, Hinesville
Hunter Army Airfield, Savannah

Fig. 3.1. Key posts in the continental United States (*note:* subject to change)

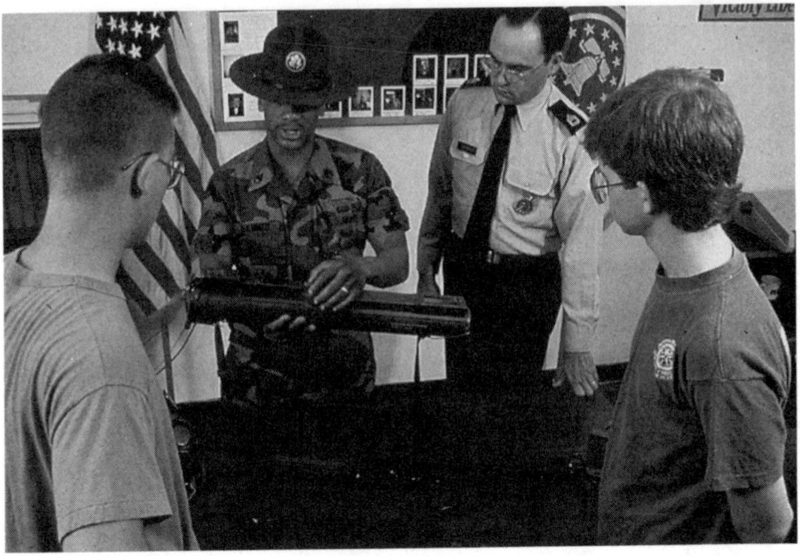

Fig. 3.2. Next stop, the reception battalion

tation to the Army. Men and women receive essentially the same initial training, including weapons instruction, but by law women cannot be assigned to direct combat. The Army believes, however, that no matter what their specialty, all soldiers must learn the basic combat skills that will give them the confidence and ability to defend themselves.

After completing your initial processing at the Reception Battalion, you will be assigned to a training company and meet your drill instructor (DI). Your DI is a seasoned noncommissioned officer (a sergeant) who has undergone a rigorous training program. He or she is the primary individual responsible for your training during BCT.

You will think your DI does an unusual amount of shouting, all of which seems directed at you. But if it is any comfort, everyone else in your training company will feel the same way. So don't let it get to you. You are not being hassled or harassed. Your DI's job is to turn you into a good soldier within a few short weeks. The shouting and toughness are all part of the process. In time, you will come to remember your DI, if not with affection, certainly with respect.

Will BCT be tough? You bet it will. Apply yourself, meet every challenge with the best you've got, listen to your instructors, and you will pass. During BCT, you will use your muscles and mind as you never have before. You will be tired and sore

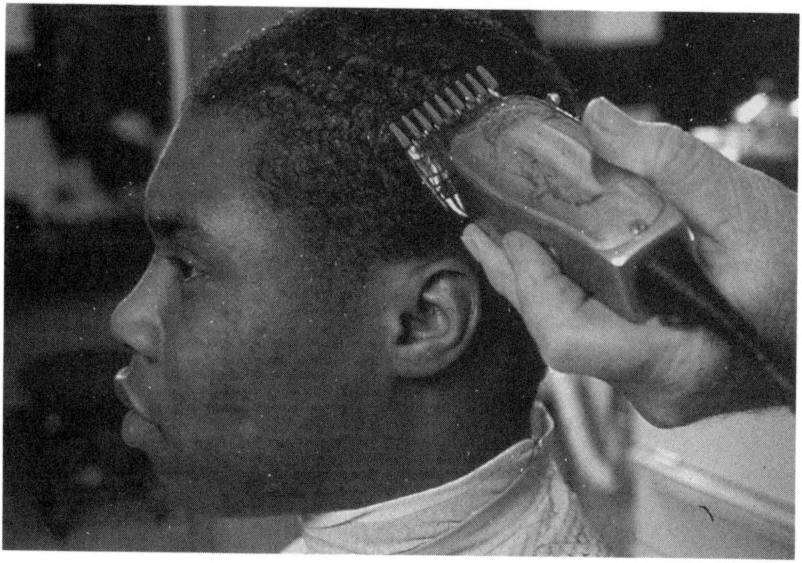

Fig. 3.3. Getting an Army haircut

at the end of each training day. But if you try hard, you will make it—a high percentage of young people who come into the Army do. The following is what you can expect during your eight weeks of BCT.

Routine

Your time in basic training will be filled with a variety of activities and classes that include:

- physical fitness training (running, calisthenics, obstacle courses, etc.)
- weapons training
- field hygiene
- military courtesies and customs
- military justice
- protective measures against nuclear, biological, and chemical weapons
- first aid
- tactical training
- Army heritage and traditions

Your daily schedule during basic training will be posted on a weekly training schedule on your company bulletin board. It will give the time, place, uniform, and instructor of specific

Fig. 3.4. Barracks maintenance

subjects that will be taught to you. The schedule will include meals, inspections, guard duty, and other events. You will be required to read the schedule daily.

A Typical Day of Basic Training

Conducted under the watchful eye of your DI, your basic training will keep you busier than you have ever been before. A typical daily schedule is highly regimented and looks like this:

0400	Reveille (wake up): Wash, make bed, clean personal area
0500	Formation; march to dining hall (Breakfast)
0600	March to barracks
0700	Formation; physical training
0800	Return to barracks, prepare for daily inspection
0900	Formation; march to classroom for instruction
1200	March to dining hall (Lunch)
1300	Formation; drill and ceremonies instruction
1500	March to classroom for instruction
1600	Return to company area; physical training
1700	March to dining hall (Dinner)
1800	Return to barracks; additional cleaning of barracks
1900	Study course material; clean rifle, shine boots
2100	Lights out

Fig. 3.5. Recruits pass through the serving line in the messhall

On Saturdays, the schedule is pretty much the same, except for a weekly inspection in ranks, followed by a full schedule of physical training and barracks maintenance. On Sundays, recruits get up an hour later than usual and can attend religious services in the base churches. After this they perform more study or maintenance work in the afternoon and evening.

First Week

During this week, your DI will introduce you to the fundamentals of Army life. You will learn about standard operating procedures (SOPs), which explain the proper way to do certain things, such as going on sick call (seeing a doctor), requesting an emergency leave, and receiving and sending mail. You will also be introduced to a daily program of physical exercise and military drill and ceremonies.

As part of orientation week you will be taught the basics about Army life. You will become familiar with the chain of command, salutes, uniforms, customs, and ceremonies; what you are expected to learn during your basic training; Army routine (over the next eight weeks you will live by a very detailed daily schedule); how to tell time the Army way; and Army terminology.

Fig. 3.6. A recruit emerges from the gas chamber

Second Week

You will continue your daily regimen of physical exercise and drill and ceremonies. In addition, your instruction will include other subject areas such as first aid, the military justice system, and the use of the gas mask as a defense against chemical warfare. During this week you will also be familiarized with the M-16 rifle, the basic infantry weapon, and other weapons, including the M-60 machine gun, the light antitank weapon (LAW), hand grenades, and the Claymore mine.

Third Week

The principal activity of the third and fourth weeks is M-16 rifle training. All recruits will "qualify" on the target range. The Army considers this to be one of the most important objectives of basic training and devotes more than 100 hours to it. Training on the M-16 rifle stresses four fundamentals: steady position for firing; proper aiming point for sights; breath control; and steady trigger squeeze. During the first four days of this training, you and the members of your company will bivouac (camp out) in tents near the rifle range.

Fig. 3.7. An instructor helps a recruit align his rifle during marksmanship training

While encamped, all recruits will be taught weapon safety and maintenance.

Fourth Week

The highlight of this week is M-16 qualification. Because M-16 rifle training is so intense, more than 90 percent of Army recruits qualify on their first try. Remedial training and retesting are given to those who fail in their initial try. During this week, while continuing your physical training and close-order drills, you will also handle, and in some cases fire, other weapons, such as the M-60 machine gun, the LAW, and the Claymore mine.

Fifth Week

This is the week you and your company will conduct a four-night tactical bivouac under simulated combat conditions. You will be taught how to construct a foxhole and other defensive positions, and how to conduct day and night patrolling. You

Fig. 3.8. An instructor works with a recruit in preparing an M-18 Claymore antipersonnel mine

Fig. 3.9. Preparing a daytime patrol

Fig. 3.10. Rope traversing on the Confidence Course

will also be tested on the Hand Grenade Assault Course, where you will be required to throw two live grenades.

Sixth Week

The major challenge you will face this week is the Infiltration Course, which is designed to simulate some of the obstacles (trenches, tree stumps, barbed wire, and so on) that a soldier might encounter on an actual battlefield. With its rope climb, cargo nets, and other challenges, this course will test your physical endurance. You will negotiate the course during both day and night. Your company will also go back to the rifle range during this week to fire at moving targets.

Seventh Week

You will return to the rifle range, where you will be taught to fire the M-16 rifle while moving on combat assaults. You will also negotiate the Confidence Course, which consists of scaling high walls, swinging on ropes, jumping from towers, and circumventing obstacles such as pits and trenches. Designed to build confidence in each soldier, this course also teaches trust and dependence on others.

Fig. 3.11. Practicing first aid

In addition to the Confidence Course, you will also be required to take a physical qualification test consisting of push-ups, sit-ups, and a 2-mile run. During this week you will perform additional drills and ceremonies.

Eighth Week

You and your company members must take and pass the End-of-Cycle Test. This is a hands-on test in which each soldier must satisfactorily perform 20 different tasks. Tasks include such things as treating a fellow soldier for shock, applying a field dressing to a wounded soldier, demonstrating the proper use of a gas mask, preparing and firing a Claymore mine, putting a LAW into action, demonstrating your map-reading ability, and moving a unit under simulated hostile fire.

After you complete this all-day test, you begin your out-processing from basic training and preparing for graduation.

BCT Graduation

Graduation is concluded as a formal military parade and review. Family and friends of graduates are invited to the cere-

Fig. 3.12. A platoon of graduating recruits passes the reviewing stand

monies. Each unit and soldier that has won honors during training is recognized. In basic training, your company will compete for a series of awards for athletic skill, scholastic achievement, military drill, inspections, and overall excellence. Flags awarded to winning training companies are carried in parades and reviews. The training company guidon (unit flag) may also carry athletic streamers. At the graduation review, any outstanding recruit awards or other special recognition certificates are presented.

Congratulations are in order when you complete basic training. You made it! You are no longer a recruit! It's been tough but you have met the challenge and are now ready for Advanced Individual Training (AIT), the next step in becoming a full-fledged soldier in the U.S. Army.

Advanced Individual Training (AIT)

After graduation, you and other members of your BCT company will go on to Advanced Individual Training. The type of AIT for soldiers depends on their enlistment agreement and the tests given during BCT.

Your AIT program will employ the most modern teaching and learning methods available. It will be a perfect blend of practical hands-on training on real equipment and classroom instruction by professionals in the field you have chosen. The quality of training you receive would be difficult to match in civilian life.

Your advanced individual skill training will build on your new assets: a new frame of reference on where you are going, new self-confidence, and new physical and mental abilities. Each AIT program is different and therefore cannot be described in detail here. Depending on the branch you have chosen, your AIT will generally range from seven to nine weeks, although some specialized MOS training can last longer.

II. Army Life

4. Being a Soldier

"Yours is the profession of arms, the will to win, the sure knowledge that in war there is no substitute for victory, that if you lose, the nation will be destroyed, that the very obsession of your public service must be duty, honor, country."
General Douglas MacArthur

What's It Like to Be a Soldier?

You have probably already talked to friends about joining the Army. Perhaps you have met soldiers, visited an Army recruiter, or spoken with relatives who once served in the Army. No doubt the answers you received helped form an opinion in your mind that was positive, or you would not be reading this book. Still, there is that big question in the back of your mind: "What is it *really* like to be a soldier?" The real expert on the latest details of all the Army programs is your Army recruiter, but this guide will also help you find some answers.

While there is much commonality in the experiences of all soldiers, especially in the first months of initial entry training, each soldier is soon on an individual path that makes the Army a unique experience for each. Jobs will be different, units will be different, locations will be different, and bosses will be different. The decisions you make along the way will steer you in your own direction and to different experiences than your fellow soldiers, yet you will share much with them.

Some of what you may have heard from others might make you think that as a soldier you will be nothing but an unimportant number, an unknown lost in a "green machine." *That's not true.* In fact, during your initial entry training you will probably receive more individual attention than you want! The Army *is* a big organization, but it is an organization of people working together as a team. Soldiers must be able to depend on one another, and it is the job of the Army instructors to insure that every soldier is fully qualified. In the Army you will meet and make the closest friends you will ever have, work together with them, and together share the Army adventure wherever it leads you.

Duty, Discipline, and Service

It is the sense of duty and discipline that sets the Army apart from civilian life. When you join the Army you are doing much more than hiring on for a job. You are joining the profession of arms—a profession of dedicated men and women who have taken an oath of service to their country. It also means you have voluntarily given up certain personal choices you had as a civilian. You become part of a special community with different rules, different patterns of behavior, even different clothes, food, and living conditions than your civilian friends.

One example will be your changes of location, or Permanent Changes of Station (PCS). Depending on the needs of the Army for your skills, you will probably move several times, and be told where and when to go. Regular moves from one Army post to another are a fact of life for all active-duty soldiers. Many career Army people spend much of their active-duty years on installations that are self-contained, small cities, where everything—including the post exchange or PX (shopping malls), the commissary (supermarket), recreational facilities, theater, and hospital—is provided by the Army. (Many Army families do, however, live off-post and are also part of their civilian communities.)

Much of your time will not be your own. Mandatory inspections and formations occur regularly in the Army, regardless of one's rank or job. Extra duty, such as working overtime or on weekends without additional pay, is also common. As you find out in basic training, physical fitness is very important throughout your Army service. Soldiers spend several mornings each week on calisthenics training before work.

If you are assigned to one of the Army's tactical units, you can expect to spend a great deal of time in field-exercise training at your home station, in other parts of the United States, and overseas. For example, if you are assigned to the 82d Airborne Division in Fort Bragg, North Carolina, you have a large military installation in which to train, but you may also participate in rapid-deployment alerts, where you board aircraft at 0200 (2:00 A.M.) and conduct a training airborne assault many hours later in a foreign country.

If you are assigned to one of the armored, mechanized, or light infantry divisions, you can expect to be sent for training with your unit at the National Training Center (NTC) in California's Mojave Desert. Light infantry, Airborne, and Ranger units also receive special training throughout the year at Fort Polk's Joint Readiness Training Center (JRTC) in Louisiana. Both the NTC and the JRTC are in isolated areas with harsh terrain.

Sometime during your Army career, you will probably have the opportunity to participate in war games with troops from foreign countries. Although many of these annual exercises are being reduced in scope, in years past thousands of soldiers were sent to Germany, Korea, and Alaska to conduct simulated combat against aggressor forces. These exercises, often conducted in the snow and rain, are designed to be as realistic as possible, with the training day lasting up to 20 hours, 7 days a week.

It is standard operating procedure (SOP) in some divisions to have each brigade within the division rotate being "on call" for a specified time. During this period, soldiers must stay close enough so that they can report, in battle gear, within a short time. If they leave the post, they have to call in periodically to make sure that a "call-out" order hasn't been issued.

Although they don't talk much about it, the old-fashioned values of honesty, courage, honor, loyalty, obedience, selflessness, and duty are very important to good soldiers. These values lie at the heart of the soldier's profession. This is what "service" means.

The Soldier's Creed

"I am an American soldier. I am a member of the United States Army—a protector of the greatest nation on earth. Because I am proud of the uniform I wear, I will always act in ways creditable to the military service and the nation it is sworn to guard.

"I am proud of my own organization. I will do all I can to make it the finest unit in the Army. I will be loyal to those under whom I serve. I will do my full part to carry out orders and instructions given me or my unit.

"As a soldier, I realize that I am a member of a time-honored profession—that I am doing my share to keep alive the principles of freedom for which my country stands. No matter what the situation I am in, I will never do anything, for pleasure, profit, or personal safety, which will disgrace my uniform, my unit, or my country. I will use every means I have, even beyond the line of duty, to restrain my Army comrades from actions disgraceful to themselves and to the uniform.

"I am proud of my country and its flag. I will try to make the people of this nation proud of the service I represent, for *I am an American soldier.*"

(TRADOC Pam 600-4)

Rank and Pay Grade

The Army is formally structured using specific ranks. Every soldier has a rank from the highest to the lowest. You will receive your first rank the day you join the Army. It is your official military title, and it also determines the amount of pay you receive. Each rank has a different level of pay called a "pay grade." A new soldier just entering the Army usually begins with the rank of Private (PV1) and the pay grade of E-1 (Enlisted Grade 1). Promotion to Private (PV2) with pay grade E-2 usually occurs after successful completion of six months' service.

Seniority between soldiers of equal rank is determined by length of time in that rank—the soldier the longest time in the respective rank is the senior. When the date of rank is the same, then the soldier longest in the Army is the senior. A chart showing the Army's ranks and pay grades is in Chapter 14.

Make no mistake about it—the Army is competitive and privileges are earned through experience and successful performance. There are several programs for accelerated promotion. The promotions and rank you earn will be shown on your uniform as stripes for all to see. It is something to wear with pride. Respect and courtesy are shown to those who have earned it. Whatever the skill in which you specialize, you will be challenged both physically and mentally to be promoted as far as possible—to be the best you can be. A more detailed discussion of promotions is in Chapter 14.

Pay and Leave

A soldier's pay is determined by Congress. Each year a pay scale is approved that directs the amount each pay grade receives. In most years there are pay raises, but not always. In addition to a soldier's basic salary, several other types of additional pay, called "allowances," are provided. Which ones you will receive depends on your particular situation. For example, a married soldier who is unable to find government-provided housing receives additional money to help pay for civilian housing for his family.

Soldiers who perform special types of dangerous duty such as parachuting, underwater diving, and disposal of explosives receive additional money called hazardous duty pay. There are also programs to pay additional money to a soldier for special skills such as speaking another language. In addition to pay and allowances, there are many other benefits a soldier and his dependents receive. Some of these programs are discussed briefly in this guide, and more information can be provided by your recruiter.

A soldier has the choice of being paid once or twice a month. The money is deposited by the Army directly into a bank account of the soldier's choice. Every time a soldier is paid a statement of payment is provided called a Leave and Earnings Statement (LES). As the name LES implies, it also includes information on the number of days of paid vacation, or leave, a soldier has earned. A soldier earns 2½ days of leave per month, or 30 days for an entire year. A detailed explanation of the LES is in Chapter 14. The current pay charts are in Appendix D.

Appearance and Clothing

The Army places a great deal of importance on the appearance and dress of its soldiers. As a uniformed service the state of discipline and morale in the Army is judged, in part, by the appearance of its soldiers and the manner in which they wear their uniform. The proper manner of wearing uniforms and other items of apparel such as eyeglasses, earrings, and jewelry is described in Army Regulations.

Soldiers wear a variety of military clothing depending on the nature of the duties they are doing and on the weather. A complete set of appropriate Army clothing will be issued when you arrive for training. The majority of time during your training you will be dressed in one of the military work uniforms. Formerly called "fatigues," these uniforms are called Battle Dress Uniforms or BDUs. The most common BDU in the states is the woodland camouflage pattern. Another variation available is the tan-brown desert pattern, similar to that worn in Operation Desert Storm. There are also white snow suits for winter and arctic camouflage.

One of the uniforms you will receive is the Army Green Service Uniform or "Army Greens." This uniform is worn during most on-duty non-field occasions, for official travel, and off-duty times. There are several combinations of shirt, tie, and coat that can be made with the Green Service uniform. These are categorized as Class A or Class B uniforms. You may also hear soldiers, both male and female, refer to their Greens coat as a "blouse." This is the old Army term that was used to distinguish it from the overcoat. More information on Army uniforms is in Chapter 6.

If their commander permits, off-duty soldiers may wear civilian clothing. Your position as a soldier, however, makes outrageous or extremes of clothing styles inappropriate. Whether you like it or not, on duty and off a soldier represents the Army. Everyone a soldier meets judges the Army by what they see. Look sharp, and keep your Army's image sharp!

Army Customs and Traditions

Customs and traditions are an inseparable part of the Army and are part of what distinguishes it from civilian life and the other military services. From the moment a soldier enters the Army, traditions are a part of the soldier's life. The uniform, the hand salute, the names of ranks, places, and things, how soldiers address one another, courtesies rendered the national flag and superiors, and even the way to tell time are all part of tradition. Some traditions go back to ancient armies and are common to military services around the world. Others are unique to your Army.

A new soldier will find it confusing at first, like learning a different language; however, within a few weeks it will all become familiar routine. Much of your instruction during your first days in basic training will concern those customs and traditions you need to know. This guide also provides a good introduction to some of the basics discussed below:

Chain of Command

The Army has an established sequence of commanders from the President of the United States as commander in chief down through the subordinate commanders to the enlisted soldiers leading the smallest Army units. This is called the chain of command. Figure 4.1 outlines this chain so you can understand it. As you can see, the chain is slightly different while you are in training, but the concept is the same.

Saluting

One of the most basic military courtesies and signs of respect a soldier performs is to salute the national flag or a higher-ranking officer. Enlisted men and NCOs must salute all officers, and officers salute all higher-ranking officers. Salutes are initiated by the junior person and answered by the senior. It is a sign of mutual respect and courtesy between members of the same profession. There are different ways to salute depending whether you are carrying a rifle or not. Instructions for proper saluting are presented in Chapter 29.

4-1: Chains of Command

BCT Company	Regular Unit
Commander in Chief	Commander in Chief
Secretary of Defense	Secretary of Defense
Secretary of the Army	Secretary of the Army
Army Chief of Staff	Army Chief of Staff
Post Commanding General	Theater Commander
Brigade Commander	Army Group Commander
Battalion Commander	Corps Commander
Company Commander	Division Commander
First Sergeant	Brigade Commander
Drill Sergeant	Battalion Commander
	Company Commander
	Platoon Leader
	Squad Leader

Honors to the Flag

The American flag is honored twice every day on Army posts around the world—once in the morning at "reveille" when the flag is raised and then again at "retreat," or the end of the day, when the flag is lowered. Reveille starts a soldier's work day and retreat normally ends it. Traditional bugle calls are played for each ceremony. On most posts all outdoor activity ceases and persons outside stop and face the direction of the flag while the ceremonies take place. You will very quickly learn to recognize the bugle calls for each. During the retreat ceremony two bugle calls are used. The first is "Retreat" followed by "To the Colors." A cannon will frequently be fired to signal that the flag is being lowered. Sometimes the national anthem is played.

Bugle Calls

In the early days of the Army the bugle acted as the soldier's clock, and as the commander's loudspeaker. It was used to tell the soldiers in a unit what duties they should perform in the garrison and on the battlefield. A system of different calls was used that a soldier learned by heart. Today the tradition of bugle calls is continued in a much reduced manner such as the ceremonial calls for reveille and retreat discussed previously. In addition, depending on the post, you will hear the familiar "Taps," which is the last call of the day, "Mess Call," which announces meal time, and others.

Army Time

The Army uses a 24-hour-per-day system of telling time. This is to prevent confusion between, for example, 6:00 A.M. and 6:00 P.M. As shown in Figure 4.2 hours of the day are numbered from 1 to 24. The time is expressed as a four-digit number, for example "1403." The first two digits show the hour and the last two the minutes. The morning hours go from immediately after midnight (0001) to 12:00 noon (1200). The afternoon hours go from immediately after noon (1201) to midnight (2400). The time between midnight and 1:00 A.M. is shown only as minutes, for example, five minutes after midnight is 0005, not 2405 hours. When writing, the word "hours" is frequently used to prevent confusion with other numbers. When speaking, the word "hours" is not normally used. Thus, for 0700 hours a soldier would say "zero seven hundred" or for 2145 hours say "twenty-one forty-five."

Dates

The military express dates in the specific sequence of day, month, and year. You will normally also see the dates abbreviated so that June 5, 1994, is expressed as 5 JUN 94. The Army has a set of three-letter abbreviations for the months that you will learn.

Army Terms

As mentioned earlier, the Army has its own manner of speaking. The words come from traditional military words, from foreign words or expressions American soldiers have picked up over the years, and from abbreviations of titles, longer words, or series of words. An Army base, no matter what its official title may be, is usually referred to by soldiers as a "post."

Fig. 4.2. Army time

Weapons systems frequently retain the name given them by the contractor making the system, or the Army may select a name. For example the Army has a tradition of naming tanks after famous generals such as Sherman, Patton, and Abrams. Soldiers also make up their own words or slang such as "GI" or "jeep."

In several cases a different name is used for the same size unit. For example a "company" in the infantry is called a "troop" in the cavalry and a "battery" in the artillery. There are too many terms to try to define them all in this guide, and new ones are added almost daily. As many as possible are used in this guide so you will become familiar with them. There is also a glossary of selected Army terms in Appendix I.

Titles

The chart at Figure 6.1 shows the rank insignia and official titles for the Army. In speaking to a soldier, however, the full rank title is not always used. Both ranks of Private are called "Private." Sergeants up to the rank of First Sergeant are all addressed as "Sergeant," or if they are Drill Sergeants as "Drill Sergeant." First Sergeants, the senior NCO in a company/troop/battery, is called by the full title "First Sergeant." The senior NCO in a battalion or larger unit is a Command Sergeant Major, who is also addressed by full title. With officers, both Second and First Lieutenants are addressed as "Lieutenant." Lieutenant Colonels and Colonels are addressed as "Colonel." Normally only warrent officers and officers are addressed as "Sir."

Unit Traditions

Some of the strongest bonds that develop in a soldier are the ones to the unit and to the other soldiers in it. It is a feeling that is impossible to explain to someone who has never experienced it. The pride and sense of belonging to a special group develops a deep loyalty. Many units express their pride in unique ways. Some units wear special badges, headgear, or other emblems on their uniforms. They greet one another with a unit motto, nickname, or slogan. Soldiers in the 7th Cavalry battalions say "Garry Owen" when they salute, while paratroopers will say "Airborne, all the way."

Soldiers of corps, divisions, separate brigades, regiments and other units are authorized to wear a cloth shoulder-sleeve insignia (SSI) on the left shoulder of their uniforms. Soldiers who serve with such a unit in a war zone are authorized to also wear the SSI of that unit on their right shoulder. In addition soldiers may wear small regimental insignia. These traditions reflect the high spirit of the units and the pride of their members. Soldiers in a unit learn to stick together, look out for one another, and to help out when another needs assistance.

For a better understanding of other Army traditions, it is recommended you go back and read again the short history of the Army provided earlier in this chapter. Many unit traditions come out of the experiences of soldiers in the past.

Family Life

A number of soldiers enter the Army already married or get married soon after joining. In addition to the money for non-government housing, the Army also provides many other benefits for a soldier's family members. On many Army posts family housing for junior soldiers is very scarce, and military families frequently must live off post in the civilian community. Of course all of the post facilities remain available no matter where you live. A discussion of these facilities is in Chapter 14.

It is the nature of the Army that soldiers must be frequently separated from their families. These may be short separations for only a day or two, or in the case of major exercises or crises for longer periods of time. When separation occurs there are support organizations, both formal and informal, to assist the family members left at home in coping with the situation and in maintaining as normal a life as possible. Each post is organized differently, but normally there is an Army Community Service office to help. In addition a soldier's unit will try to provide basic guidance and support. The Army recently started a test program called Army Family Team Building to assist Army families in being more self-reliant. If you have a family with you, you should find out what is available as soon as you arrive at a post. There are many agencies ready to help, but it is your responsibility to insure your family will be able to properly cope with your absence.

Military Training

While on active duty, you will have many opportunities for different types of training. Training is the Army's top priority because it is the cornerstone of combat readiness. A "battle focus" concept is used to derive peacetime training requirements from wartime missions. These requirements guide the planning, execution, and assessment of each Army organization's training program. The goal is to ensure that soldiers train as they are going to fight.

During your Army service, you will progress through various training stages. First is your Initial Entry Training (IET)—Basic Combat Training (BCT) and Advanced Individual Training (AIT)—that allows you to perform in your specific military occupational specialty (MOS). IET also prepares you for training at your first duty station.

Because a soldier needs to know different skills at different ranks, the Army has organized the training of individual soldiers into various skill levels. IET, combined with subsequent training in a unit, qualifies a soldier at Skill Level 1—those skills, proficiencies, and abilities typically needed to perform efficiently up through the rank of corporal or specialist. The next four skill levels are taught through the Noncommissioned Officer Education System (NCOES). Skill Level 2 concerns sergeant; Skill Level 3 staff sergeant; Skill Level 4 platoon sergeant; and Skill Level 5 master sergeants through command sergeant major. To make a promotion a soldier needs to be constantly preparing for the next higher skill level.

Army Jobs

There are more than two hundred fifty specific jobs, called Military Occupational Specialties (MOS) in the Army. These include everything done in the Army from finance accounting to helicopter repair. The similar MOSs are organized into thirty-one groups called Career Management Fields (CMF). When you enlist, you are guaranteed training in the MOS you choose from those for which you are qualified. A listing of the MOSs by CMF is at Appendix E.

5. Personnel Matters

Enlisted Service Records

During your Army service, there will be two important service records that will be kept on you: your Military Personnel Records Jacket (MPRJ) and your Individual Training Record (ITR). Your MPRJ will include such documents as:

- Enlistment and reenlistment contracts.
- Assignment orders to permanent duty stations or temporary duty to military or civilian schools.
- Orders assigning you a military occupational specialty (MOS).
- Initial entry training.
- Promotion or reduction orders.
- Performance ratings.
- Awards or decorations.
- Letters of appreciation or commendation.
- Emergency data, such as your next of kin.
- Servicemen's Group Life Insurance coverage you may carry.
- Certificate of release or discharge from active duty.

Your ITR reflects Basic, Advanced, and One Station Unit Training that you receive. This information is placed inside your MPRJ. The purpose of the ITR is to record the training performance and standards achieved by soldiers.

The following information, as a minimum, will be included in your ITR:

- Weapons qualification.
- Hand grenade qualification.
- Army physical fitness test results.
- Code of Conduct and Law of Land Warfare class performance.

Your service records are very important both during and after your Army service. One of your unit's personnel specialists can tell you the procedures for reviewing them to make sure that they are accurate and answer any questions you may have.

Career Management Fields

The use of CMFs allows the Army to better manage a soldier's assignments, schooling, and advancement. The number and specific MOSs comprising a CMF change as new equipment and technology are added to the Army.

In managing the career of enlisted soldiers, Army personnel specialists' objectives are to:

- Ensure efficient use of soldiers in accomplishing the Army's basic mission to fight and win in combat.
- Place soldiers in positions that require skills, knowledge, and abilities compatible with their MOS.
- Strengthen and broaden a soldier's MOS qualifications and prepare him or her for career progression, greater responsibility, and a diversity of assignments (AR 600-200, p. 14).
- See Appendix E for the current CMFs for active duty soldiers.

Promotion

Advancing in your Army career means increased pay, greater responsibilities, more status, and recognition. The Army is a pyramidical, or hierarchical, organization. Everybody has a boss immediately above him or her in the pyramid. As a beginning enlisted person, you will be way down the pyramid, but remember, one advantage of the Army promotion system is that everyone has an equal opportunity to achieve higher rank. In the Army, it doesn't matter whom you know, where you come from, or your family's social status. In the Army the only criterion used in getting ahead is your character as a soldier and how well you perform your duty.

Army Regulation 600-20, *Enlisted Ranks Personnel* establishes five objectives of the Army promotion system:

- Fill authorized enlisted spaces with qualified soldiers.
- Provide for career progression and rank that is in line with a soldier's potential.
- Recognize the best qualified soldier who will attract and retain the highest caliber soldier for a career in the Army.
- Preclude promoting the soldier who is not productive or not best qualified.
- Provide an equitable system for all soldiers.

Your rank in the Army describes the level of achievement you have attained. Promotions are important to every soldier. The primary qualification for promotion in the Army is in mastering the skills needed to perform the duties in the new grade. Technical expertise in the soldier's field of specialization is a consideration in the promotion process, but personal traits, professionalism as a soldier, and leadership are also important. Before you can expect to be promoted, you must be highly proficient in your present grade and level of responsibility.

Active Army enlisted soldiers normally begin their service as Private (PV1) pay grade E-1 and are advanced to the rank of Private (PV2) pay grade E-2 when they have satisfactorily completed six months of service. The promotion from Private (PV1) to Private (PV2) is probably the easiest in the Army. Unless a soldier has been placed in non-promotable status for some reason, this first promotion is almost automatic. Promotion to Private First Class (PFC/E-3) normally comes after twelve months in the Army and four months in the pay grade of E-3. Criteria for promotion to Corporal (CPL/E-4) or Specialist (SP4/E-4) is twenty-four months in the Army and six months in grade of E-3. These promotions are on the authority of the unit commander. There are programs that provide faster than normal, or "fast-track," promotion. Your Army recruiter has the details on these programs.

Soldiers being considered for promotion to the rank of Sergeant (SGT/E-5) or Staff Sergeant (SSG/E-6) must appear before a promotion board, compete for promotion only in their MOS, and meet certain educational requirements. These are completion of the eighth grade (or an equivalency test) or higher for promotion to Sergeant. Promotion to Staff Sergeant, requires a high school diploma (or equivalency test) and associate or higher degree. Promotion to Sergeant and Staff Sergeant is made using a promotion point system. The Army determines how many Sergeants and Staff Sergeants in each MOS. Based on this need the promotion point cut-off scores are determined, authorizing commanders to promote the best qualified in each MOS. Time in grade and time in service for promotion to Sergeant are normally eight months in pay grade E-4 and three years of service in the primary MOS. For promotion to Staff Sergeant, a soldier must have served ten months in pay grade E-5 and have seven years of service.

A centralized promotion system is used for the promotion to Sergeant First Class (SFC/E7), Master Sergeant (MSG/E-8), and Sergeant Major (E-9). Eligibility for promotion to these ranks is based on date of rank. In addition, promotion to Master Sergeant and Sergeant Major requires a set length of cumulative enlisted service. The criteria for promotion for each grade are announced by Headquarters, Department of the Army (HQDA) prior to each selection board.

Promotion Board

Boards are the standard method of the Army for the selection of the best-qualified individuals for promotions and some awards. In addition to promotion boards, local boards are held to recommend soldiers for Soldier or NCO of the Month and to attend schools. Boards are convened at HQDA to consider senior NCOs for promotion, schools, separation, and assignments.

Every board is different. In addition to reviewing a soldier's records and qualifications, many boards will interview candidates and ask professional questions. Questions normally fall into three broad areas: general military subjects, MOS job/skill knowledge, and current events. Refresher study on these topics and staying abreast of what is being reported in the newspapers and professional publications as the *Army Times* will help your appearance before the board to be a successful one.

6. Uniforms

The reference for Army uniforms is Army Regulation 670-1, *Wear and Appearance of Army Uniforms*. It will provide you with the necessary information regarding commonly worn Army uniforms.

The Army is a uniformed service wherein discipline is judged, in part, by the manner in which the individual soldier wears the prescribed uniform. Uniforms are to be properly fitted, clean, serviceable, and pressed as necessary.

Soldiers must project a military image that leaves no doubt that they live by a common military standard and are responsible to military order and discipline.

There are a number of uniforms worn by soldiers, including a variety of maternity uniforms. Some of the more common uniforms you will see are the Army green uniform (figures 6.3 through 6.4) and the battle dress uniform (BDU) (figure 6.5). Other Army uniforms you will see are shown in figures 6.6 through 6.10. For details of branch colors and scarves, see Chapter 17, table 17.1.

Insignia of Rank and Branch

Army insignia of rank for officers, warrant officers, and enlisted personnel are shown in figure 6.1. When wearing the Army green uniform, officers wear their rank insignia on the shoulder loop of their jacket, and enlisted personnel wear their's on the sleeve of their jacket. Branch insignia is worn by both officers (see Appendix G) and enlisted personnel (see figure 6.3) on the lapel of their Army green uniform jacket. Enlisted soldiers do not wear their branch insignia on the collar of their BDU; however, officers do.

On the BDU uniform, officers wear their rank insignia on the right collar and branch insignia on the left collar. Enlisted soldiers wear their rank insignia on both collars.

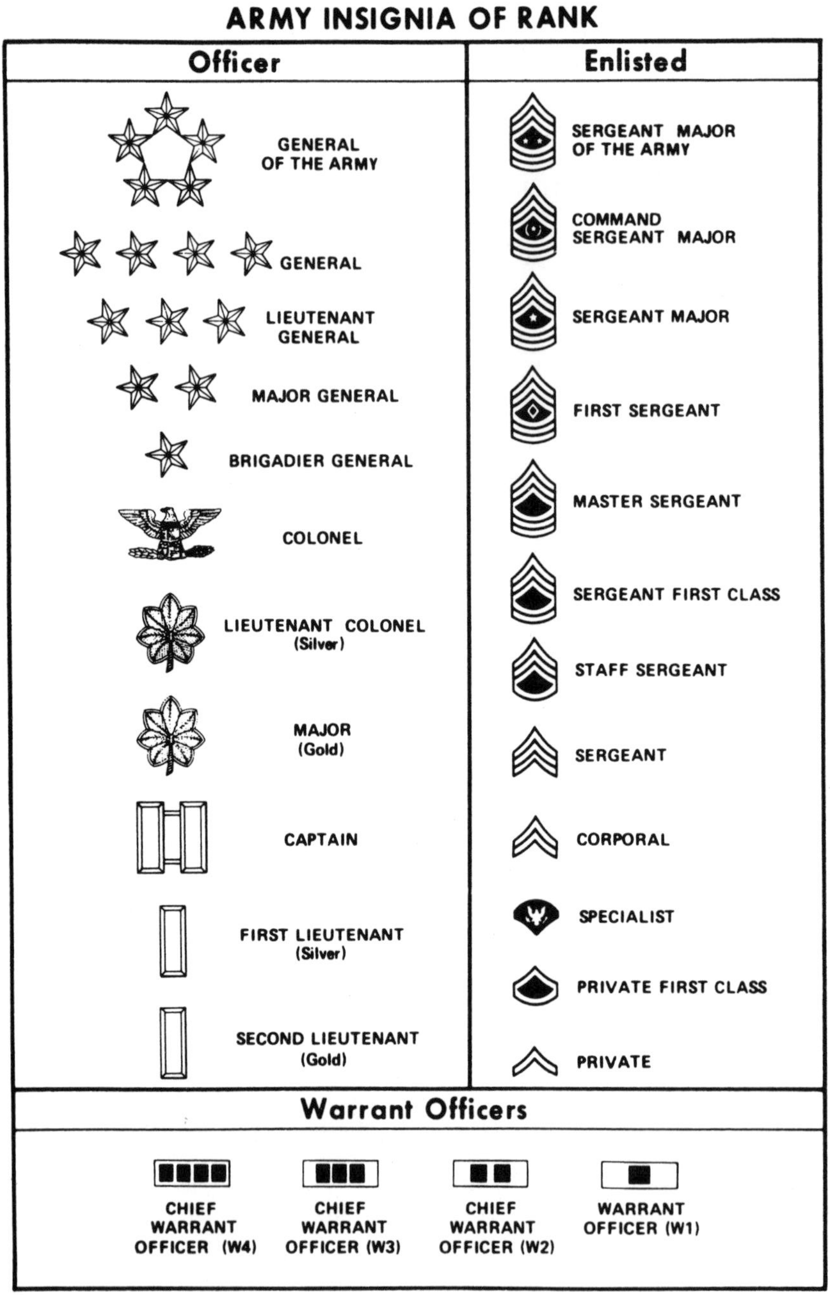
ARMY INSIGNIA OF RANK
Officer
Enlisted
GENERAL OF THE ARMY
GENERAL
LIEUTENANT GENERAL
MAJOR GENERAL
BRIGADIER GENERAL
COLONEL
LIEUTENANT COLONEL (Silver)
MAJOR (Gold)
CAPTAIN
FIRST LIEUTENANT (Silver)
SECOND LIEUTENANT (Gold)
SERGEANT MAJOR OF THE ARMY
COMMAND SERGEANT MAJOR
SERGEANT MAJOR
FIRST SERGEANT
MASTER SERGEANT
SERGEANT FIRST CLASS
STAFF SERGEANT
SERGEANT
CORPORAL
SPECIALIST
PRIVATE FIRST CLASS
PRIVATE
Warrant Officers
CHIEF WARRANT OFFICER (W4)
CHIEF WARRANT OFFICER (W3)
CHIEF WARRANT OFFICER (W2)
WARRANT OFFICER (W1)

Fig. 6.1.

Headgear

There are several types of service caps, hats, berets (headgear), and helmets authorized for wear by soldiers.

The two most commonly worn caps are the service cap and garrison cap. Both are dark green to match the Army green uniform. The service cap for males has a flat round top and is sometimes called the "flying saucer." The service cap for females is a different design. Generals and other officers over the rank of captain have gold oak leaves embroidered on the visors of their service caps. All other officers and soldiers have black leather visors. Different-colored service caps are worn with different uniforms. For example, a dark blue service cap is worn with the Army dress blue uniform. The cap insignia with an American eagle is worn on the front, but the design is different for officers, warrant officers, and enlisted soldiers.

The garrison cap for male and female enlisted soldiers is similar in form, and insignia on it are worn in the same manner. The garrison cap is sometimes called the "overseas cap" because it is easily folded and stored and is most frequently worn when traveling. The garrison cap of officers has a narrow gold (generals) or gold and black piping or band on its edges. Officers wear the insignia of their rank on the left side of the cap, while enlisted soldiers wear the Distinctive Unit Insignia (DUI) of their unit. Figure 6.2 illustrates some of the Army's headgear.

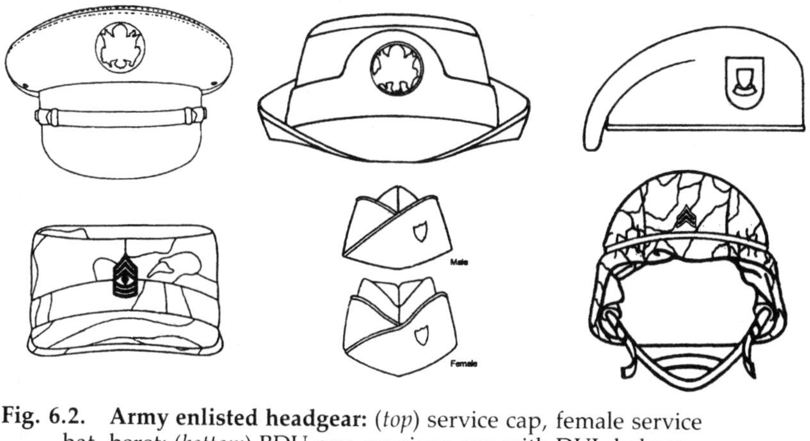

Fig. 6.2. Army enlisted headgear: (*top*) service cap, female service hat, beret; (*bottom*) BDU cap, garrison cap with DUI, helmet

Other headgear authorized for Army personnel include the following:

Black beret (Rangers)
Green beret (Special Forces)
Maroon beret (Airborne)
Drill sergeant hat
Female white or blue service hat

Service Stripes

Enlisted personnel wear gold-colored service stripes, or "hashmarks," on the outside bottom half of the left sleeve of the Army green uniform jacket. Each stripe signifies completion of three years of active federal service, active reserve service, or combination thereof. Service need not have been continuous, and a tenth stripe is authorized after 29½ years.

Overseas Service Bars

The overseas service bar is a gold-colored bar worn on the outside bottom half of the right sleeve of the Army green uniform coat. One bar is authorized for each six months of active Army service outside the United States during periods specifically designated by the Army. These periods include World War II, Korean War, Vietnam War, Dominican Republic, Laos, Cambodia, and the Persian Gulf. There will no doubt be other periods designated in the future.

Shoulder Sleeve Insignia

Current Organization

Full-color shoulder sleeve insignia (SSI) of an individual's current organization are worn centered on the left sleeve ½ inch below the top of the shoulder seam on Army green coats. Subdued versions are worn on the BDU uniform. SSI are frequently called "shoulder patches" by soldiers.

Former Wartime Service

At an individual's option, the SSI worn in wartime service may be worn on the right sleeve of all Army green uniform coats. A subdued version may be worn on the field and work uniform coats and shirts.

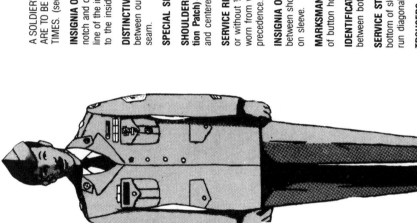

GARRISON CAP—Worn with front vertical crease of cap centered on forehead in a straight line with nose. Cap will be slightly tilted to the right, but will not touch ear.

BLACK FOUR-IN-HAND TIE

US INSIGNIA—Approximately 1″ above notch and centered on collar with centerline of insignia bisecting the notch and parallel to the inside edge of the lapel.

SHOULDER SLEEVE INSIGNIA/FORMER WARTIME ORGANIZATION—½″ down from shoulder seam and centered.

UNIT AWARD EMBLEM—centered ⅛″ above pocket.

NAMEPLATE—on flap of pocket centered between top of button and top of pocket.

INSIGNIA OF GRADE—same as other side.

OVERSEA BARS (Hershey Bars)—4″ above and parallel to the bottom of the sleeve and centered.

IDENTIFICATION TAGS (Dog Tags)—Worn when engaged in field training, when traveling in aircraft, and when outside CONUS.

BELT—1¼″ black web or woven elastic web with a black or brass tip. The tip will pass through the buckle to the wearer's left; the brass tip only will extend beyond the buckle.

BUCKLE—1¾″ x 2¼″ oval shaped, plain-faced, solid brass.

Army Green Uniform

A SOLDIER'S HAIR, SIDEBURNS, AND MUSTACHE ARE TO BE KEPT IN A NEAT MANNER AT ALL TIMES. (see AR 670–1 for guidelines.)

INSIGNIA OF BRANCH—Approximately 1″ above notch and centered on collar with the centerline of the insignia bisecting the notch and parallel to the inside edge of the collar.

DISTINCTIVE UNIT INSIGNIA (crest)—Centered between outside edge of button and shoulder seam.

SPECIAL SKILL BADGE—¼″ above ribbons.

SHOULDER SLEEVE INSIGNIA (Current Organization Patch)—½″ down from shoulder seam and centered.

SERVICE RIBBONS—⅛″ above pocket with or without ⅛″ space between rows and will be worn from wearer's right to left in order of precedence.

INSIGNIA OF GRADE (Stripes)—centered halfway between shoulder seam and elbow and centered on sleeve.

MARKSMANSHIP BADGE—centered between top of button hole and top of pocket.

IDENTIFICATION BADGE—centered on pocket between bottom of flap and bottom of pocket.

SERVICE STRIPES (Hash Marks)—4″ above bottom of sleeve and centered on sleeve (stripes run diagonally).

TROUSERS—will reach top of instep (may have a slight break in front), and cut diagonally to midpoint between top of heel and top of shoe at the rear.

Fig. 6.3. Army green uniform for male personnel

BERET—Worn tilted slightly to back of head with insignia centered on the forehead and not forward of forehead hairline (insignia will be placed 3/4″ from bottom edge of Beret front, parallel to floor and centered on eyelet).

US INSIGNIA—Bottom of disk centered approximately 5/8″ up from notch with center line of insignia parallel to inside edge of lapel.

SHOULDER SLEEVE INSIGNIA—FORMER WARTIME ORGANIZATION—1/2″ down from shoulder seam and centered.

UNIT AWARD EMBLEM—Centered with bottom edge 1/8″ above top of nameplate.

INSIGNIA OF GRADE (STRIPES)—Centered halfway between shoulder seam and elbow and centered on sleeve.

NAMEPLATE—Centered 1-2″ above top edge of top button.

OVERSEA SERVICE BARS (Hershey Bars)—4″ above and parallel to bottom of sleeve and centered.

SKIRT—Not more than 1″ above or 2″ below crease in back of knee.

STOCKINGS—Unpatterned/non-pastel materials of sheer or semi-sheer, with or without seams.

PUMPS—Black Service, untrimmed, closed toe heel, heel 1″ to 3″ and sole thickness 1/2″ max.

IDENTIFICATION TAGS (Dog Tags)—Worn when engaged in field training, when traveling in aircraft, and when outside CONUS.

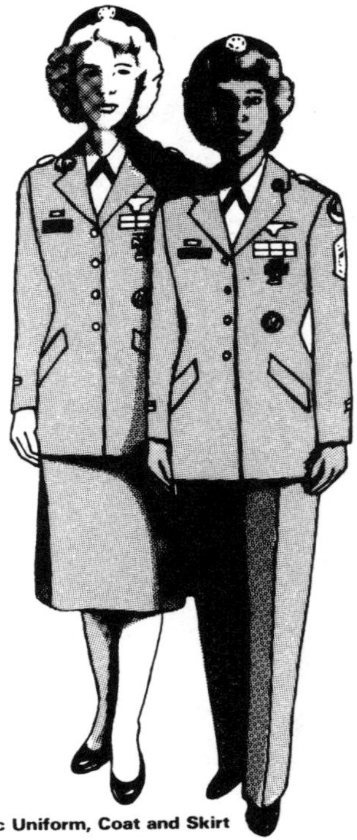

Classic Uniform, Coat and Skirt

Classic Uniform, Coat and Slacks

INSIGNIA OF BRANCH—Same as US Insignia.

DISTINCTIVE UNIT INSIGNIA (Crest)—Centered between outside of button and shoulder seam.

SPECIAL SKILL BADGE—1/4″ above ribbons.

SHOULDER SLEEVE INSIGNIA (current organization)—1/2″ down from shoulder seam and centered.

SERVICE RIBBONS—Centered with bottom line positioned parallel to bottom edge of nameplate.

MARKSMANSHIP BADGE—Centered parallel to top edge of top button 1/4″ below service ribbons. (Slight adjustment to conform to individual figure differences authorized.)

IDENTIFICATION BADGE—Centered with top edge of badge parallel to top edge of third button from top.

SERVICE STRIPES (Hash marks)—4″ above bottom of sleeve and centered (stripes run diagonally).

SOCKS—Optional plain black cotton or cotton nylon may be worn with black oxford shoes or Jodhpur boots, when worn with slacks.

SHOES—Black Oxford leather (nonpatent) with maximum of 3 eyelets, closed toe and heel (heel no higher than 2″).

JEWELRY: EARRINGS—Screw-on or post-type on optional basis with service, dress, and mess uniforms only.
NECKLACE: A purely religious medal on a chain is authorized as long as neither is exposed.
A WRIST WATCH AND NOT MORE THAN TWO RINGS ARE AUTHORIZED.

Fig. 6.4. Army green uniform for female personnel

HAIR—Neatly groomed and will not present an extreme, ragged, or unkempt appearance. Hair will not extend below bottom edge of collar, nor be cut to appear unfeminine. Styles will not interfere with the proper wearing of military headgear.

INSIGNIA OF GRADE—Subdued pin-on, or sew-on, will be centered on each collar bisecting the collar 1″ from the point.

SHOULDER SLEEVE INSIGNIA—FORMER WARTIME ORGANIZATION—½″ down from shoulder seam and centered (subdued only).

INSIGNIA NAMETAPE—Centered, immediately above and parallel to top of pocket.

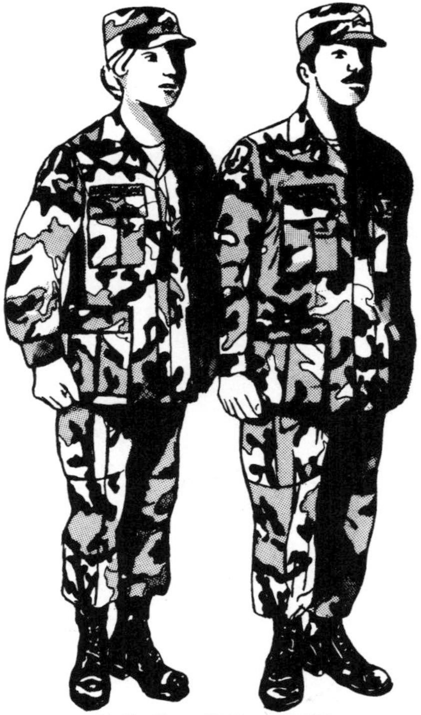

Battle Dress Uniform (BDU)

CAMOUFLAGE CAP—Straight on head so that cap band creates a straight line around the head parallel to the ground. (subdued insignia of grade ONLY and centered from top to bottom, right to left)

UNDERSHIRT—Army Brown or Green is authorized.

SHOULDER SLEEVE INSIGNIA—Current Organization—½″ down from shoulder seam and centered. (subdued only)

'US ARMY' DISTINGUISHING INSIGNIA—Centered immediately above and parallel to top edge of pocket.

BLACK BOOTS—Clean and shined at all times (no patent leather).

SOCKS—ONLY Olive Green, shade 408, is authorized for wear with combat or organizational boots.

BLACK BUCKLE & BLACK TIPPED BELT ONLY COMBINATION AUTHORIZED.

Fig. 6.5. Battle dress uniform (BDU)

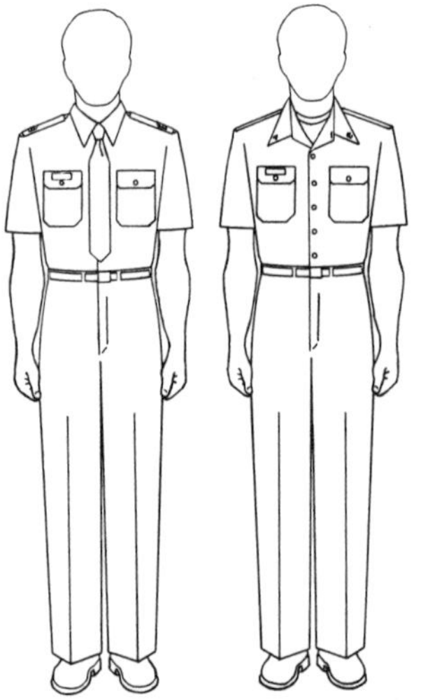

Fig. 6.6. Class B Army green uniform for male personnel

Combat Leader's Identification

The combat leader's identification insignia is a green cloth loop, 1⅝ inches wide, worn in the middle of both shoulder loops of the Army green uniform coat and cold weather coat (field jackets). The specific leaders in units authorized to wear

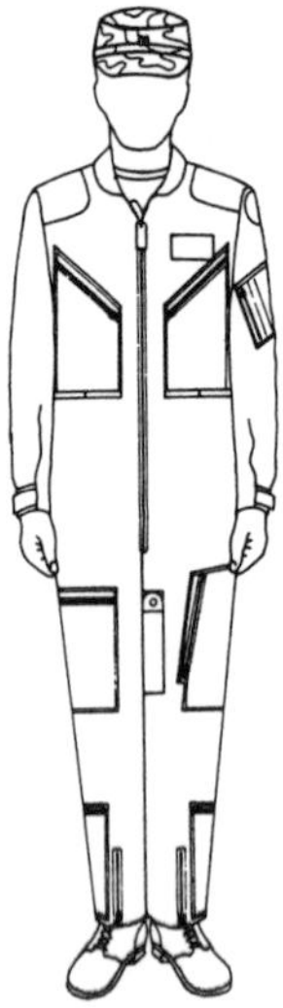

Fig. 6.7. Flight uniform

Fig. 6.8. Cold weather uniform

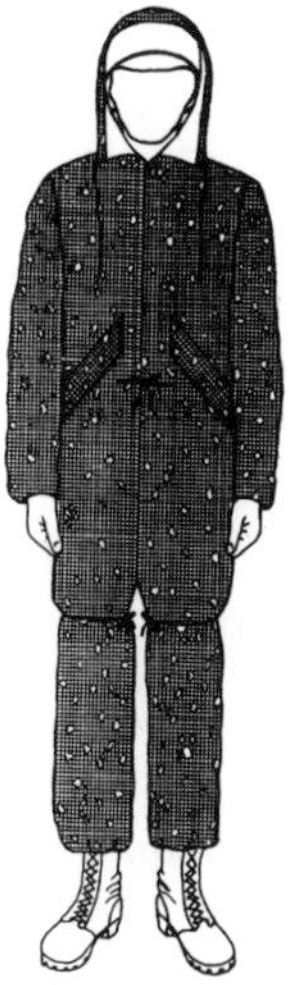

Fig. 6.9. Desert battle dress (night) uniform

the combat leader's identification insignia are commanders, deputy commanders, platoon leaders, command sergeants major, first sergeants, platoon sergeants, section leaders (when so designated), squad leaders, tank commanders, and rifle squad fire team leaders.

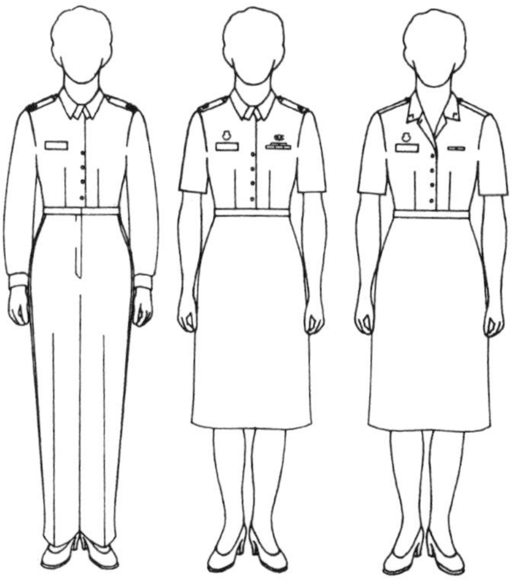

Fig. 6.10. Army Class B Army green uniform for female personnel

Nameplate

This is a 1-by-3-by-1⁄16-inch piece of black laminated plastic with a white border. Nameplates are worn on the right side of various Army uniforms and also on the Army green shirt and the black pullover sweater (see figure 6.11).

Distinctive Unit Insignia and Heraldic Items

Distinctive unit insignia (informally called "unit crests") are made of metal or metal and enamel and are usually based on elements of the design of the coat of arms or historic badge approved for a specific unit. They serve as identifying devices, promote esprit de corps, and are based on the lineage and battle honors of the unit. A complete set of distinctive unit insignia consists of three pieces: one for each shoulder loop and one for headgear.

Distinctive unit insignia are worn by soldiers on various Army uniforms and the black pullover sweater.

Distinctive Items—Infantry

Infantry personnel are authorized to wear the following additional distinctive items in recognition of the particularly hazardous and demanding duties of their branch. These are:

1. an infantry blue shoulder cord worn on the right shoulder of the Army green, blue, and white uniform coats and shirts; passed under the arm and through the shoulder loop; and secured to the button on the shoulder loop.
2. an infantry blue disk worn beneath the branch of service and the "U.S." insignia.

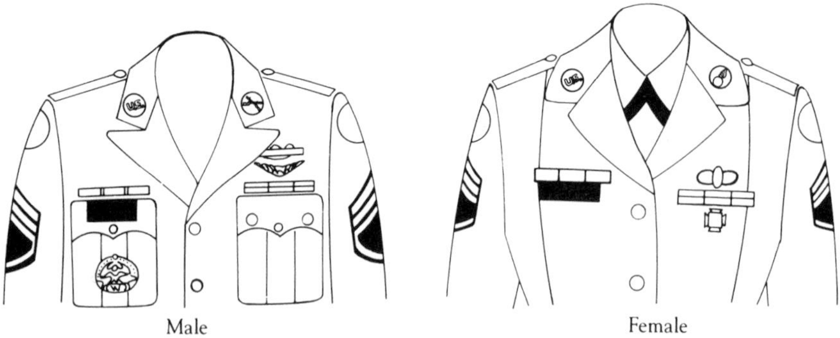

Fig. 6.11. Placement of nameplate on Army green uniform jacket

3. an infantry blue disk worn beneath the insignia on the green and blue service caps and drill sergeant hat.

Distinctive Items—Other Than Infantry

Organizational Flash
This is a shield-shaped, embroidered cloth patch of the unit colors, approximately 2¼ inches long and 1⅞ inches wide, worn centered on the stiffener of the beret by personnel authorized to wear one of the organizational berets (Ranger, Special Forces, Airborne).

Airborne Background Trimming
This is a small oval, usually cloth, embroidered with the unit colors. It is worn as a background behind the parachutist or air assault badge on the Army green coat and shirt by soldiers assigned to those type units.

Airborne Insignia

This is a round cloth insignia composed of a white parachute and glider on a blue disk with a red border, approximately 2¼ inches in diameter. It is worn by all personnel of the 101st Airborne (Air Assault) Division, and airborne-qualified personnel serving as Army recruiters, at brigade or lower level at IET, and in jump positions in non-airborne units. Enlisted personnel wear the insignia on the left side of the garrison cap, one inch from the front fold, with the glider facing forward. Officers wear it on the right side. See figure 6.12.

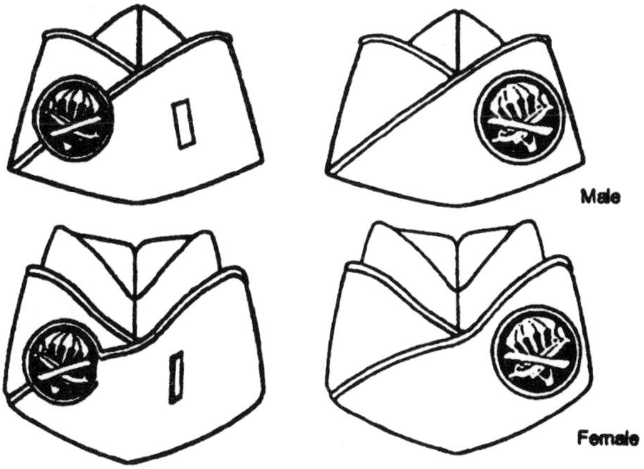

Fig. 6.12. Airborne insignia on garrison cap, officer and enlisted

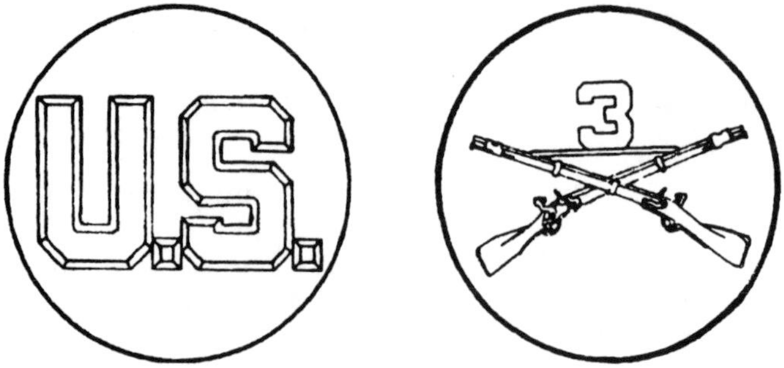

Fig. 6.13. U.S. and branch collar insignia

Enlisted Collar Lapel Insignia

Enlisted soldier collar lapel insignia for the Army green uniform consist of "U.S." insignia and insignia of branch mounted on a 1-inch diameter disk of gold-colored metal. During basic combat training, you will wear the "U.S." insignia on both lapels. Upon award of an MOS, you wear the appropriate branch insignia on the left lapel of prescribed uniforms. These insignia are called "brass."

Regimental Collar Lapel Insignia

Soldiers affiliated with Infantry, Armor, Field Artillery, Air Defense Artillery, Cavalry, or Aviation regiments are authorized to wear their branch collar insignia with their regimental number on it. All Special Forces soldiers, no matter which SF group they may be in, are members of the 1st Special Forces, and therefore do not wear any number on their collar branch insignia. See figure 6.13 for an example of regimental insignia.

Awards and Decorations

"Award" is an all-inclusive term referring to any decoration, medal, badge, ribbon (a 1⅜-inch-by-⅜-inch colored bar that is worn in lieu of a medal), or appurtenance (a device affixed to a ribbon) given to a soldier or unit.

The purpose of the Army's awards and decorations program is to provide recognition for acts of valor, exceptional service or achievement, special skills or qualifications, and acts of heroism not involving actual combat. Individual soldiers may

Fig. 6.14. This is how the Silver Star, Purple Heart, and Army Commendation Medal would look to someone facing you

receive decorations and service awards. A *decoration* is given for an act of gallantry or meritorious service. A *service award* is given for participation in designated wars, campaigns and expeditions, or for fulfilling a specific service requirement.

A *unit award* is given to a unit for an act of gallantry or meritorious service. It is worn permanently by members of the unit who participated in the action. Other soldiers may also wear some unit awards while they are assigned to the unit. Units may also receive service credit, such as for participating in a war or campaign. A streamer is placed on the unit flag to represent the award or service performed. Streamers are discussed in Appendix B.

Individual U.S. awards are worn above the left breast pocket or centered on the left side of the prescribed uniform with the exception of the Medal of Honor, which may be suspended around the neck. Awards are worn with the highest displayed above and to the wearer's right of the others. A soldier authorized the Silver Star (SS), the Purple Heart, and the Army Commendation Medal (ARCOM) would display them left to right (Figure 6.14).

SS PH ARCOM

The order of precedence in wearing Army service ribbons representing decorations and service medals is shown in Appendix H. (See also AR 670-1 and AR 672-5-1, *Awards and Decorations* for more details.) Many awards from foreign governments may be worn in the order of their receipt after all U.S. awards.

Badges and Tabs

Badges and tabs are awarded to soldiers for the purposes of identification, in recognition of attaining special skills or proficiency, or as a member of a special unit.

Combat and Special Skill Badges

These are awarded to denote proficiency in performance of duties under hazardous conditions and circumstances of extraordinary hardship, as well as special qualifications and successful completion of prescribed courses of training. Listed below, grouped in order of precedence, are the combat and special skill badges authorized for wear on the Army uniform:

Group 1. Combat Infantryman and Expert Infantryman badges
Group 2. Combat Medical and Expert Medical badges
Group 3. Army Aviator, Flight Surgeon, and Aircraft Crewman badges
Group 4. Glider, Parachutist, Combat Parachutist, Pathfinder, Air Assault badges, and the Ranger and Special Forces metal tab replicas
Group 5. Diver, Driver and Mechanic, and Explosive Ordnance Disposal badges

Special Skill Tabs of cloth are also worn to indicate Ranger and Special Forces qualifications.

Marksmanship Badges and Tabs

These are awarded to indicate the level to which an individual has qualified in prescribed weapons' firing courses or events. They include the Expert, Sharpshooter, and Marksmanship qualification badges, the U.S. Distinguished International Shooter Badge, Distinguished Pistol Shot, and the President's Hundred Tab.

Identification Badges

These are worn to denote service performed in special assignments. They include the Presidential Service Badge, Vice Presidential Service Badge, Office of the Secretary of Defense Identification Badge, Joint Chiefs of Staff Identification Badge, Army General Staff Identification Badge, Army Student Nurse Program Identification Badge, Drill Sergeant Identification Badge, U.S. Army Recruiter Badge, the Career Counselor Badge, Army National Guard Recruiter Badge, and the U.S. Army Reserve Recruiter Badge.

Other Special Skill Badges

Some commanders have authority to approve temporary local wear of special skill badges that in the commander's judgment have a beneficial impact on soldier morale, unit training, and esprit de corps. These consist of subdued cloth badges and patches worn on the field and work uniform. They reflect attainment of a high degree of skill, proficiency, and excellence.

There are numerous U.S. and foreign badges and tabs that may be worn in addition to those in this guide. The most common special skill badges are discussed below. See AR 675-2-1 for more details.

Infantryman Badges

To earn the Expert Infantryman Badge (see figure 6.15), you have to pass a battery of tests that are both physically and mentally challenging. The wreath means the badge was earned in combat (see figures 6.16 through 6.18).

Medical Badges

As shown in figures 6.20 through 6.22, these are awarded to members of the Army medical team who demonstrate outstanding ability and proven skill in the field. Again, the wreath signifies the badge was earned in combat.

Diver Badges

To become a diver in the Army, you need an athlete's conditioning and reflexes. To earn distinction as a diver is to earn a special kind of respect. As you progress in proficiency, your badge will show it (see figures 6.23 and 6.24).

Air Assault and Pathfinder Badges

The soldier who wears the Air Assault Badge (see figure 6.25) has mastered the many skills necessary for airmobile warfare, including the art of rappelling from a hovering helicopter. Pathfinders (see figure 6.26) are the soldiers who arrive on the scene first to establish drop zones and landing zones for Airborne and airmobile operations. That explains their motto, "First in, last out."

Parachutist Badges

When you graduate from Airborne school, you don't get a diploma—you get parachute or "jump" wings (see figure 6.27).

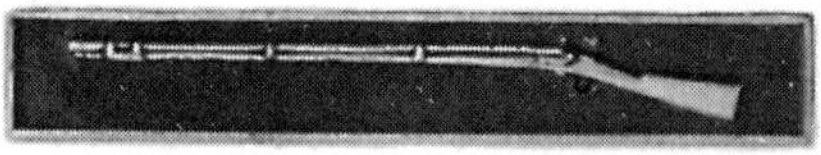

Fig. 6.15. Expert Infantryman Badge

Fig. 6.16. Combat Infantryman Badge, first award

Fig. 6.17. Combat Infantryman Badge, second award

Fig. 6.18. Combat Infantryman Badge, third award

Fig. 6.19. Expert Field Medical Badge

Fig. 6.20. Combat Medical Badge, first award

Fig. 6.21. Combat Medical Badge, second award

Fig. 6.22. Combat Medical Badge, third award

Fig. 6.23. Salvage Diver

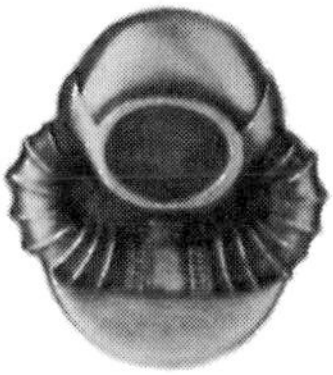

Fig. 6.24. Scuba Diver

Fig. 6.25. Air Assault Badge

Fig. 6.26. Pathfinder badge

Fig. 6.27. Parachutist

Fig. 6.28. Senior Parachutist

Fig. 6.29. Master Parachutist

Fig. 6.30. Aircraft Crewman

Fig. 6.31. Senior Aircraft Crewman

Fig. 6.32. Master Aircraft Crewman

Fig. 6.33. Army Aviator

Fig. 6.34. Senior Army Aviator

Fig. 6.35. Master Army Aviator

Fig. 6.36. Explosive Ordnance Disposal Badge

Fig. 6.37. Senior Explosive Ordnance Disposal Badge

(As you might guess, it's no ordinary school. The final exam is given at 1,250 feet and it is literally a big step forward!) To earn the Senior Parachutist Badge, you need at least 30 jumps under your belt; for Master, at least 65 jumps and additional training (see figures 6.28 and 6.29). The Army recently added two new badges—Military Free Fall Parachutist and Jumpmaster in Special Operations. Drawings were not available at press time.

Aviation Badges

With over 8,000 aircraft, the Army has a large flying fleet. These are the insignia of the people who keep the Army in the air. Enlisted soldiers can earn Crewman badges (see figures 6.30 through 6.32); Aviator badges are worn by officers and warrant officers (see figures 6.33 through 6.35).

Explosive Ordnance Disposal Badges

Soldiers who deal with explosives need a cool head, a steady hand, and many hours of special training in a field where normal means hazardous conditions. Skill is only one requirement (see figures 6.36 through 6.37).

Marksmanship Badges

These badges signify the level of skill: Marksman, Sharpshooter, or Expert (see figures 6.38 through 6.40). The clasps shown in figure 6.41 signify the weapon.

Driver and Mechanic Badges

The Army moves on wheels—from sedans and HUMMWVs to pickups, buses, and tractor-trailers. The badges in figure 6.42 are awarded to the soldiers who demonstrate a high degree of skill in operating or maintaining the Army's vehicles.

Special Forces, Ranger, and Airborne Tabs

Both the Ranger and Special Forces Tabs are Group 4 Special Skill badges. Individuals authorized both the Ranger and Special Forces tabs may choose which one they desire to wear. For exact details on how these tabs are worn, see AR 670-1.

Earning a *Ranger* tab (figure 6.43) is a proud and uncommon accomplishment. And it doesn't come easily. First, you have

Fig. 6.38. Marksman

Fig. 6.39. Sharpshooter

Fig. 6.40. Expert

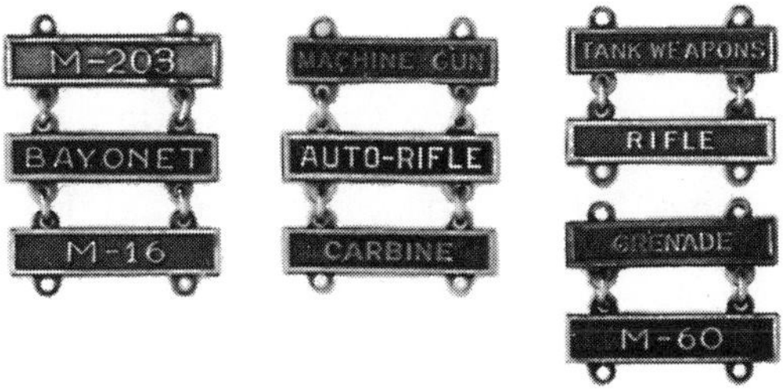

Fig. 6.41. Marksman qualification clasps

Fig. 6.42. Driver/Mechanic and clasps

Fig. 6.43. Tabs—Ranger, Special Forces, Airborne

to qualify for Ranger School. Then, you have to complete nine weeks of the toughest training the Army has to offer.

It takes a special kind of person to earn the right to wear the tab of *Special Forces* (figure 6.43): someone who is eager for challenge and hungry for responsibility, someone who doesn't think courage, pride, honor, and integrity are simply words, but a code by which to live. If you're that kind of person, the Special Forces tab might be tailor-made for you. And you can wear your Special Forces or Ranger tab throughout your Army career.

The *Airborne* tab is worn as part of a unit's shoulder sleeve insignia and is reserved for soldiers who are assigned to airborne positions. Do you have what it takes to step out of the door of a flying aircraft, day or night, and land safely on the ground ready to fight? If you've got the spirit for this kind of challenge, you're the right person for an airborne unit and the pride of wearing the *Airborne* tab with your shoulder sleeve insignia.

Appurtenances

Appurtenances are devices affixed to service ribbons. They are worn to denote additional awards, participation in a specific event, or other distinguished characteristics of the award. Examples include "V" for valor, oak or silver clusters for second or succeeding awards, and an arrowhead to denote participation in an airborne, air-landed, or amphibious assault onto enemy-held territory.

BRONZE OAK LEAF CLUSTER

The bronze oak leaf cluster represents second and subsequent entitlements of awards.

SILVER OAK LEAF CLUSTER

A silver oak leaf cluster is worn for the sixth, 11th, or in lieu of five bronze oak leaf clusters.

BRONZE SERVICE STAR

The bronze five-pointed service star represents participation in campaigns or operations, multiple qualification or an additional award to any of the various ribbons on which it is authorized.

SILVER SERVICE STAR

Worn in the same manner as the bronze star, but each silver star is worn in lieu of five bronze service stars.

WINTERED OVER

For wintering over on the Antarctic continent, a clasp for Antarctica Service Medal, suspension ribbon and a disc for the service ribbon of bronze for first winter, gold for second winter, silver for third winter.

"V" (VALOR) DEVICE

This metallic bronze letter "V" represents valor and does not denote an additional award. Only one may be worn on any ribbon.

HOURGLASS

Issued for each succeeding award of the Armed Forces Reserve Medal.

GERMANY AND JAPAN CLASPS

Worn on the suspension ribbon of the Army of Occupation Medal.

GOOD CONDUCT MEDAL CLASP

Number of loops and color denote number of awards of Good Conduct Medal. Bronze, second–fifth awards; silver, sixth–10th; gold, 11th–15th.

BRONZE ARABIC NUMERAL

Denotes subsequent awards of the Air Medal, Multinational Force and Observers Medal, Overseas Service Ribbon and Army Reserve Components Overseas Training Ribbon and level of non-commissioned officer professional military education.

ARROWHEAD

Awarded for participation in an initial assault landing. Worn on the service and suspension ribbons of the appropriate campaign or service medal. Only one may be worn on any ribbon.

The above display represents the correct order of precedence for ribbons most likely to be worn today on the Army uniform. Devices worn on these ribbons must be worn in a specific manner and are used to denote additional awards or participation in a specific event. For additional information about the proper order of display, placement of devices or about ribbons not shown, refer to AR 670-1.

Fig. 6.44. Appurtenances

7. Discipline and Military Justice

Discipline

Service in the U.S. Army carries with it a responsibility to the U.S. government and the American people that occasionally restricts a soldier's private and public activities, such as the use of government property and off-duty employment. Field Manual 27-14, *Legal Guide for Soldiers,* discusses restrictions and responsibilities in the conduct of your personal affairs and your rights as a soldier.

In the Army, discipline is the standard of personal and ethical conduct, courtesy, and appearance that enables a soldier to perform with optimum efficiency.

Discipline is essential to the successful accomplishment of a military mission because each mission requires a team effort.

Army Regulation 600-20 defines discipline as a function of command. However, meaningful discipline exists only when soldiers obey the rules that govern their conduct because they know and accept the rules. Saluting, for example, should not be viewed as a burden or a chore, but a willing acceptance of the rank of the individual being saluted.

There are times in the Army, however, when discipline fails and punishment may be required. The most familiar measures in the Army to enforce discipline are Article 15 of the Uniform Code of Military Justice (UCMJ) and the court-martial. Both of these measures are discussed at length later in this chapter. A brief outline of the UCMJ is in Appendix C.

In the case of poor duty performance or minor misconduct, a unit commander has the authority to withhold many of your privileges, such as pass privileges or the use of the post service club. Often these nonpunitive, administrative actions have a rehabilitative effect on soldiers, thus benefiting both the soldier and the Army.

Uniform Code of Military Justice

The Uniform Code of Military Justice (UCMJ) is a federal law that establishes the present system of U.S. military criminal justice. It describes what conduct is criminal for military personnel and the types of courts and basic procedures used to process military criminal cases.

The UCMJ provides that, as a member of the U.S. Armed Forces, if you are suspected of a crime, you may not be forced to speak against yourself. Before questioning, you must be advised of your right to remain silent. Also, if you are in custody, you must be told that you have the right to speak to a lawyer and have a lawyer present during questioning if you choose to answer questions.

Soldiers and units in the Army Military Police Corps, in addition to many other duties, are responsible for crime prevention and investigations, the operation of Army confinement and correctional facilities, control of vehicles and personnel, and physical security operations.

A soldier may be punished under Article 15, UCMJ, for minor offenses, such as insubordination or disrespect of superior authority. This punishment is termed "nonjudicial" because it is given by the commander instead of by a court-martial.

The procedures that must be followed for punishment under Article 15, UCMJ, and the rights that a soldier has under this form of punishment are discussed in detail in FM 27-14.

Courts-Martial

The Army's court-martial system tries soldiers accused of violations of the punitive articles of the UCMJ (Articles 77 through 134; see Appendix C).

Just as in other U.S. criminal courts, Army courts-martial are adversary proceedings; that is, the government and the accused each present matters that apply to their sides and must follow certain rules in doing so.

There are three levels of courts-martial.

- Summary Court-Martial (SCM). This is the lowest level of court-martial and is issued for minor crimes. It is composed of one commissioned officer who tries minor crimes. The maximum punishment depends on a soldier's rank but may not exceed confinement for one month, forfeiture of two-third's pay for one month, and reduction in rank. A soldier may consult a lawyer concerning the case but is not entitled to have an appointed military lawyer present at the trial. You have the right to refuse trial by SCM.

- Special Court-Martial (SPCM). Three court members comprise the SPCM. The defense counsel must be a lawyer. A military judge is normally appointed for the trial. The maximum sentence that a SPCM can impose is confinement for six months, forfeiture of two-third's pay per month for six months, and reduction in rank to the lowest enlisted grade. In some instances, the sentence may include a bad conduct discharge.
- General Court-Martial (GCM). The highest of the three levels of court-martial is the GCM. It tries the most serious offenses, such as murder, rape, robbery, and desertion. A GCM consists of at least five court members and a military judge.

Both the prosecuting (trial) counsel and the defense counsel must be lawyers. A formal investigation must occur before the trial. The GCM judge may sentence a soldier to any punishment authorized by law.

Don't take punishment under UCMJ lightly. It is serious business. Disciplinary action can be detrimental to a soldier's career, affecting promotions, assignments, and reenlistment and civilian employment once you have left the Army.

Homosexuality

The issue of homosexuality in the military is a complex problem for which all of the military services are still seeking satisfactory resolution.

The Army defines a homosexual as a person, regardless of gender, who engages in, desires to engage in, or intends to engage in homosexual acts. A homosexual act means bodily contact, actively undertaken or passively permitted, between persons of the same sex for sexual satisfaction (AR 635-200, p. 58).

The Department of Defense policy released in February 1994 maintains the fundamental principle that homosexual conduct is incompatible with military service. However, a person's sexual orientation is considered a personal and private matter. Homosexual orientation is not a bar to service entry or continued service unless there is homosexual conduct. Homosexual acts by soldiers are prohibited by the UCMJ and are punishable by court-martial or administrative discharge. Potential recruits will not be asked about sexual orientation. New soldiers are fully briefed on the latest Army policies concerning this issue.

Code of Conduct

The Geneva Convention Relative to the Treatment of Prisoners of War, 12 August 1949, is an international agreement to protect the human rights of POWs. These rights include:

- sufficient food and housing to ensure your health;
- medical care;
- religious freedom; and
- the right to keep your personal property, to prisoner representation, and to send and receive mail.

As a prisoner of war (POW), a soldier faces what could be the most difficult challenge of his life. To assist American military personnel who are taken prisoner, the Department of Defense created the Code of Conduct—a product of the U.S. experience in the Korean War.

Under the Geneva Convention, you are required to provide minimal information, such as name, rank, service number, and date of birth, to the enemy. This information is to be used in communications and repatriation efforts between warring parties. You are also required to obey POW camp regulations and perform whatever labor is appropriate for the welfare and protection of prisoners.

The Code of Conduct, written in 1955 and amended in 1977, is a recommended standard of behavior for American POWs. It reminds the soldier, as well as other U.S. service members, that by fulfilling their duty and continuing to resist the enemy, they are more likely to survive with honor and self-respect.

The six articles of the Code of Conduct are identified below.

> I. I am an American. I serve in the forces which guard my country and our way of life. I am prepared to give my life in their defense.
>
> II. I will never surrender of my own free will. If in command, I will never surrender my men while they still have the means to resist.
>
> III. If I am captured, I will continue to resist by all means available. I will make every effort to escape and aid others to escape. I will accept neither parole nor special favors from the enemy.
>
> IV. If I become a prisoner of war, I will keep faith with my fellow prisoners. I will give no information nor take part in any actions that might be harmful to my comrades. If I am senior, I will take command. If not, I will obey the lawful orders of those appointed over me and will back them up in every way.
>
> V. When questioned, should I become a prisoner of war, I am required to give only name, rank, social security number, and date of birth. I will evade answering further questions

to the utmost of my ability. I will make no oral or written statements disloyal to my country and its allies or harmful to their cause.

VI. I will never forget that I am an American, responsible for my actions, and dedicated to the principles that made my country free. I will trust in my God and in the United States of America.

Knowing the principles of honor and courage expressed in the Code of Conduct provides a soldier the moral foundation for survival if captured by the enemy.

The convention is meant as a protection of your rights as a prisoner, and the rights of those you may take prisoner. As an American soldier you are legally responsible to follow the convention in the treatment of your prisoners, and you will be held accountable for violations.

8. Military Courtesy and Custom

Courtesies Toward Officers and NCOs

During basic combat training (BCT), you will receive classes on military courtesies, customs, and ceremonies.

Here are some rules that will benefit you to know from the outset in dealing with officers and noncommissioned officers (NCOs).

- Always address and refer to officers by their rank, such as "Captain" or "Lieutenant." You should address and refer to NCOs as "Sergeant." The senior sergeant in your company is called "First Sergeant." The senior sergeant in your battalion is "Sergeant Major."
- When talking to an officer, stand at attention unless given the order "At ease." When you are dismissed, or when the officer departs, come to attention and salute.
- When an officer enters a room, the first soldier to see the officer calls the soldiers in the room to attention but does not salute. A salute is rendered only when a soldier is reporting to an officer.
- When accompanying a soldier who is senior to you in rank, walk on his or her left.
- When entering or exiting a vehicle from the passenger side, the junior ranking soldier is the first to enter, and the senior in rank is the first to exit.
- When an officer or NCO enters a crowded hallway where soldiers are taking a break or standing in a line, the first soldier to see the officer or NCO should call "At ease" and "Make way" so those present will move to the sides of the hallway and allow passage. (The officer or NCO may state, "Carry on." This means the soldiers should continue with whatever they were doing previously.)

- When outdoors and approached by an NCO, you should stand (if seated) and greet the NCO by saying, "Good Morning (or Afternoon), Sergeant."

Hand Salutes

One of the military customs that you will learn in BCT is that, as a soldier, you salute to show respect toward an officer, the U.S. flag, and our country (represented by the national anthem). You will be taught the proper way to give a hand salute. Chapter 29 of this guidebook introduces you to the basic steps for performing a proper salute, and also contains an illustration. Your BCT instructor will teach you the correct procedure in detail. It may seem complicated at first, but you will see most of it is common sense. To help make it less confusing, you may want to learn some of the rules for saluting before you report to BCT. The best rule to follow, however, is the old Army saying for new recruits, "When in doubt, salute." You can't go far wrong with that approach.

You may want to learn some of the following rules for saluting before reporting to BCT.

- When you meet an officer outside, salute when approximately six steps away. Accompany the salute with an appropriate greeting, such as "Good morning, sir," or "Good afternoon, ma'am."
- Salute all officers that you see in official vehicles identified by special plates or flags.
- Salute only on command when in a formation.
- The salute is always initiated by the subordinate.
- It is not customary for enlisted soldiers to exchange salutes, except in some ceremonial situations.
- When the U.S. flag is being raised in the morning (reveille) or lowered in the evening (retreat), you should come to attention on the first note of the national anthem or "To the Color," ("Color" usually refers to the U.S. flag but can also include your unit flag) and give a hand salute. (Full details on flag courtesies can be found in AR 840-10.)
- If you are in a car when the flag is being raised or lowered, dismount, face the flag, and salute.
- A soldier in civilian clothes still honors the flag by placing his or her right hand over the heart.

Gun Salutes

A national salute of 21 guns is fired on Washington's Birthday, Memorial Day, and Independence Day, and to honor the President of the United States and heads of foreign states. The number of guns fired for other dignitaries will vary as determined by protocol.

Army Customs and Traditions

Customs and traditions are an inseparable part of the Army and help distinguish it from civilian life, and the other military services. From the moment a soldier enters the Army, the Army's customs and traditions are a part of the soldier's life. The uniform, the hand salute, the names of ranks, places, and things, how soldiers address one another, courtesies rendered the national flag and superiors, and even the way to tell time—these are all part of it. Some traditions go back to ancient armies and are common to military services around the world. Others are unique to your Army.

As a new soldier, you will find it confusing at first, like learning a different language. However, within a few weeks it will all become familiar routine. Much of your instruction during your first days in basic training will concern the customs and traditions you need to know. This guide also provides a good introduction to some of the basics discussed below.

Unit Flags

Flags are very important to soldiers. They are more than mere bits of cloth—to a soldier a flag represents the essence of the unit or nation. In wars past, many soldiers have given their lives carrying and defending their unit and national flags on the battlefield. Most Army units from battalion up to the highest level have a unit flag, or "color," of the familiar rectangular shape. A company, troop, or battery has a smaller flag with twin tails called a guidon. By the colors and symbols used on the various flags a soldier can identify the unit.

The headquarters of each brigade of a division has a distinguishing flag with a background divided into two equal vertical stripes of the same colors as the division flag—red and blue for all types of infantry divisions (infantry, mechanized, light, and airborne), red and yellow for armored and cavalry divi-

Fig. 8.1. Brigade flag (1st Brigade, 1st Armored Division)

sions. The shoulder sleeve insignia of the division is in the upper center of the flag, where the colors meet, and below it is the number of the brigade. This combination of colors, insignia, and numerals identifies the type of division, specific division, and specific brigade. Figure 8.1 shows a brigade flag of the 1st Armored Division.

Each battalion has a flag with a background color of the branch of the battalion, or in the case of multibranch service battalions, a combination of the two branch colors. In the center of the flag is the national eagle, the coat of arms of the parent regiment, or the battalion insignia on a shield over the eagle's breast. In the eagle's mouth is a scroll with the unit's motto. Under the eagle is another scroll with the official designation of the unit. In the case of a regimental battalion, the number of the battalion is shown in a small circle in the upper outer corner of the flag. Figure 8.2 shows the flag of an armor battalion.

The National Flag

Most respected of all flags is the United States flag, or National Color. It is honored twice every day at all Army posts. Honors are given in the morning at "reveille" to start the day. This is when the American flag is raised for the first time. Honors are again rendered at the end of the working day, or "retreat,"

Fig. 8.2. Battalion flag (1st Battalion, 81st Armor)

when the flag is lowered. Reveille starts a soldier's work day and retreat normally ends it.

Traditional bugle calls are played for both of these daily ceremonies. On most posts all outdoor activity ceases and persons outside stop, face the direction of the flag, and render the appropriate salute while the ceremonies take place. During the retreat ceremony two bugle calls are sounded. The first is "Retreat" followed by "To the Color." A cannon, or "evening gun," will frequently be fired to signal that the flag is being lowered. As an alternative to "To the Color" the National Anthem may be played.

Bugle Calls

In the early days of the Army the bugle acted as the soldier's clock and as the commander's loud speaker. It was used to tell the soldiers in a unit what duties they should perform in the garrison and the commands they were to follow on the battlefield. A system of different calls was used that a soldier learned by heart. Today the tradition of bugle calls is continued in a much reduced manner. There are the ceremonial calls for reveille and retreat discussed previously. In addition, depending on the post you are at, you will hear "Tattoo" to signal "lights out" at night, the familiar "Taps," which is the last call of the day, "Mess Call," which announces meal time, and others.

Regiments and Distinctive Unit Insignia (DUI)

As discussed earlier in the history of the Army, other than a few exceptions, mostly armored cavalry regiments, the regiment no longer exists as a separate unit in the Army. While many soldiers may wear a small metal insignia called a Distinctive Unit Insignia (DUI)—commonly called a "unit crest"—of a regiment, most regiments do not have an active headquarters. These regiments are represented in the Army by their battalions, which retain their regimental names and flags. If the battalions serve under a higher headquarters, it is usually a brigade. However, the Army feels it is important to maintain the link between today's soldiers and the traditional Army regiments of the past. This is done through the battalion designations and the wearing of the DUI. The Army has reduced in size so much that only a small portion of the total number of historic regiments can be represented in the active force. Every effort is made to retain the maximum number of the oldest and most distinguished regimental names on the active list. It is common, therefore, for the Army to have only one battalion of a regiment serving.

Traditional regiments, as well as many other Army units have a coat of arms that is unique to that unit. The coat of arms usually contains symbols relating to significant events in a unit's past, or which describe in symbolic terms the mission and capabilities of the unit. Nonregimental units such as division headquarters, support battalions, aviation, transportation, and medical battalions, and other types of units may also have a DUI. As a general rule, if a unit has a flag (not a guidon), it has a DUI.

A DUI normally is only a portion of the full coat of arms of a unit. Figure 8.3 shows the DUI for the 8th Cavalry Regiment. A DUI is based on a unit's coat of arms. It may be taken from the "crest," which is the part over the top of the shield, or from another part of the arms. For example, both the 5th Artillery and 3d Armored Cavalry DUIs come from the crest, while the others obviously do not. It is a common error to call the DUI "a unit crest." Some units, such as the 3d Infantry Regiment, wear more than one type of DUI. More information on DUIs is provided in Chapter 6.

Special Unit Traditions

Soldiers show their pride in unit membership in many ways. Some soldiers may wear special headgear, badges, or other emblems on their uniforms. They may greet one another with

Fig. 8.3. Distinctive unit insignia (8th Cavalry)

a unit motto, nickname, or slogan. In one regiment's battalions, one day a year, the NCOs are given full charge of the unit. This is done to commemorate a time in the unit's past when all of the officers were killed or wounded, and the NCOs had to take command.

These traditions reflect the high spirit of the units and the pride of their members. Soldiers in a unit also have a tradition to look out for one another, and to help out when another needs assistance. Remember that you will be a part of the traditions for the soldiers of the future.

9. Security of Information

Classified Information

Upon your entry into the Army, you will be given an initial security briefing and thereafter receive annual security awareness briefings. You will also receive a security briefing prior to any foreign travel and upon termination of your Army service. Your initial briefing will acquaint you with material presented in AR 380-5, *Department of the Army Information Security Program*.

It is important for you to know that certain information you will be dealing with in the Army has been determined "classified information." This is information or material that requires protection against unauthorized disclosure (a communication or physical transfer of classified information to an unauthorized recipient) in the interest of U.S. national security. As a soldier, it is your personal, moral, and legal responsibility to protect classified information.

Security Classification Designations

Classified information is given a level of protection based on the amount of damage that would occur if the information were subjected to unauthorized disclosure. There are three levels of classification. From lowest to highest, they are: CONFIDENTIAL, SECRET, and TOP SECRET.

Materials classified as Confidential are those documents or equipment whose unauthorized disclosure could reasonably be expected to cause "damage" to national security. Examples of damage include:

- the compromise of information that indicates strength of ground, air, and naval forces in the United States and overseas;

- disclosure of technical information used for training, maintenance, and inspection of classified munitions of war; and
- revelation of performance characteristics, test data, design, and production data on munitions of war.

The unauthorized disclosure of materials designated at the Secret level of classification could be reasonably expected to cause "serious damage" to national security. Examples of serious damage include:

- disruption of foreign relations significantly affecting the national security;
- significant impairment of a program or policy directly related to the national security;
- revelation of significant military plans or intelligence operations;
- compromise of significant plans or intelligence operations; and
- compromise of significant scientific or technological developments relating to national security.

"Exceptional grave damage" to national security could occur when material designated as Top Secret is disclosed to unauthorized persons. Examples of exceptional grave damage include:

- armed hostilities against the United States or its allies;
- disruption of foreign relations vitally affecting national security;
- the compromise of vital national defense plans or complex cryptologic and communications intelligence systems;
- the revelation of sensitive intelligence operations; and
- the disclosure of scientific or technological developments vital to national security.

Classified information is marked at the top and bottom of each page with the highest level of classification on that page. It is only used by persons that have been granted a personnel security clearance equal to or greater than the level of classified information they are to work with.

Those persons granted access to classified information have a "need to know" in order to perform their assigned duties. Further, they must have the ability to properly protect the classified information.

Soldiers and civilian employees of the Department of the Army (DA) who require access to classified information to perform their assigned duties have a responsibility to adhere to the standards of conduct required of persons holding positions of trust. They must avoid personal behavior that could cause them to be ineligible for access to classified information within their knowledge, possession, or control.

You must notify your supervisor or security manager when you become aware of information that could affect the security program of your unit or that involves the trustworthiness of someone with access to classified information.

Classified information should not be discussed over unsecured telephone lines or in any other way that an unauthorized person might overhear or see.

The Army's Vulnerability

As an American soldier you are a prime target for foreign intelligence and terrorist elements that may act in a manner detrimental to the interests of U.S. national security.

The Army is vulnerable to espionage, sabotage, subversion, sedition, and terrorism both within and outside the United States. The dissolution of the Warsaw Pact and the retreat of communism have not lessened the threat of espionage. The increasing need for foreign governments to collect American technology, which they target through their intelligence services; the targeting of U.S. installations and personnel by countries that sponsor terrorism; and the increasing opportunities for travel and contact with foreign citizens all underscore the necessity for all soldiers to remain security-conscious.

Army Regulation 381-12, *Subversion and Espionage Directed Against the U.S. Army (SAEDA),* provides guidance and establishes procedures and responsibilities for the Army's counterintelligence (CI) awareness, education, and reporting program. The goal of the SAEDA program is to secure the assistance of every soldier in the deterrence and detection of foreign intelligence and terrorist threats to the Army.

CI is concerned with identifying and countering the threat to security posed by foreign intelligence services or organizations, or by individuals engaged in espionage, sabotage, subversion, or terrorism. It does not include, but may complement, personnel, physical, information, and communication security programs.

Once you are in the Army, you will learn about a number of programs designed to counter threats against the Army. At this point, however, the following definitions may prove helpful to you.

Espionage is the act of obtaining, delivering, transmitting, communicating, or receiving information in respect to national defense with an intent or reason to believe that the information may be used to the detriment of the United States or to the advantage of any foreign nation.

Sabotage is an act or acts with intent to injure, interfere with, or obstruct the national defense of a country by willfully injuring or destroying, or attempting to injure or destroy, any national defense or war matériel, premises, or utilities, including human and natural resources.

Subversion is advocating, causing, or attempting to cause insubordination, disloyalty, mutiny, or refusal of duty by any member of the armed forces of the United States or by Department of Defense civilian personnel with the intent to interfere with, impair, or influence the loyalty, morale, or discipline of such armed forces.

Terrorist activity is any activity that uses violence or the threat of violence to attain political, religious, or ideological goals. This is done through intimidation, coercion, or instilling fear. Terrorism involves a criminal act that is often symbolic in nature and intended to influence an audience beyond the immediate victims.

Persons with Special Vulnerability

Certain persons in the Army, by virtue of their position, travel, duties, access, and associations, present attractive targets to foreign intelligence.

Historically, foreign intelligence agents have targeted persons with access to sensitive compartmented, cryptographic, and special program information. Those who occupy positions of special interest to foreign intelligence also include soldiers, as well as DA civilians, involved in research and development; classified document custodians; and persons working in the scientific, technical, communications, and intelligence fields.

Individuals seeking information on Army activities may offer money or ask favors as they establish what might appear to be an innocent friendship or a legitimate professional relationship. They later use extortion, blackmail, payment of money, or punishment of relatives living in their country. Foreign intelligence agents may present themselves in a variety of roles, such as students, tourists, diplomats, or business people. If you are contacted by a foreign national, you must report that contact to your security manager or to the CI office nearest your duty location.

Reporting Requirements

All Army units have security plans and checklists that comply with the Army's information security program and deal with your unit's unique work environment regarding classified information access, safekeeping and storage, and disposal and destruction. You will become familiar with them once you join your unit.

Major points that you should remember from this chapter are:

- Persons are granted access to classified information because they have a need to know.
- You are responsible to protect classified information.
- You are required to report the following to your security manager:
  1. Possible loss or compromise of classified material.
  2. Information that could reflect adversely on the trustworthiness of an individual who has access to classified information.
  3. Attempts by foreign nationals to cultivate a friendship that one would not normally be able to reciprocate or that involves offering money payments or bribery to obtain classified information or information that could have potential intelligence value.

10. Hygiene, First Aid, and Fitness

Personal Hygiene

Because of the close living and working quarters frequently found in an Army environment, personal hygiene is extremely important. Disease or illness can spread rapidly and can affect your entire squad, platoon, or company, making you and your fellow soldiers unfit for duty.

Uncleanliness or disagreeable odors affect the morale of fellow soldiers in the barracks as well as in the field. A daily bath or shower whenever possible is necessary to maintain cleanliness and prevent body odor and will aid in preventing common skin diseases. Medicated powders and deodorants help keep the skin dry.

Dental Hygiene

Your teeth are intended to last a lifetime, and they can with proper care. Daily use of a toothbrush and dental floss after meals is essential. You should also have regular dental checkups and cleanings. This care may prevent gum disease, infection, and tooth decay.

One of the major causes of tooth decay and gum disease is plaque. Plaque is an almost invisible film of decomposed food particles and millions of living bacteria. To prevent dental diseases, you must effectively remove plaque from your teeth.

If you notice any of the following warning signs, you should see a dentist immediately.

- Gums that bleed easily
- Permanent teeth that are loose or separating
- Any change in the way your teeth fit together when you bite

Remember, one of the many advantages you enjoy in the Army is free dental care. For active-duty family members, a dental insurance program is available at a minimal cost, and emergency dental care is authorized for family members on a space-available basis at military dental facilities.

Field Hygiene

During peace, the mission of the Army is to prepare units to perform their wartime missions. For most soldiers, this will mean spending a great deal of time in the field conducting training exercises. Your unit's ability to train properly and to perform its assigned mission increases if you are free from disease. There are several simple things you can do to prevent disease to yourself and others while on field exercises. Army Field Manual FM 21-100, *Field Hygiene and Sanitation* provides detailed instructions. The following are just a few suggestions to help you get started. You will be taught many other aspects of field hygiene in BCT and from your unit leaders. All units have standard procedures established that you will learn.

Follow Waste Disposal Procedures in the Field

The main reason for burying waste is to prevent the breeding of flies. Flies can spread diarrhea and dysentery. Procedures for waste disposal are as follows:

1. Use the unit latrine for body waste or dig your own "cat hole." A cat hole is a hole 1 foot deep and 1 foot wide. Cover it with dirt when you are finished.
2. Use the garbage pit for other waste or dig your own garbage pit. Dig it deep enough to allow 4 inches of dirt to cover the garbage when you are finished filling the hole.

Prevent Skin Infections

You must bathe frequently in the field. If showers or baths are not available, use a washcloth daily to wash your genitals, armpits, feet, and other areas where you sweat or that become wet, such as between the thighs or (for females) under the breasts. You can also use talcum powder in these areas to keep your skin dry.

Proper foot care is essential for all soldiers and a few simple, common-sense steps can prevent serious foot problems. Wash and dry your feet thoroughly, especially between your toes.

Attend promptly to common medical problems such as blisters, ingrown toenails, and fungus infections like athlete's foot.

You should also wear proper clothing. Wear loose-fitting uniforms because they allow for better ventilation. Tight-fitting uniforms reduce blood circulation and ventilation. Don't wear nylon or silky undergarments. Cotton undergarments are more absorbent and allow the skin to dry.

Wash Your Hands Before Eating

Your hands will come into contact with many sources of bacteria while you are in the field. Some of these sources are insect repellent, the latrine door, weapons and ammunition, and dirt.

Protection Against Respiratory Disease

The air you breathe and the things you touch carry many diseases. Most of these diseases, such as colds, will simply make you miserable and make doing your job more difficult. Others, such as the flu, can be severe enough to kill. To keep from getting respiratory diseases, do the following:

1. Avoid soldiers who are sick, if possible. Talk them into going to sick call for treatment.
2. Avoid using towels, caps, cigarettes, radios, or anything else that others have handled.
3. Provide an opening for fresh air into your fighting position or shelter.
4. Wash your hands as often as possible.

Substance Abuse

The Army considers abuse of any substance a serious problem. It may cause serious health complications, mental incapacitation, and even death. The Army life is an active one filled with physical and mental demands in the performance of potentially hazardous machines and activities. Safety and success requires a soldier to be in top condition and to remain alert. Substance abuse adversely affects the health and job performance of the individual soldier and also places at risk the safety of other soldiers. In training and in combat the success of the entire mission and the lives of the soldiers could be jeopardized.

Abuse of any substance, drugs or alcohol, never solves problems. It just postpones or compounds them. Soldiers who abuse substances run the risk of an addiction that creates new troubles and makes old problems worse.

The Army Alcohol and Drug Abuse Prevention and Control Program

The Army has a vigorous and effective program called the Army Alcohol and Drug Abuse Prevention and Control Program (ADAPCP). Voluntary entry into the program is strongly encouraged. Soldiers who enter this program can seek and receive help without an adverse effect on their career. ADAPCP is designed to prevent substance abuse, identify and assist the abuser as early as possible, and restore that soldier to duty. Detailed information is available from ADAPCP counselors and Army Regulation AR 600-85.

The objectives of the ADAPCP are to

1. prevent alcohol and other drug abuse;
2. identify alcohol and drug abusers as early as possible;
3. restore both military and civilian employee abusers to effective duty or identify rehabilitation failures for separation from government service;
4. provide for program evaluation and research;
5. ensure that effective awareness education is provided at all levels;
6. ensure that adequate resources and facilities are provided to accomplish the ADAPCP mission;
7. guarantee that all personnel assigned to ADAPCP staffs are appropriately trained and experienced to accomplish effectively the ADAPCP mission; and
8. achieve maximum productivity in job performance, reduced absenteeism, and lower attrition among Department of the Army civilian employees by preventing and controlling abuse of alcohol and other drugs within the civilian work force.

Sexually Transmitted Diseases

Sexually transmitted diseases (STDs), also known as venereal diseases, are caused by organisms normally transmitted by an infected person through sexual activity. Some STDs, Hepatitis B and AIDS for example, can also be transmitted through the exchange of body fluids such as blood. Although AIDS is by far the most deadly of these diseases and has received widespread publicity, the other diseases also are a serious health threat, in some cases fatal, and must not be ignored. With the exception of the AIDS virus, modern drugs have proven effective against most of the common STDs if they are treated in a timely manner.

Following responsible sexual practices such as the use of condoms, washing the genitals, and urinating immediately after intercourse is a major step in prevention of infection. Some of the more serious STDs are:

- nonspecific urethritis (chlamydia)
- gonorrhea
- syphilis
- Hepatitis B
- Acquired Immunodeficiency Syndrome (AIDS)

Currently, the Department of Defense tests its uniformed services personnel for the presence of the HIV antibody to the AIDS virus. The military feels this procedure is necessary because the uniformed services act as their own blood bank in a combat situation.

HIV-antibody-positive soldiers may not be assigned overseas including Alaska and Hawaii. They must be rechecked every six months to determine if the disease has become worse. If the disease has progressed, they are discharged from the Army. The Army also requires that all soldiers receive annual education classes on AIDS.

First Aid

First aid is the emergency care given to the sick, injured, or wounded before being treated by medical personnel. The Army Dictionary defines first aid as "urgent and immediate lifesaving and other measures which can be performed for casualties by nonmedical personnel when medical personnel are not immediately available." In basic training, you will receive hands-on first aid training in such techniques as mouth-to-mouth resuscitation and bandaging wounds. Once you join your unit, you will receive additional first aid instructions. Army Field Manual FM 21-11, *First Aid for Soldiers,* will also help you remain skilled in the correct procedures for giving first aid. The following examples of first aid are provided to give you an idea of the nature and extent of first aid knowledge soldiers must have.

Fundamental Criteria for First Aid

Normally, every squad, team, or crew will have one member who is a "combat lifesaver"—a nonmedical soldier who has been trained to provide emergency care.

However, you must be prepared to depend on your own first aid knowledge and skills to save yourself or other soldiers in a critical situation. You may be able to save a life, prevent permanent disability, or reduce long periods of hospitalization by knowing what to do, what not to do, and when to seek medical assistance.

In basic training you will be taught three essential criteria regarding first aid.

- Check for *Breathing*. Lack of oxygen intake (through a compromised airway or inadequate breathing) can lead to brain damage or death in very few minutes.
- Check for *Bleeding*. Life cannot continue without an adequate volume of blood to carry oxygen to tissues.
- Check for *Shock*. Unless shock is prevented or treated, death may result even though the injury would not otherwise be fatal.

Every soldier is issued a first aid case with a first aid dressing encased in a plastic wrapper for his own use. If you administer first aid to another soldier, remember to use the injured person's dressing. You may need your own later.

Climatic Injuries: Heat and Cold

Climate-related injuries are usually preventable. Prevention is both an individual and leadership responsibility. As a soldier in training and on active duty you will be exposed to all types of weather and living conditions. You may have to live in the field for long periods or perform routine duties outside for extended periods. While the Army provides the best clothing and shelter possible, it is ultimately the responsibility of each soldier to take whatever protective measures are possible to prevent a weather injury.

In your training you will learn many preventive techniques and measures to take, warning signs of impending injury, and first aid steps should an injury occur. Climatic injuries can occur in almost every season of the year depending on the temperature and the moisture conditions. The two most dangerous seasons, however, are summer and winter, when soldiers are exposed to extremes of temperatures. Pay attention to your instructors and FM 21-11. Implement what they teach in self-care and in the care for any soldiers for whom you may be responsible.

10-1: Wet Bulb Globe Temperature Index

Criteria		PMM	
Heat Condition/ Category	WBGT Index (°F)	Water Intake (quarts/hour)	Work/Rest Cycle (minutes)
1*	78–81.9	At least 1/2	Continuous
2	82–84.9	At least 1/2	50/10
3	85–87.9	At least 1	45/15
4	88–89.9	At least 1-1/2	30/30
5†	90 and above	More than 2	20/40

*MOPP gear or body armor adds at least 10°F to the WBGT index.

†Suspend physical training and strenuous activity. If operational (nontraining) mission requires strenuous activity, enforce water intake to minimize expected heat injuries.

Note: "Rest" means minimal physical activity. Rest should be accomplished in the shade if possible. Any activity requiring only minimal physical activity can be performed during "rest" periods. Examples include: training by lecture or demonstration, minor maintenance preocedures on vehicles or weapons, and personal hygiene activities such as skin and foot care.

Sun and Heat Injuries

In the summer the combination of high temperature and high humidity can cause fatal heat injuries. This potentially deadly combination is measured by a device called the wet bulb globe. To protect soldiers doing outside duties during the summer, the Army uses the Wet Bulb Globe Temperature Index to determine a heat condition. Based on that condition soldiers are notified to take protective measures, such as increasing water intake, loosening uniforms, and rest periods. While you will not be taking such measurements yourself, you should understand what is meant by the index and the precautions necessary.

Cold and Wet Injuries

Cold injuries are most likely to occur when an unprepared or careless soldier is exposed to winter temperatures. The type of cold weather and the nature of combat operation or training in which the soldier is involved, a soldier's clothing, physical condition, and mental makeup are all determining factors.

Cold injuries, however, can normally be prevented. Well-disciplined, properly equipped, and well-trained soldiers can be protected even in the most adverse conditions. Soldiers must know the importance of personal hygiene, exercise, care of the feet and hands, and the proper use of protective clothing. They must know how to take care of themselves and others to prevent injuries and to treat injuries if they should occur.

10-2: Windchill Factor

Estimated wind speed (mph)	Actual temperature reading (°F)											
	50	40	30	20	10	0	-10	-20	-30	-40	-50	-60
	Equivalent chill temperature (°F)											
calm	50	40	30	20	10	0	-10	-20	-30	-40	-50	-60
5	48	37	27	16	6	-5	-15	-26	-36	-47	-57	-68
10	40	28	16	4	-9	-24	-33	-46	-58	-70	-83	-95
15	36	22	9	-5	-18	-32	-45	-58	-72	-85	-99	-112
20	32	18	4	-10	-25	-39	-53	-67	-82	-96	-110	-121
25	30	16	0	-15	-29	-44	-59	-74	-88	-104	-118	-133
30	28	13	-2	-18	-33	-48	-63	-79	-94	-109	-125	-140
35	27	11	-4	-20	-35	-51	-67	-82	-98	-113	-129	-145
40	26	10	-6	-21	-37	-53	-69	-85	-100	-116	-132	-148

(Wind speeds greater than 40 mph have little additional effect.)	LITTLE DANGER in less than one hour with dry skin. Maximum danger of false sense of security.	INCREASING DANGER Danger from freezing of exposed flesh within one minute.	GREAT DANGER Flesh may freeze within thirty seconds.
	Notes: 1. Trench foot and immersion foot may occur at any point on this chart. 2. °F = 9/5 °C + 32		

FM 21-11 identifies cold and wet injuries, the signs/symptoms associated with these types of injuries, and appropriate first aid procedures.

Physical Fitness Training

The Army places a high priority on physical fitness training. The fitness of each individual soldier has a significant influence on his or her comrades and the unit mission. If one soldier is not "fit to fight," it can have a devastating effect on fellow soldiers and the ultimate outcome of the unit's mission. Thus, the Army's physical fitness program is as comprehensive as possible. It encompasses exercise, weight control, diet and nutrition, and stress management.

Army Physical Fitness Test

The Army's Physical Fitness Test (APFT) consists of three events: push-ups, sit-ups, and running. These three events are designed to test a soldier's endurance, strength, and cardiorespiratory efficiency. Participating in a regular exercise program

Fig. 10.3. Physical training

will help you improve your test performance. The APFT standards for men and women, by event and age group, are shown in tables 10.4 and 10.5, respectively. The first number in each pair of requirements is the minimum time or number of repetitions a soldier must achieve to earn a minimum passing score of 60 points. The second number indicates the score needed to earn the maximum score of 100 points.

TABLE 10.4. Minimum/Maximum Standards for the Army's Physical Fitness Test for Men

Age	*Push-ups (min/max)*	*Sit-ups (min/max)*	*Two-Mile Run (min/max)*
17–21	42/82	52/92	15:54/11:54
22–26	40/80	47/87	16:36/12:36
27–31	38/78	42/82	17:18/13:18
32–36	33/73	38/78	18:00/14:00
37–41	32/72	33/73	18:42/14:42
42–46	26/66	29/69	19:06/15:06
47–51	22/62	27/67	19:36/15:36
52+	16/56	26/66	20:00/16:00

TABLE 10.5. Minimum/Maximum Standards for the Army's Physical Fitness Test for Women

Age	*Push-ups (min/max)*	*Sit-ups (min/max)*	*Two-Mile Run (min/max)*
17–21	18/58	50/90	18:54/14:54
22–26	16/56	45/85	19:36/15:36
27–31	15/54	40/80	21:00/17:00
32–36	14/52	35/75	22:36/18:36
37–41	13/48	30/70	22:36/19:36
42–46	12/45	27/67	24:00/20:00
47–51	10/41	24/64	24:30/20:30
52+	09/40	22/62	25:00/21:00

Weight Control

The Army places a very high priority on weight control. Reenlistment or extension to a current enlistment can be barred for soldiers not meeting minimum Army standards. Tables 10.6 [Male] and 10.6A [Female] reflect the maximum weight for a soldier, based on height, age group, and gender. Involuntary separation from the Army can also be enacted if a soldier has been unsuccessful in meeting Army weight standards after spending six months in the Army Weight Control Program (AWCP). In addition, overweight soldiers will not be considered for promotion and will not be authorized to attend professional military or civilian schooling until they meet Army weight standards. The AWCP is aimed at ensuring that all soldiers are physically able to perform under the most strenuous combat conditions and that all soldiers maintain a trim military appearance.

All soldiers must be weighed at the time of the APFT or at least every six months. In addition, body-fat composition testing is required whenever a supervisor feels that a soldier's appearance suggests excessive body fat. Although all soldiers are encouraged to strive for a low percentage of body fat (for example, age group 17–20 is 24 percent for males and 30 percent for females), a more lenient maximum allowable body-fat percentage has been established by age group and sex (see table 10.7).

Soldiers who exceed either the maximum weight limit or maximum body-fat composition must enter a weight-control program that includes nutritional training and exercise programs administered by Army health officials. Weight-loss and body-fat goals are established, and monthly weigh-ins are required. Few exceptions to these standards are allowed.

TABLE 10.6. Military Acceptable Weight (in Pounds) as Related to Age and Height for *Males*—Initial Army Procurement

Height (inches)	*Minimum weight any age*	*Maximum Weight by Years of Age*			
		17–20	*21–27*	*28–39*	*40 and over*
60	100	139	141	143	146
61	102	144	146	148	151
62	103	148	150	153	156
63	104	153	155	158	161
64	105	158	160	163	166
65	106	163	165	168	171
66	107	168	170	173	177
67	111	174	176	179	182
68	115	179	181	184	187
69	119	184	186	189	193
70	123	189	192	195	199
71	127	194	197	201	204
72	131	200	203	206	210
73	135	205	208	212	216
74	139	211	214	218	222
75	143	217	220	224	228
76	147	223	226	230	234
77	151	229	232	236	240
78	153	235	238	242	247
79	159	241	244	248	253
80	166	247	250	255	259

NOTE: If a male exceeds these weights, percent body fat will be measured per the method described in AR 600-9. If a male also exceeds this body fat (table 10.7), he will be rejected for service.

TABLE 10.6A. Military Acceptable Weight (in Pounds) as Related to Age and Height for *Females*—Initial Army Procurement

Height (inches)	Minimum weight any age	Maximum Weight by Years of Age: 17–20	21–27	28–39	40 and over
58	90	112	115	119	122
59	92	116	119	123	126
60	94	120	123	127	130
61	96	124	127	131	135
62	98	129	132	137	139
63	100	133	137	141	144
64	102	137	141	145	148
65	104	141	145	149	153
66	106	146	150	154	158
67	109	149	154	159	162
68	112	154	159	164	167
69	115	158	163	168	172
70	118	163	168	173	177
71	122	167	172	177	182
72	125	172	177	183	188
73	128	177	182	188	193
74	130	183	189	194	198
75	133	188	194	200	204
76	136	194	200	206	209
77	139	199	205	211	215
78	141	204	210	216	220
79	144	209	215	222	226
80	147	214	220	227	232

NOTE: If a female exceeds these weights, percent body fat will be measured per the method described in AR 600-9. If a female also exceeds this body fat (table 10.7), she will be rejected for service.

TABLE 10.7. Body-Fat Composition Standard

Age Group	*Sex*	*Percentage of Body Fat*
17–20	M	24
	F	30
21–27	M	26
	F	32
28–39	M	28
	F	34
40+	M	30
	F	36

11. Training

The Key Element to Success

For the Army to fulfill its mission—to deter war, or, if deterrence fails, to reestablish peace through victory on the battlefield—quality training is essential and is a top priority in the Army.

Training is the cornerstone of combat readiness and must focus on the individual, the units, and their leaders. It is vital to the Army Team—the active Army, the Reserve components (the U.S. Army Reserve and the Army National Guard), and Department of Army civilians.

Soldiers spend the majority of their time training. The Army's training programs are guided by the doctrine, philosophy, and principles that are discussed in FM 25-100, *Training the Force,* and FM 25-101, *Battle-Focused Training.* Tough, demanding, and realistic conditions; high standards; and a focus on each unit's peacetime and wartime missions characterize the Army's training programs. The proficiency developed by quality training includes basic soldier skills such as marksmanship and land navigation, but there is more than basic skills in being a soldier today.

Technical competency in specific job areas and in unit operations is also vital. As today's Army continues to modernize, individual skills in communications, computers, aviation, and other high-technology areas increase in importance. The emphasis and investment that the Army places on training paid great dividends in Operation Desert Storm in 1991 with a rapid, overwhelming victory over Iraqi forces. As the Army builds down to a smaller force, it will be essential to maintain its focus on training. Unit readiness is the objective of all Army training.

Although major reductions to the Army force structure and its resources are taking place, one fact remains constant: training is the glue that holds the Army together.

Fig. 11.1. Soldiers rappell from a UH-1 Huey helicopter.

As a first-term enlistee or a soldier with many years of experience, you should be interested in Army training for a very personal reason: your survival on the battlefield!

Training prepares soldiers, leaders, and units to fight and win in combat—the Army's basic mission. It is the key element to ensure success in battle. Through realistic and demanding training, the Army develops the basic war-fighting spirit, skills, and techniques to win on the battlefield. Highly skilled soldiers with modern war-fighting equipment are the only formula for victory.

How the Army Trains

The Army is firmly committed to tough, demanding, and realistic training. In basic combat training (BCT), you are taught the basic skills of soldiering. BCT will give you a new frame of reference, new confidence in yourself, and new physical and mental abilities.

In advanced individual training (AIT), depending on the branch you chose, you receive training in one of the combat arms branches or one of the hundreds of Military Occupational Specialties (MOS) offered by the Army in the combat support or combat service-support branches. Your training will employ the most modern teaching and learning methods available. It will be a perfect blend of practical, hands-on training on real equipment and classroom instruction by professionals in the field that you have chosen. The quality of training you receive in the Army will be difficult to match in civilian life. Your training begins from the moment your drill sergeant instructs you in the facing movements of close-order drill (left face, right face, etc.), and it is ongoing while you are on active duty.

There are a few things you need to know about how the Army trains its soldiers.

1. First and foremost, soldiers are taught their individual skills.
2. Soldiers are trained physically so that they have stamina on the battlefield.
3. The importance of psychological training is not overlooked, for the trauma of the battlefield is very powerful. Soldiers must be trained to handle the fear associated with battle.
4. Army training is *made* interesting because the result of uninteresting training is boredom, which would force many soldiers out of the Army.
5. Army training *is* interesting because it is realistic, thorough, challenging, and constructive.

Like many soldiers, you may not know early in your first enlistment if the Army will be your career. That's okay. A solid foundation in one of the Army's training programs will help launch a successful career for you either in the military or after you return to civilian life.

Training to Fight and Win

Remember that in the Army training is the cornerstone of success. It is a full-time job for the soldier in peacetime and continues in wartime as well. On the day of the battle, soldiers and their units will fight as well or as poorly as they were trained in the days leading up to the battle.

Even though soldiers receive a great deal of training during their BCT and AIT, most of their training is conducted in their units, where they learn more about their individual skills, and also train as members of teams under conditions that approx-

Fig. 11.2. A soldier wearing a protective mask and multiple integrated laser engagement system (MILES) gear performs immediate action on his jammed M-60 machine gun during an exercise.

imate battle. Special emphasis is given to simulators and training simulations to enhance combat realism and as a cost-effective alternative to field training and live ammunition usage.

The complexities of modern-day warfare make it increasingly important to concentrate on training programs for small-unit (squad and platoon) leaders. These leaders direct the employment of weapons and small units. Thus, they must be competent in their use. Small-unit skills are difficult to learn and require constant practice to maintain.

Once you complete small-unit training, you will undergo your annual company and battalion training at one of the combat training centers (CTCs)—the National Training Center (NTC), Fort Irwin, California; the Combat Maneuver Training Center (CMTC), Hohenfels, Germany; or the Joint Readiness Training Center (JRTC), Fort Polk, Louisiana.

Individual Training in Units

The Individual Training Evaluation Program (ITEP) provides a formal structure for a soldier's ongoing training. It consists of

Fig. 11.3. Jungle training

three components: Common Task Training (CTT), the Self-Development Test (SDT), and the Commander's Evaluation (CE).

CTT emphasizes basic combat survival skills (for example, map reading and communication procedures) that all soldiers must successfully perform in order to maintain an acceptable level of proficiency. Soldiers are tested each year on their ability to perform these skills.

The SDT is a written test of MOS skills, training, and leadership knowledge. Soldiers at Skill Level 2—sergeants and higher—take the SDT annually.

The CE is a hands-on test administered by each command. It is designed to help the commander and others in the chain of command assess overall proficiency of soldiers in a unit on individual tasks critical to the unit's mission. In developing a mission essential task list (METL) that relates to his organization's wartime mission, the commander and unit leaders determine the level of proficiency each soldier has achieved in relationship to the standards outlined in various manuals. FM 25-100 discusses the METL development process.

Commanders and unit leaders are also responsible for ensuring that their unit is trained to perform collective tasks.

Fig. 11.4. An AH-1G Cobra fires 2.75-inch rockets during a training exercise.

They use various training manuals to develop a unit training strategy.

Noncommissioned Officer Education System (NCOES)

Another phase of enlisted training is the NCOES. The goal of the NCOES is to train NCOs to be trainers and leaders. It is designed to prepare soldiers to perform their duties at the next higher skill level. NCOES courses in leadership and technical training are conducted in service schools and NCO academies both within the Continental United States (CONUS) and overseas. There are four levels of training within NCOES: the Primary Leadership Development Course (PLDC); the Basic NCO Course (BNCOC); Advanced NCO Courses (ANCOC); and the U.S. Army Sergeants Major Academy (USASMA). A brief description of these courses follows:

PLDC. This is a four-week, non-MOS-specific leadership course that emphasizes the fundamentals of how to lead and train and the duties, responsibilities, and authority of the NCO.

BNCOC. The length of this course varies according to MOS. First priority to attend this course goes to soldiers selected for promotion to Staff Sergeant.

ANCOC. These courses stress MOS-related tasks with emphasis on technical and advanced leadership skills and knowledge of the military subjects required to train and lead other soldiers at the platoon or comparable level. Course length varies with the requirements of the particular MOS.

USASMA. This is a 22-week course that prepares Master Sergeants and First Sergeants for troop and staff assignments as Sergeants Major throughout the Army. It is a great honor to be selected for this course and is a big step in an NCO's career.

12. Duty Assignments

Where Will You Be Assigned?

Travel! Adventure! New people and places! That's what the Army offers you. The opportunity of seeing different, sometimes exotic foreign lands is a primary reason many young men and women join the Army. But foreign lands aren't the only travel destinations you can reach in the Army. There are many posts spread across the United States for you to see. They range from metropolitan areas like Washington, D.C., to smaller areas like Columbus, Georgia; Leavenworth, Kansas; and Colorado Springs, Colorado. Altogether there are over 30 major Army bases and posts in the United States and dozens more smaller installations. Whether you want an overseas assignment or duty in the United States, the possibility is great you will get something you want.

Moving is still an essential part of Army life. With the proper attitude, it can be the greatest adventure of your military service. You will have experiences and see things both in the United States and overseas that most civilians only dream about.

Enlisted Personnel Assignment System

The task of putting the right soldier in the right job belongs to the Army's Enlisted Personnel Assignment System. Its primary mission is to meet personnel requirements for the Army. Secondary goals are to

1. equalize desirable and undesirable assignments by reassigning the most eligible soldier from those of similar MOS and grade;
2. equalize the hardship of military service;

3. meet the personal desires of the soldier as indicated on DA Form 2635, "Enlisted Preference Statement"; and
4. assign each soldier so that he or she will have the greatest opportunity for professional development and promotion.

Soldiers become available for reassignment when they are awarded an initial or a new MOS, volunteer for reassignment, finish schooling or training, or complete an overseas tour or a "normal" assignment in the United States. Each MOS has an established period that is considered "normal" for a soldier to spend in the United States before being assigned to an overseas position. The Enlisted Distribution Assignment System (EDAS) matches available soldiers against requisitions based on grade, MOS, skill level, and the expiration of their terms of service (ETS). Other factors considered include the number of months since a soldier's last official move and the months since serving in an overseas area.

Taking Your Family with You

Other than training, most assignments in the United States are for three years. When you go overseas, your tour of duty will vary by location. Appendix I lists a sample of selected Army overseas tour lengths. A complete list of overseas tours is found in AR 614-30, Appendix B.

Depending on the location, you may be able to take your family along with you on an assignment. There are a variety of pays and allowances associated with moving a soldier and family that are available depending on the situation. Soldiers must discuss their move with the servicing military travel office to determine what they are authorized to receive. In general, the government will pay for your family's moving expenses. A job for your spouse and the availability and expense of housing to accommodate your family are other factors that you will have to consider.

During your initial time in the Army, you may find it impossible or impractical to take your family with you to your first training assignments. Normally these training assignments are for only a few weeks or months and much of your time will be spent studying or in the field. The training also may be at several different locations, so you could be moving frequently. Since short periods of time at a location are not considered your permanent assignment or station, they are called "temporary duty" or TDY. In a TDY status you will receive money for travel and food, but family members will not. It is pre-

Fig. 12.1. Fort Greely, Alaska

sumed they remain at your permanent home, or wait and join you at your station after you are settled.

Frankly, during BCT and AIT you will be living in a barracks or in the field, and will not have much time for other than military duties. First, you have to go to basic training, then advanced individual training, and perhaps further specialized training. Separation from your family can be tough, but there is an advantage: you can devote more time to training, learning new skills, and getting set in your new job and assignment without the concern of also trying to settle your family in a new location. They can join you when the situation is more favorable for them.

Overseas Service

The primary role of soldiers stationed overseas is the same as that of their statewide counterparts, that is, to fulfill mission requirements. Overseas assignments are an integral part of Army life, but with changes in the international situation since the late 1980s, requirements to keep large numbers of Army forces permanently based abroad have diminished. The United States, however, must continue to maintain capable and cred-

12-2: Household Goods Weight Allowance

Rank	Limit in pounds for shipping or storing: Without dependents	With dependents
E-9	12,000	14,500
E-8	11,000	13,500
E-7	10,500	12,500
E-6	8,000	11,000
E-5	7,000	9,000
E-4 (> 2 years)	7,000	8,000
E-4 (< 2 years)	3,500	7,000
E-3	2,000*	5,000
E-2	1,500*	5,000
E-1	1,500*	5,000

Source: Per Diem, Travel and Transportation Allowance Committee
*E-3s, E-2s, and E-1s married to E-3s, E-2s, or E-1s are entitled to a combined weight allowance of 5,000 pounds when both are without dependents.

ible Army forces forward-deployed in Europe, Asia, and in other areas of vital strategic interest to our country.

For many soldiers, an overseas assignment will be the first time that they have traveled abroad. Unlike other Americans who visit foreign countries for a short vacation, a soldier's overseas assignment is normally for two or three years. When you are assigned overseas will depend largely on your Military Occupational Specialty (MOS). If you have a combat arms or military intelligence MOS, you are a likely candidate for overseas duty during your first term of enlistment.

Soldiers who are outgoing and adventurous have a great time during their overseas tours. Take, for example, eating new foods. Your assignment could lead to a new experience sampling Japanese teriyaki, or trying kimchi in Korea, or enjoying bratwurst in Bavaria. Experiencing new cultures can be an adventure in itself.

Deferments, Deletions, and Curtailments

Deferments are temporary delays in the PCS date, usually for less than 90 days. *Deletions* of an overseas assignment are longer delays. When a deletion is approved, the soldier normally will be stabilized at the present assignment for up to one year or until the problem for which the deletion was approved has been resolved.

Quite logically, the Army desires to keep deferments, deletions, and curtailments of overseas assignments to a minimum because these actions tend to adversely affect personnel readiness. They will, however, be granted occasionally, mostly for compassionate reasons.

When a family member requires hospitalization of less than 90 days, deferments can be granted. In more severe cases, when hospitalization is expected to extend beyond 90 days, a deletion can be approved. Terminal illness of a family member, where death is expected within a year, is another reason for deletion.

Once a soldier is overseas, the tour can be curtailed for some of the same reasons approved for deferment or deletion. The death of an immediate family member can be cause for curtailment, as can urgent health problems of a family member living with the soldier overseas.

Volunteering

Instead of waiting for the Army to assign you to an overseas post, you may choose to volunteer for such an assignment. Although volunteering doesn't guarantee an assignment, it does increase your chance of getting an assignment that suits your needs and desires. The Army benefits from its volunteer program by identifying soldiers who are highly motivated about their new assignments.

Once overseas, you may also volunteer for an extension of your tour and for intertheater and intratheater transfers. An *intertheater transfer* is an overseas transfer from one theater to another; an *intratheater transfer* is from one location to another within the same theater. Overseas theaters encompass the following geographic locations: Africa and Middle East/Asia area (AMEA); Europe area (EURA); Far East and Pacific area (FEPA); and South America and Caribbean area (SACA).

Homebase and Advance Assignment Program (HAAP)

The Homebase and Advance Assignment Program (HAAP) reduces family dislocation and the expenditures of Army funds in reassigning soldiers to new duty stations. Sergeants and above are eligible to participate in the HAAP. Under HAAP, a soldier's current stateside assignment is considered the homebase. When the individual receives an overseas assignment to a 12-month, short-tour, dependent-restricted area, the soldier

Fig. 12.3. On the move in South Korea

is returned to the homebase area once the overseas assignment is completed, when at all possible. If a return to the homebase is not possible, the soldier is at least informed of the assignment that will follow the overseas short tour before leaving the overseas location. For a more detailed discussion of the HAAP, see AR 614-200.

Assignment of Married Service Couples

Army requirements and readiness goals are paramount when considering soldiers for assignment. Special consideration can be afforded to married couples when both individuals are members of the Army. Specifically, the Army has established a voluntary Army couples program (the Married Couples Program [MACP]), which provides consideration for joint assignments. Such joint assignments, of course, must be consistent with the needs of the Army. Soldiers married to members of other branches of the military are not eligible for the MACP.

Reporting to a New Duty Station

A new assignment other than short periods less than 179 days is called a permanent change of station (PCS). The orders assigning you to a new duty station include a date, a no-later-than time, and a destination where you should report.

You should make travel arrangements so that you arrive during the morning hours. This may require your spending a night in a local motel or making arrangements to stay on post at visitors' quarters the night before reporting for duty.

Make sure you have copies of your orders and a recent haircut and that your uniform is clean and well-pressed. You want to make a favorable impression.

Just like your basic combat and advanced individual training, reporting to your first unit will be organized for you. You will receive an indoctrination and information package that will be of tremendous value in helping you learn about your new duty station. Records that you have with you will be turned over to a personnel specialist, and you will complete forms that will allow you to collect travel allowances.

As you adjust to your new PCS, you will want to study a map of the post and locate the post exchange, recreational facilities, and training areas.

Fig. 12.4. Maneuvers in Central America

13. Educational and Commission Opportunities

Soldier and Student

When you put on an Army uniform, you become a part of a unique learning system. From the beginning, your Army experience will challenge you, push you, and help you improve beyond anything you ever imagined. Being a soldier means sharpening your mind and toughening your body, getting a sense of who you are and what you can do. The Army is one of the smartest routes to getting an advanced education. In the Army, learning is a way of life.

The Army believes that education is one of the keys to building a successful future. Professional training and challenging experiences, combined with a wide range of educational opportunities, can make you a better soldier and person.

As a soldier, you will have access to programs at accredited colleges, universities, and vocational schools around the world. You can also take correspondence courses. Many courses are designed to accommodate your busy schedule. Offered either on post or within commuting distance, classes are scheduled to fit into your off-duty time on weekends, and evenings. Many of the schools available to you grant college credits for your military training and experience.

Professional Army education counselors are available to help you set educational goals and outline the academic or vocational courses you will need to achieve those goals. Your counselor will help you balance training, on-the-job experience, and self-development initiatives, thus allowing you to work toward credentials that will enhance your leadership abilities and support continued development in your Army specialty.

Educational and Commission Opportunities

Young men and women who want to learn and improve themselves have wide opportunities in the Army today. The majority of soldiers in the Army are already high school graduates. Those who have not completed high school can earn an equivalency certificate. Those who qualify can take a full four-year college course for a bachelor's degree or, through selection for Reserve officer training programs (ROTC), earn a commission in the Army while also earning a college degree.

The time you spend in the Army is time well spent. As you continue learning and accepting new responsibilities, you will be gaining self-confidence, determination, and discipline, characteristics that money can't buy and that spell success in any field of endeavor. Your breadth of experience and maturity will be easily recognized. You will be clearer about your career aims and more realistic about the short-term effort needed to achieve your long-term goals.

What can you personally get from the Army's commitment to professional training and education? Four things come to mind:

- Technical school training
- On-the-job training
- Continuation training and education
- College credits and a degree

Technical School Training

After basic training, some soldiers will report to a military technical school to receive initial training in their chosen career field or occupational specialty. These schools start from scratch; that is, they begin with the very basics of knowledge and proceed to teach people complex tasks and skills. So if you are worried that you can't learn a seemingly complex skill in mechanics or electronics, for example, set your worries aside. The Army will fully train you even if you have no prior experience in the subject in which you are interested. Some examples of the courses taught in service schools are:

- Radar
- Satellite communications
- Data processing
- Medical administration
- Vehicle and helicopter maintenance
- Missile mechanic

On-the-Job Training

Some soldiers go straight to their first unit after basic training. There, they begin an on-the-job (OJT) training program. Others who arrive at their first unit even after advanced individual training or technical school must still be trained in their specific duties. They also begin an OJT or apprenticeship program.

Your supervisor will not expect you to know everything about your new job. He or she would be shocked if you did. All that your supervisor will ask of you is that you do your best to learn, a step at a time and apply the knowledge to help the unit. As you learn your job, your progress will be recorded. Eventually you will be tested on what you know; when you have achieved skilled status, you will receive appropriate certification.

This certification is valuable. It lets your leaders—the military chain of command—and civilian employers know that you have passed a thorough learning program and are fully qualified at your occupation. Some colleges and vocational schools will give you credit or advanced standing in classes based on your military skill certification.

You should also know that the Army has arranged with the U.S. Department of Labor (DOL) a terrific Apprenticeship Program. Any Army recruiter can fill you in on the details. The following is a list of skills in the Army Apprenticeship Program:

- Air defense
- Armor
- Artillery
- Engineer
- Intelligence
- Missiles and munitions
- Ordnance
- Quartermaster
- Signal
- Transportation

While it's easy to sign up for the program, completing it requires steady, hard work. When you have successfully completed the Apprenticeship Program, you will receive a Certificate of Completion of Apprenticeship from the DOL. This will mean a lot to civilian employers when you are job hunting.

Continuation Training and Education

The Army recognizes that in today's world of rapidly changing technology soldiers must keep abreast of new ideas and knowledge in their career field and specialty. Therefore, the Army has come up with an impressive system of short courses that you can take to improve your skills after your initial training is completed. For example, a helicopter engine repairman may be sent to a technical school course to learn how to repair a new helicopter that is just coming into the Army.

Regardless of what your Military Occupational Specialty (MOS) is—automotive repair, legal specialist, military policeman, or radio repairman—there will be plenty of courses to help you stay up-to-date. These courses, coupled with additional educational courses, will broaden your horizons and improve your knowledge. Education makes you well-rounded, flexible, and more able to meet everyday challenges both in the Army and in the civilian workplace.

Army Education or Learning Center

Most Army installations have both an Education Center and a Learning Center. While these centers vary in size and program offerings on different Army posts, they are available so you can take advantage of the many educational opportunities the Army has to offer.

At the Education and Learning Centers, you will find an education counselor who will help you identify your educational and professional goals. If you are unsure about your goals, your counselor can help you determine what your interests and abilities are and recommend what to do next. A few minutes with your counselor can ensure that you are on the right career track with a plan that is manageable, fulfilling, and tailored to meet your anticipated needs. Your counselor can help you select courses and programs relevant to your career field. Counseling services include academic and vocational planning, testing, college application processing, and financial aid advice.

The Education and Learning Centers also offer and administer standardized tests used for college admission and for awarding college-level credit. Frequently, these tests are given at no cost to the soldier. In addition, you will also find at many of the centers a variety of multimedia resources ranging from computer programs to reference libraries of military books and technical pamphlets designed to help you learn more about your Army specialty. Most Education and Learning Centers also have language labs complete with audiotapes and workbooks for learning foreign languages. Based on space availability, most of these resources are open to spouses.

Correspondence Courses

Regardless of where you are assigned, there are numerous correspondence courses available to you from fully accredited civilian colleges and universities.

This is how correspondence courses work. After enrollment, you receive course materials by mail. You complete reading assignments and exercises, submit the work by mail for evaluation, correspond with a professor, and in the end, take one or more examinations through the Education Center. Credits earned through correspondence courses equal those earned by other students in a normal classroom environment. The major difference is the extra discipline required by you to work diligently at the assignments without the benefit of specific deadlines and the watchful eye of a professor. Tuition assistance for correspondence courses is determined by the same rules that apply to standard college courses. An Army recruiter is one of the education counselors located on an Army post who can give you the specifics.

Tuition Assistance

Most soldiers are eligible for some amount of tuition assistance. Tuition assistance does not require you to incur additional service obligation, nor does receiving tuition assistance reduce other educational benefits that may be available to you. However, if a soldier withdraws from a course, neglects to make up an incomplete grade within 120 days, or fails a course due to nonattendance, the Army will require the soldier to pay back the tuition.

The federal government also supports higher education through student aid programs that include grants (money that does not have to be repaid) and loans. A counselor at the Education and Learning Centers is in the best position to provide you with current information on these programs, as well as on various scholarships from military and veterans' organizations that may be available to you.

Money for College

The Congress and the Army offer soldiers programs to help pay for college education. Two of them are the Montgomery

GI Bill (MGIB) and the Army College Fund (ACF). These programs are available to help pay for college once you have completed two or more years of active service. You must have a high school diploma or equivalent by the end of your first enlistment term to take advantage of this special educational incentive program.

The MGIB is available to every soldier entering the Army, regardless of the Military Occupational Specialty. A three-year enlistment could help you through the MGIB program to accumulate up to $14,400 for college. Through the ACF, you may also be eligible to receive an additional $10,600 for your college education. To qualify for the ACF, you must be a high school graduate and score 50 or higher on the Armed Forces Qualification Test (AFQT). You must also enlist in one of more than 55 specialties reserved for this program. For additional details on the MGIB and the ACF, you should talk with an Army recruiter.

Commission Opportunities

If a commission as an officer in the Army is your goal, you should know about a number of programs that can help you get one. A brief discussion of these programs follows.

Officer Candidate School (OCS)

Enlisted personnel on active duty may be eligible to apply for OCS training. Applicants must meet the following criteria:

1. Be between 19.5 and 29 years of age upon enrollment,
2. Not be assigned to a COHORT unit,
3. Have completed at least 2 years (60 semester hours) of college, and
4. Achieve a minimum score of 90 on the Officer Selection Battery test.

During their training at OCS, candidates are paid at the E-5 level unless they held higher rank prior to their assignment to OCS. You should know that the 14-week course is rigorous, requiring a high level of physical fitness, mental fortitude, and dedication to succeed. Upon successful completion of the course, graduates are commissioned as second lieutenants.

The U.S. Military Academy (USMA)

Soldiers who wish to attend the USMA may seek direct nominations under the provision of Army Regulation AR 351-12 if

Fig. 13.1. An aerial view of the South Post at the U.S. Military Academy

the individual is able to meet the entrance requirements without further study. The U.S. Military Academy Preparatory School (USMAPS), located at Fort Monmouth, New Jersey, provides an alternative for soldiers who need additional academic preparation to compete successfully for an appointment to the USMA. A soldier continues to receive full pay and benefits, is provided housing and meals, remains eligible for promotion, and incurs no additional service obligation while attending USMAPS.

To qualify for admission to USMAPS, a soldier must meet the following criteria:

1. Be a U.S. citizen,
2. Be at least 17 but not yet 21 years of age on 1 July of the year entering USMAPS,
3. Be single and without dependents,
4. Hold a high school diploma, and
5. Have high morals.

Reserve Officers' Training Corps (ROTC)

Another option for the enlisted soldier to become an officer is to separate from the Army under a special ROTC scholarship

Fig. 13.2. ROTC cadets prepare to use M-136 light anti-armor weapons.

program, earn a college degree, be commissioned a second lieutenant, and return to active duty. The Army provides for a small number of soldiers annually to be discharged early to attend college full-time under the Army ROTC program. This program offers two- and three-year scholarships for active-duty enlisted personnel. Returning to active duty as a Regular Army second lieutentant, however, is not guaranteed. Based on the needs of the Army, some ROTC cadets are commissioned as second lieutenants in the U.S. Army Reserves.

To be considered for one of the scholarships, a soldier must have completed at least one year but not more than two years of college. Scholarships cover the time remaining to finish the degree. To be eligible, the soldier must

- Be a U.S. citizen.
- Be on active duty at least until 1 June of the year in which he or she will begin full-time college study in September.
- Be less than 25 years of age on 30 June of the year in which he or she will receive a commission.
- Be medically qualified.
- Demonstrate strong leadership potential.
- Have a GT Aptitude Area score of at least 115.

- Have a minimum accumulative grade point average of 2.0 on a 4.0 scale for all college work completed thus far.
- Have passed the Army Physical Fitness Test within the past year with a minimum score of 180 and a minimum of 60 points in each event.
- Be accepted as an academic junior for the two-year scholarship, or as an academic sophomore for the three-year scholarship, by an institution offering Army ROTC.

Warrant Officer Entry Course (WOEC)

Warrant officers are highly specialized experts and trainers who operate, maintain, administer, and manage the Army's equipment, support activities, and technical and tactical systems. The career progression of warrant officers is designed to encourage them to seek in-depth knowledge of certain systems and activities and maintain proficiency in their particular skills.

The Warrant Officer Entry Course (WOEC), located at Fort Rucker, Alabama, trains selected enlisted personnel in the fundamentals of leadership, ethics, personnel management, and tactics. Following completion of the rigorous six-week course, the warrant officers go to additional specialized training in their particular MOS. Although warrant officers may serve in a variety of MOS, there is an emphasis on maintenance and aviation specialties. (For additional information, see Department of the Army Pamphlet 350-1.)

To qualify for entry to the WOEC, a soldier must

- Be a sergeant or higher.
- Have earned a high school diploma or General Educational Development (GED) equivalency.
- Have served three years of active service prior to appointment.

14. Army Pay and Benefits

The Army Pay System

Army pay accounts for active-duty soldiers are handled by the Defense Finance and Accounting Center, Fort Benjamin Harrison, Indiana. Your Army pay is computed each month. You may elect to be paid once a month—at the end of the month—or twice a month—at mid-month and the end of the month.

On 21 November 1988, the Under Secretary of the Army approved adoption of a new military pay system software to pay active-duty and Reserve component soldiers of the Army. This system is called Joint Uniform Military Pay System/Joint Service Software (JUMPS/JSS). Changes under this system include a revised "Leave and Earnings Statement" (LES, as seen in figure 14.3) and a new form called the "Net Pay Advice" (NPA, as seen in figure 14.2).

Figures 14.1 through 14.8 provide explanations of each block on the LES and NPA forms.

Understanding Your Pay Statements

Each LES is personalized. Because your monthly LES contains a great deal of information on you and your progress in the Army, you should know and understand the form. The LES shows all entitlements to pay that you have earned and the deductions, allotments, and pay changes made during the period covered by the statement. It also records everything that affects your leave (vacation) account for the period of the LES. The LES helps you check the accuracy of your entitlements and manage your financial affairs more effectively. Any discrepancies should be brought immediately to the attention of the local finance and accounting officer (FAO) through your chain of command.

AIR FORCE/ARMY LEAVE & EARNINGS STATEMENT (ACTIVE & RESERVE FORCES)

ID	NAME (LAST, FIRST, M)	SOC.SEC.NO.	GRADE	PAY DATE	YRS SVC	ETS	BRANCH	ADSN/DSSN	PERIOD COVERED
	SIMPSON, EDWARD C.	303-85-7978	E3	870715	02	910714	ARMY	5053	1 - 31 MAR 90

	ENTITLEMENTS TYPE	AMOUNT		DEDUCTIONS TYPE	AMOUNT		ALLOTMENTS TYPE	AMOUNT	
A	BASE PAY	889	80	FITW	118	47	CHARITY	2	00
B	BAQ	215	70	FICA	68	07	DEP SUP	200	00
C	BAS	183	21	STATE TX	10	99			
D				SGLI	4	00			
F				USSH		50			
F				MM	442	34			
G									
H									
I									
J									
K									
L									
	TOTAL	1288	71		644	37		202	00

SUMMARY

AMT FWD +		
TOT ENT +	1288	71
TOT DED -	644	37
TOT ALMT -	202	00
NET AMT =	442	34
CR FWD -		
EOM PAY =	442	34

LEAVE	BEG BAL	ERND	USED	NEW BAL	BAL TO ETS	LV LOST	LV PAID	USE/LOSE BAL
	13.5	15.0	027	1.5	40.5			

FED TAXES	FED WAGE PERIOD	FED WAGE YTD	FED M/S	FED EX	FED TAX ADD'L	FED TAX YTD
	889.80	2,669.40	S	O		356.41

FICA TAXES	FICA WAGE PERIOD	FICA WAGE YTD	FICA TAX YTD
	889.80	2,669.40	204.21

STATE TAXES	STATE CODE	ST WAGE PERIOD	STATE WAGE YTD	STATE M/S	STATE EXEM	ST TAX ADD'L	ST TAX YTD
	CA	889.80	2,669.40	S	O		33.67

PAY DATA	BAQ TYPE	PRIMARY DEPN	VHA ZIP	RENT AMT	SHARE NR	RENT STAT	JFTR LOC	COLA DEPNS	2D JFTR LOC	BAS TYPE	CHARITY YTD	TPC	PACIDN
	SINGLE									B	6.00		AAKØNRAA

REMARKS

EXAMPLE ONLY

Fig. 14.1. Air Force/Army Leave and Earnings Statement.

AIR FORCE/ARMY NET PAY ADVICE (ACTIVE & RESERVES)

The amount in block 6 is your net pay for the pay day indicated in block 4 and was sent to the financial organization in block 7 for credit to your account. Financial organizations identified with an "A" preceding your account number participate in the Direct Deposit Check Program. When cashing a personal check at your financial organization on payday, advise your teller you are a participant in the Direct Deposit program. It will help you with better service. If you are paid once a month or you do not have your pay sent to a financial organization for direct deposit, information in blocks 5 through 7 will not be present and this form is intended to provide you with the remarks information only

1. MEMBER'S NAME AND ADDRESS	2. SSN	3. ADSN/DSSN	4. PAY DATE
SIMPSON, EDWARD C. AAIØNRAA	303-85-7978	5053	900315
	5. ACCOUNT NUMBER A-001-JUMPS-AC		6. NET PAY AMOUNT 442.34
	7. Your Net Pay was Forwarded to: Merchants Bank, Fin Ctr Br Indianapolis, IN 46249		

REMARKS
INVEST IN THE FUTURE - BUY US SAVINGS BONDS!

EXAMPLE ONLY

Fig. 14.2. Air Force/Army Net Pay Advice.

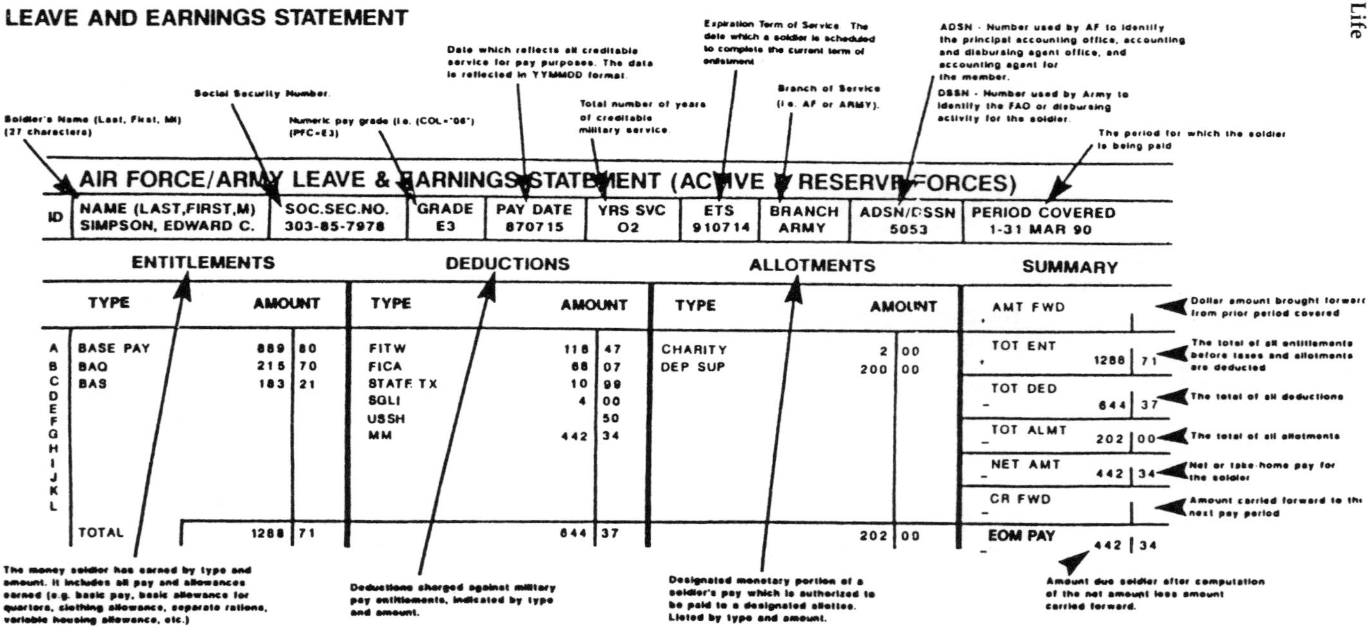

Fig. 14.3. Illustrative Leave and Earnings Statement (LES)

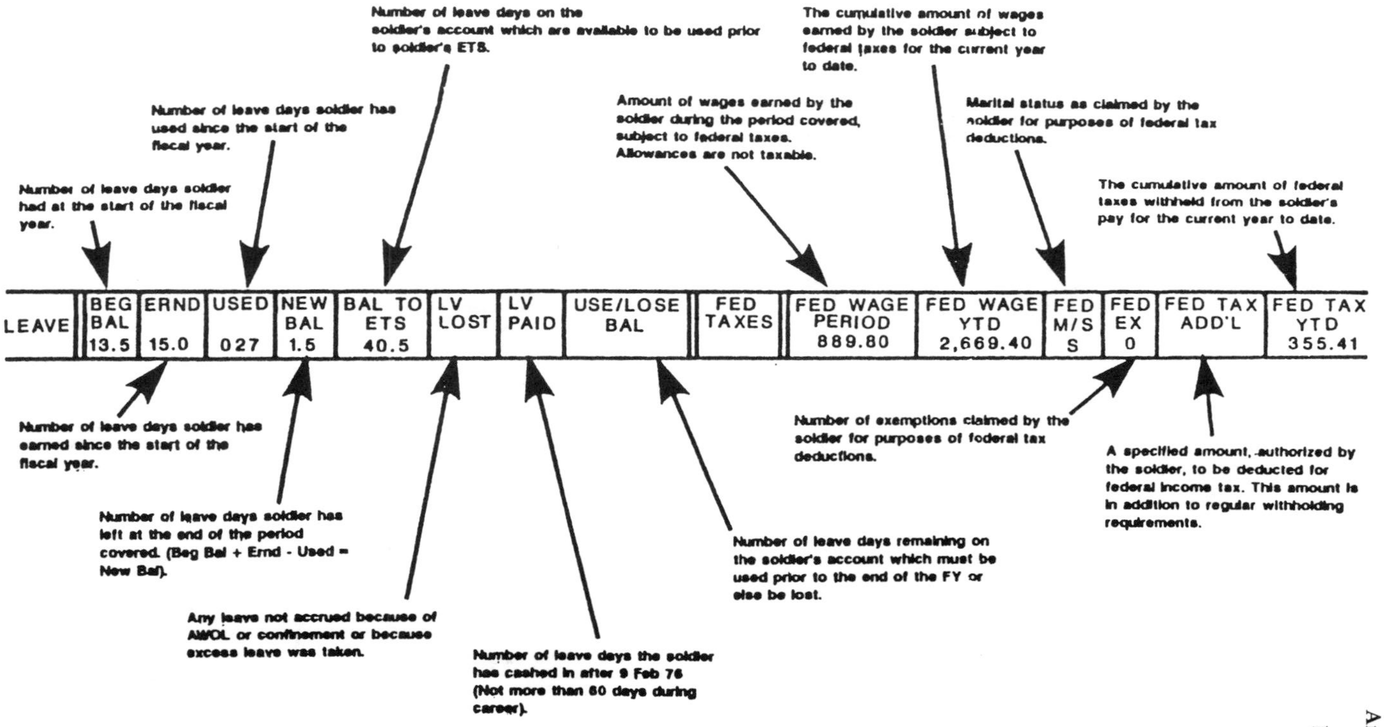

Fig. 14.4. LES explained: leave and federal taxes

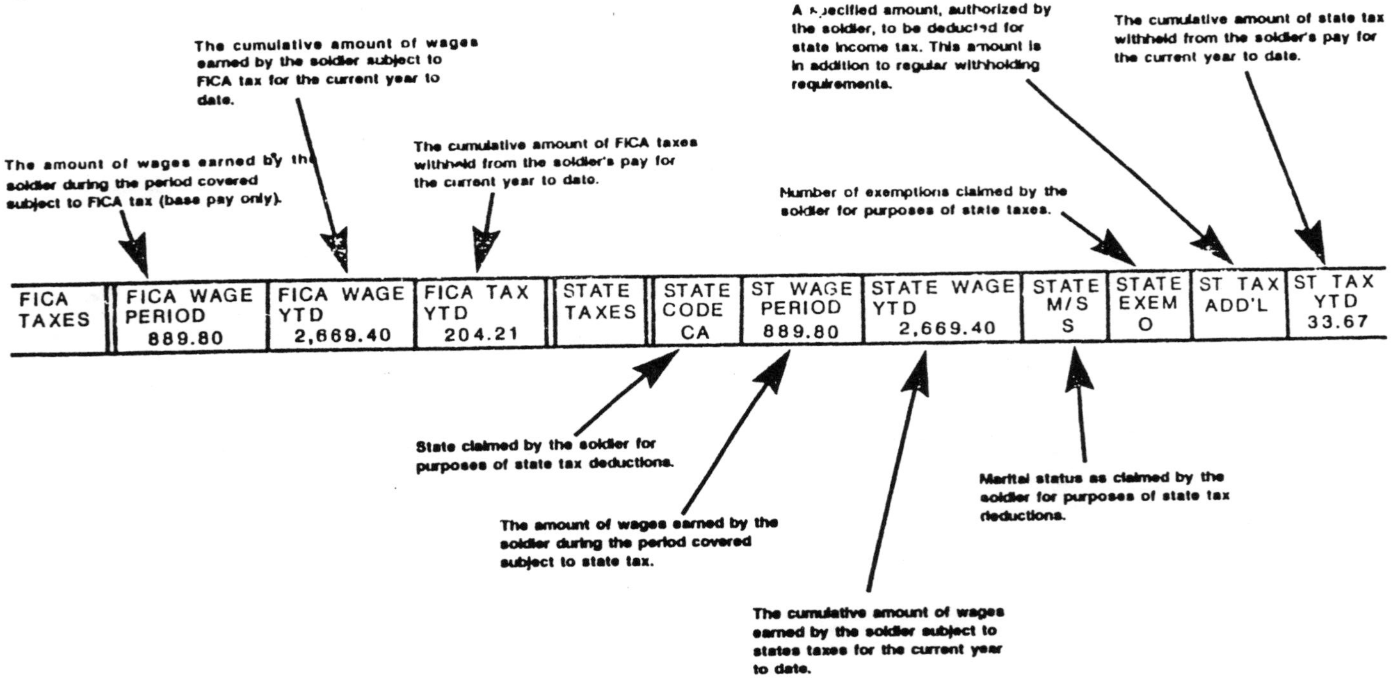
The amount of wages earned by the soldier during the period covered subject to FICA tax (base pay only).
The cumulative amount of wages earned by the soldier subject to FICA tax for the current year to date.
The cumulative amount of FICA taxes withheld from the soldier's pay for the current year to date.
Number of exemptions claimed by the soldier for purposes of state taxes.
A specified amount, authorized by the soldier, to be deducted for state income tax. This amount is in addition to regular withholding requirements.
The cumulative amount of state tax withheld from the soldier's pay for the current year to date.
FICA TAXES
FICA WAGE PERIOD 889.80
FICA WAGE YTD 2,669.40
FICA TAX YTD 204.21
STATE TAXES
STATE CODE CA
ST WAGE PERIOD 889.80
STATE WAGE YTD 2,669.40
STATE M/S S
STATE EXEM O
ST TAX ADD'L
ST TAX YTD 33.67
State claimed by the soldier for purposes of state tax deductions.
The amount of wages earned by the soldier during the period covered subject to state tax.
The cumulative amount of wages earned by the soldier subject to states taxes for the current year to date.
Marital status as claimed by the soldier for purposes of state tax deductions.

Fig. 14.5. LES explained: FICA and state taxes

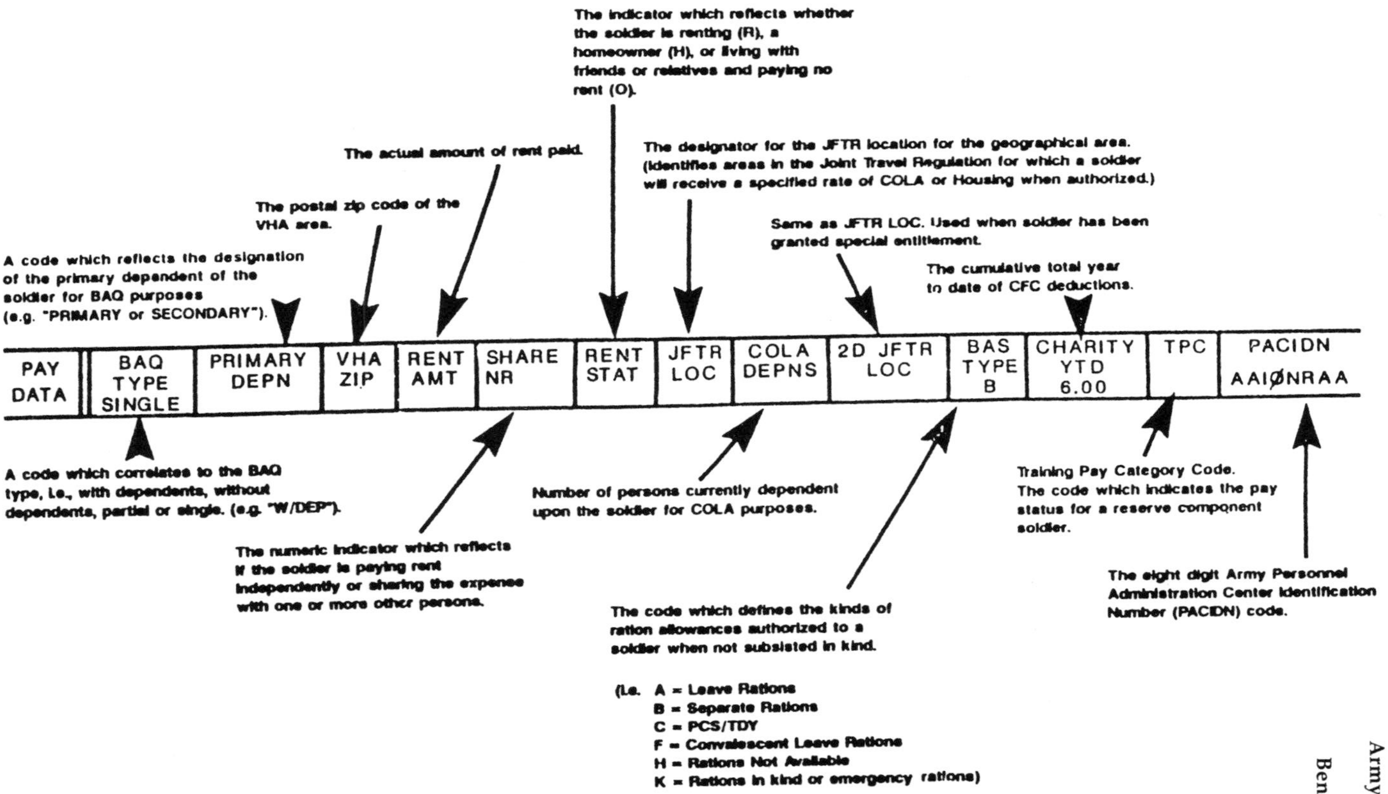

Fig. 14.6. LES explained: pay data

REMARKS

REMARKS

If there is a run over from the entitlements, deductions, or allotments from the columnar display area, it will be printed as the first priority in the remarks section.

Bank name and account number will be printed in the remarks section.

Recurring Remarks:

Debt Bal Due US - An amount owed to the government (i.e. reimbursement of advanced pay).

Held Pay Balance - Amount of monies elected for accrual by the soldier or local commander. Monthly amount will appear in the deductions column. This is Army equivalent for Accrued Pay-Balance.

Bond Data - A remark that indicates the Bond # (relating to the Bond # in the allotment section of the LES), the purchase price, and the deduction to date. Example:

BOND #1 PURCHASE PRICE $25.00; DEDUCTED TO DATE $15.00
BOND #2 PURCHASE PRICE $100.00; BOND ISSUED THIS MONTH.

Other remarks explaining changes to current month entitlements, deductions, allotments, etc. will appear in remarks.

NOTES:

Mid-month payment will be listed in the deductions column as MM.

CRA Balance will no longer be shown as a recurring monthly amount. Total (accrued) amount will be displayed in the entitlements column with an explanatory remark in the REMARKS section during month of payment only.

Fig. 14.7. LES explained: remarks

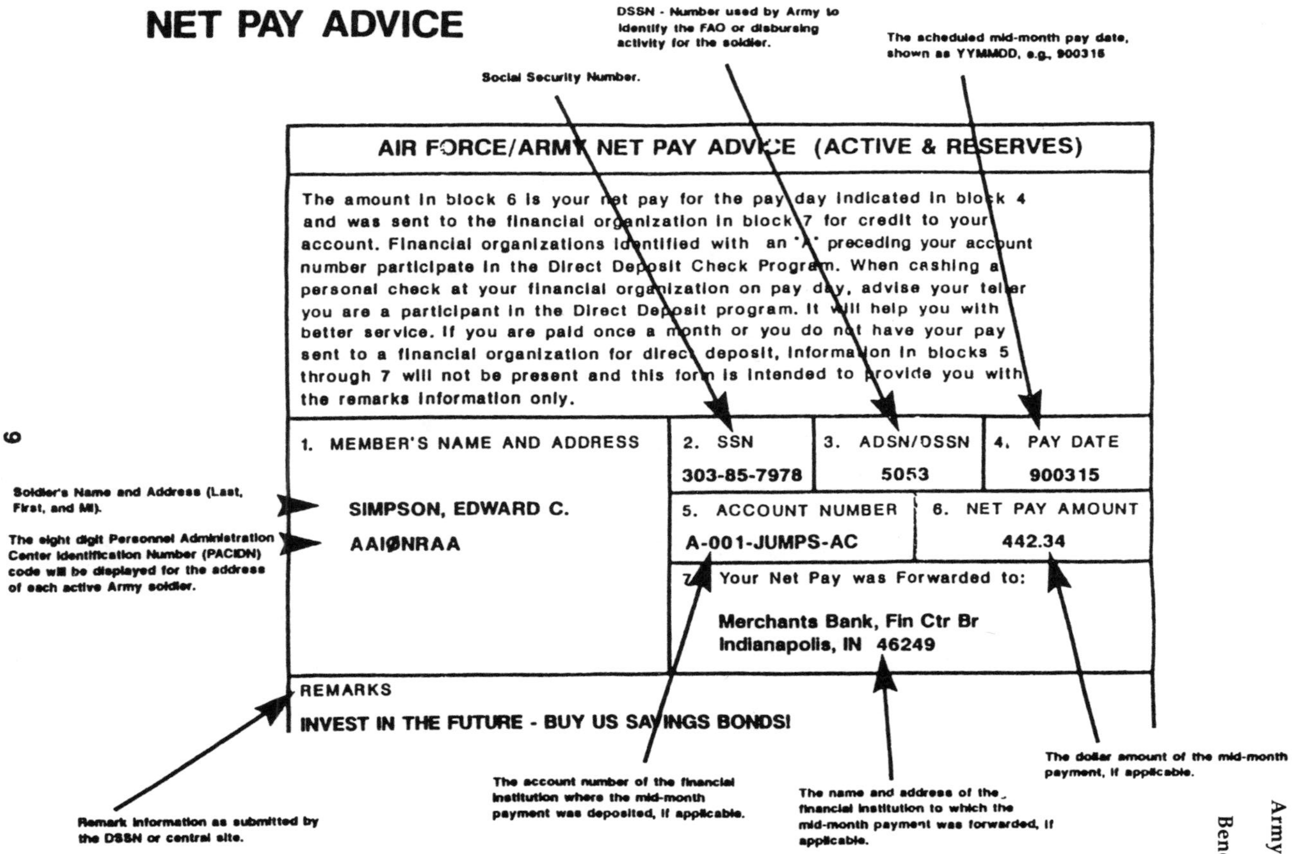
NET PAY ADVICE
DSSN - Number used by Army to identify the FAO or disbursing activity for the soldier.
The scheduled mid-month pay date, shown as YYMMDD, e.g., 900315
Social Security Number.
AIR FORCE/ARMY NET PAY ADVICE (ACTIVE & RESERVES)
The amount in block 6 is your net pay for the pay day indicated in block 4 and was sent to the financial organization in block 7 for credit to your account. Financial organizations identified with an "A" preceding your account number participate in the Direct Deposit Check Program. When cashing a personal check at your financial organization on pay day, advise your teller you are a participant in the Direct Deposit program. It will help you with better service. If you are paid once a month or you do not have your pay sent to a financial organization for direct deposit, information in blocks 5 through 7 will not be present and this form is intended to provide you with the remarks information only.
1. MEMBER'S NAME AND ADDRESS
SIMPSON, EDWARD C.
AAIØNRAA
2. SSN
303-85-7978
3. ADSN/DSSN
5053
4. PAY DATE
900315
5. ACCOUNT NUMBER
A-001-JUMPS-AC
6. NET PAY AMOUNT
442.34
7. Your Net Pay was Forwarded to:
Merchants Bank, Fin Ctr Br
Indianapolis, IN 46249
REMARKS
INVEST IN THE FUTURE - BUY US SAVINGS BONDS!
9
Soldier's Name and Address (Last, First, and MI).
The eight digit Personnel Administration Center Identification Number (PACIDN) code will be displayed for the address of each active Army soldier.
Remark information as submitted by the DSSN or central site.
The account number of the financial institution where the mid-month payment was deposited, if applicable.
The name and address of the financial institution to which the mid-month payment was forwarded, if applicable.
The dollar amount of the mid-month payment, if applicable.

Fig. 14.8. Air Force/Army Net Pay Advice explained

The NPA reflects your name, Social Security number, mid-month pay date, net pay amount that you received, the name and address of the financial institution where your pay was forwarded, if applicable, and other administrative and financial accounting information. As with your LES, errors should be brought to the attention of the FAO through your chain of command.

Types of Military Pay

Your Army pay is more complex than that of civilians. Instead of a simple salary, your pay is composed of several different types of payments. First is base pay, which constitutes the largest part of your pay while on active duty. In addition to your base pay, you may also receive enlistment and reenlistment bonuses. Moreover, a soldier may receive one or more types of additional pay called allowances. The two most important allowances are for housing (Basic Allowance for Quarters, or BAQ) and food (Basic Allowance for Subsistence, or BAS).

There are many other special and incentive pay and allowances, such as for recruiters, drill sergeants, and career counselors; foreign service pay; clothing maintenance; flight pay; hazardous duty pay; overseas incentive pay; diver's pay; and hostile-fire pay. A soldier must meet specific criteria to be eligible for these special payments. As we discuss these different types of pay, you should keep in mind that all the figures used are based on the pay scales and public laws in effect as of 1995 (see Appendix D). Military compensation is subject to continuous change. An Army recruiter can give you the most current data.

Base Pay

Your base pay depends on your pay grade. It will increase with promotions, accumulated time in service, and periodically through general pay raises given by Congress to all military services. For example, as of 1 January 1995, a Private (E-1) with less than two years of service is paid $854.40 per month. With promotion to Private (E-2), normally after six months of active duty, your pay increases to $957.60 per month. As a Private First Class (E-3), you would make $1049.70 per month (see table D.10).

Your base pay is taxable income. You will have to pay federal income tax and perhaps state income tax also. Soldiers are also subject to Social Security deductions just as with civilian pay. But the other major components of your pay, housing and food allowances, are nontaxable. In addition, some states do not tax pay when the individual is not stationed in the state. This means more money in your pocket.

Housing Allowance

All Army active-duty personnel receive a housing (quarters, or BAQ) allowance or free housing. Again, the amount depends on your rank and which one of the three following categories you fall into.

1. *Soldier with dependents*—If government housing is not provided for the soldier and family, BAQ is awarded to help offset the cost of renting (or buying a home) in the civilian community. When government quarters on post are provided to families, a soldier forfeits the BAQ.
2. *Soldier without dependents living in government barracks or quarters*—A small BAQ is provided to compensate partially for the inconvenience of living in a barracks situation. This token BAQ is called a partial rate.
3. *Soldier without dependents living off-post*—BAQ is less than the rate for soldiers of the same rank who have dependents; it is considerably more, however, than the partial rate.

For Army couples, when both spouses are service members, the guidelines change somewhat. If the couple has children, the soldier with the highest rank receives BAQ at the "with dependents" rate; the spouse receives BAQ at the "without dependents" rate. If the couple does not have children, each spouse receives the BAQ "without dependents" rate.

In addition to the BAQ, there is also a variable housing allowance (VHA) paid only to Army personnel who live off-post. The VHA is designed to help with the extraordinary housing costs some soldiers have because they live in a high-cost-of-living area. The amount of the VHA varies according to where you live. If you are stationed in Kansas, where housing costs are relatively low, your VHA payment may be only a few dollars a month or nothing. On the other hand, living in the Washington, D.C., area, where housing is quite expensive, you would receive a higher amount of VHA to offset your housing cost.

Food Allowance (Rations)

If you are single, enlisted, and required to live on post (most new Army personnel are), you will not be given a subsistance (eating) allowance. Instead, you will be given a meal card that entitles you to eat free in one of your post's military dining halls. If you decide to eat elsewhere, that's fine, but you will not get a food allowance or be paid for the meals you pass up in the dining hall.

When a government dining hall is not available, and no rations (food) are provided to a soldier, then an additional pay allowance called Basic Allowance for Subsistence (BAS) is provided. This is informally referred to as "separate rations." This allowance is also provided when a soldier is authorized to live off-post, is on leave, or on authorized travel to a new duty station. BAS rates effective for 1995 are shown in Appendix D.

Special and Incentive Pay and Other Allowances

The Army offers a number of special monthly pay entitlements to compensate soldiers for special skills, for enduring hardships, for exposure to danger, to maintain their uniforms, to serve as an incentive for reenlistment in a critical MOS, and for performance of hazardous duty. The compensation for these entitlements varies and is reflected on your LES. A discussion of some of these special payments follows.

Special Duty Assignment Pay: $110.00–$275.00
Recruiters, drill sergeants, and career counselors receive special duty assignment pay for the service they render to the Army. While these MOS require some special qualifications, these assignments are volunteer duties.

Foreign Duty Pay: $8.00–$22.50
When enlisted soldiers are assigned to arduous duty stations outside the United States, they receive extra compensation in the form of foreign-duty pay.

Foreign-Language Proficiency Pay: $100.00
Soldiers who hold an MOS requiring proficiency in a foreign language are entitled to additional pay to enhance their proficiency in that language.

Imminent-Danger Pay: $150.00
While in the Army, soldiers may become subjected to immediate danger in those areas designated as a hostile-fire area. As partial compensation for this danger, a soldier receives imminent-danger pay.

Flight Pay: $100.00–$200.00
Enlisted soldiers serving as either crew members or noncrew members with flying status are eligible for flight pay. This is considered a form of hazardous-duty incentive pay (HDIP).

Parachute Pay: $55.00 or $110.00
Soldiers also receive HDIP for performing the duties of a parachutist or being involved in parachute maintenance, testing, or packing and rigging.

Demolition Pay: $110.00
Soldiers whose primary duty assignments involve the demolition of explosives are eligible for demolition pay.

Enlistment Bonuses: Up to $8,000.00
Certain Army skills have a very high priority. If you qualify and enlist for training in one of these critical MOSs, you could earn a substantial cash bonus when you complete your advanced training in this specialty.

Selective Reenlistment Bonus: Up to $20,000.00
The selective reenlistment bonus (SRB) is a retention incentive paid to soldiers who reenlist or voluntarily extend their enlistment in Army-designated MOSs, the majority of which are highly technical.

Clothing Allowance: $82.80–$144.40
Initially the Army will provide you with a complete set of uniforms. After this initial uniform issue, you will have to buy your own clothing and accessories; however, the Army does provide you with an annual clothing maintenance allowance. This allowance is paid on the anniversary of your enlistment. It differs for males and females and the number of years of service (less than or more than three years).

Other Benefits

All the things we have discussed above—base pay, housing and food allowances, special pay, and bonuses—make up your Army "salary." But when you consider any job or career, it's smart to look at the overall financial package being offered. It is often just as important as how many dollars of take-home pay are earned. The Army has a very competitive compensation package to offer. The Army's other benefits for soldiers are free medical and dental care; special discount stores (post exchange and commissary); recreational facilities; special clubs; paid vacation; low-cost life insurance; free legal assistance; service organizations; and moving allowances.

Medical and Dental Care

From your first day at basic training, you receive free medical and dental care. In the Army, both the soldier and dependent family members receive outpatient care at military hospitals and clinics at no cost to the soldier. There is a nominal charge for inpatient care of family members.

For families not located near military health facilities, the Civilian Health and Medical Program for the Uniformed Services (CHAMPUS) is operated by the Department of Defense to pay approximately 80 percent or more of your bill if you receive medical care. CHAMPUS is a cost-sharing program; it pays part of the cost of your medical treatment and you pay the remainder. CHAMPUS reimbursement rates depend upon the amount of deductible you choose as well as the maximum cost approved by CHAMPUS for different types of medical care. The Department of Defense provides information, and there are CHAMPUS counselors to advise soldiers on the program.

Dental care is provided for active-duty soldiers at no cost. The family members of active-duty soldiers, however, are charged. A dental insurance plan is available as a voluntary program to provide preventive dental services and basic dental care at a minimal cost. Emergency dental care for the soldier's family members is still authorized on a space-available basis at a military dental facility.

Recreational Facilities

Most large Army installations offer a variety of recreational facilities for soldiers and their family members. Many activities are free or involve minimal charges. The types of facilities that are usually available to you include swimming pools, golf courses, tennis courts, gymnasiums, movie theaters, libraries, auto centers, and art and crafts centers. Outdoor recreational equipment ranging from camping equipment and canoes to scuba gear and bicycles are available for rental at a very low rate.

Enlisted Club

Most Army posts have enlisted clubs, where soldiers can relax and enjoy themselves during off-duty hours. These clubs offer a variety of musical entertainment, fine dining, and special activities. The prices go easy on your wallet.

Vacation (Leave)

Every soldier earns 30 days' paid vacation, or "leave," each year. This is in addition to the holidays and weekends you are normally off duty. Active-duty and retired soldiers are authorized to use military air flights to fly to various destinations. Seats are offered on a space-available basis first-come, first-served within several priority categories. Soldiers traveling on official business, for example, have a higher priority than retired soldiers.

Post Exchanges and Commissaries

To help stretch your dollar, prices at stores and leisure activities on post are usually below those in the nearby civilian community. Most Army installations have their own department stores called post exchanges (PX) or AAFES (Army–Air Force Exchange System). The PX carries a variety of merchandise that sells at prices comparable to many civilian discount stores.

An Army commissary is similar to and carries the same items you would expect to find in most supermarkets. You will find that the prices at the commissary, however, are normally lower than your civilian supermarket.

Legal Assistance

On most Army posts, a legal assistance office is present to provide Army lawyers who understand the Army and being a soldier. With flexible office hours that can be adjusted to accommodate your busy schedule, free legal advice is just a phone call or office visit away. Army Family Law attorneys can provide you with a range of professional services that include:

- Power of attorney
- Wills and estate planning
- Personal finances (indebtedness, insurance)
- Rental leases and sales agreements
- Notarizations
- Tax advice
- Family and domestic relations (adoptions, name changes, and so forth)

Life Insurance

Low-cost life insurance is provided to all active-duty soldiers by the government through a program called Servicemen's Group Life Insurance (SGLI). Enrollment is done automatically on enlistment, and can be set for various amounts up to a maximum of $200,000. Under current regulations, all soldiers are automatically put at the $100,000 level unless they decline it in writing. It can be increased in increments of $10,000 up to the maximum. The cost is extremely cheap, only $9.00 per month per $100,000. Compared to most civilian occupations, the Army is a high-risk environment. All soldiers, especially those married or with others depending on them for support are strongly encouraged to take advantage of this good deal. The insurance remains in effect for 120 days after leaving active duty without further payment. A proposal has been in Congress to raise the automatic enrollment to the full $200,000 maximum in 1995.

Veterans can apply during the 120-day period for a follow-on life insurance program called Veteran's Group Life Insurance (VGLI) for amounts similar to the SGLI without a physical exam. Premium costs for VGLI should be compared to other possible insurance programs before a decision is made.

Service Organizations

Many organizations provide assistance and services to soldiers and their families. Three of the most important follow.

Army Emergency Relief (AER)

AER is a private, nonprofit corporation that serves as the soldier's emergency financial assistance organization. It assists Army personnel and their families, Reservists on active duty, and needy widows and orphans of deceased Army members. AER provides emergency loans to eligible recipients who are faced with unforeseen, urgent situations requiring immediate financial attention. In special situations, grants (requiring no repayment) may also be provided. Most assistance, however, must be repaid.

American Red Cross (ARC)

The ARC supplies financial aid to Army personnel, does medical and psychiatric casework, and provides recreational services for the hospitalized. It also performs services in connection with dependency discharge, humanitarian transfer, emergency leave, leave extension, and family welfare reports.

Army Community Services (ACS) Center

The ACS Center provides a different but vital type of assistance to the soldier and his family. Counselors provide referral services to the military family, as well as in-house counseling on such matters as budgeting and personal or family problems; services available in the civilian community (libraries, parks, and recreation programs); special education needs for gifted or handicapped children; and assistance for the nonmilitary spouse seeking employment in a new community. Almost all ACS centers also maintain a lending closet with such items as bedding, dishes, and other household goods that may be needed to help set up your household when you first arrive at a post.

15. Re-up or Get Out?

The Reenlistment Decision

Many soldiers who enlist in the Army choose not to make a full career in the Army. As you approach the end of your first enlistment, you must decide whether to reenlist in the Army or to return to civilian life to pursue other goals. Reenlistment, however, is not an automatic right but a privilege. To re-up, you must be recommended by your commanding officer, be physically qualified, and meet certain standards of performance in your duties.

Types of Discharge

The type of discharge that you will receive from the Army is based on your military record. If you are separated for administrative reasons other than for completion of term of service, you may receive the following types of discharge.

- *Honorable.* This type of discharge depends on your proper military behavior and performance of duty. Isolated incidents of minor misconduct may be disregarded if your overall service record is good.
- *General Discharge under Honorable Conditions.* This discharge is appropriate for those whose military records are satisfactory but are not good enough to warrant honorable discharge. You may have had frequent nonjudicial punishment or may have been a troublemaker, but your conduct does not warrant less than a general discharge.
- *Discharge under Other Than Honorable Conditions.* Discharge from the Army under other than honorable conditions is the most severe of the administrative discharges you can receive. It may result in your loss of veteran's benefits, as determined by the Department of Veterans' Affairs. Such a discharge will

usually be given to those who have shown, for example, one or more incidents of serious misconduct.
- *Entry-Level Separation.* This discharge applies if you are within 180 days of continuous active duty and your records do not warrant a discharge under other than honorable conditions.

Planning a Second Career

Prior to retirement from the Army, planning for a second career is an important step that you must consider. In examining your Army career, you should identify those areas that will support your job aims in civilian life. Don't limit yourself to work that is directly related to your Army skills. Your training and experience as an officer or NCO is important to a new employer.

There will be a social and psychological shock that comes from leaving the structured and defined confines of the Army and entering the civilian world. This transition will not happen overnight. It may take many months for you to finally make the adjustment. Don't panic! Others have made it, and so can you!

Retirement

Soldiers are eligible to retire with retirement pay after completing 20 years of active honorable federal service. The amount of retirement pay is determined by a soldier's final rank and pay grade plus the total number of years and months of service. After completing 20 years soldiers can receive 40 percent of the average of their highest three years (called Hi-3) of base pay, and that increases for each additional year on active duty up to a maximum of 75 percent after 30 years. Under current laws most soldiers are required to retire on reaching a total of 30 years' active federal service.

The Army also offers assistance to retiring soldiers through the Army Career and Alumni Program (ACAP). This program provides information, briefings, and counseling to retiring soldiers to insure they are aware of their benefits, and entitlements. The ACAP Transition Assistance Office of an Army post also helps with civilian career preparation, job-search skills, and access to electronic job networks. This service is provided free and is available to all honorably discharged soldiers. Retirement planning must start before your retirement date if it is to be the most effective.

The Financial Package

In looking at the total financial package, you will see that the Army has quite a bit to offer you.

- Good pay
- Bonuses
- Room and board at no cost
- No-/low-cost medical and dental care
- No-/low-cost recreational facilities
- Low-cost enlisted clubs
- 30-day annual paid vacation
- Low-cost (military) travel
- Low-cost post exchanges and commissaries
- No-cost legal assistance
- Educational opportunities and financial assistance
- Low-cost life insurance
- Retirement after completing 20 years of Army service.

This is a unique and attractive financial compensation package. Check it out with your local Army recruiter.

16. Army Reserve Components

The Reserve Component Team

The Reserve Component element of America's Army is composed of the Army National Guard (NG) and the U.S. Army Reserve (USAR). In 1973, the Department of Defense introduced the Total Force Policy. The purpose of the policy was to integrate the active and reserve components in a manner that would strengthen the capability of the Army to respond to Cold War emergencies, and also give the reserve components the training and funding they needed to match the readiness to the active force. The plan worked, and a high-quality Total Army met the challenges of Grenada, Panama, and Kuwait. Now, with the end of the Cold War, the Army must prepare itself to answer a variety of potential commitments even while it is growing smaller. The answer to this dilemma is to build on the component integration concept even more, and to build mixed units of active and reserve elements. This is the blueprint for America's Army of the twenty-first century. You can be an important part of this plan whether you are an active Army or Reserve component soldier.

The Reserve Component Mission

The mission of the Resource Component (RC) is to provide trained, well-equipped units and individuals for active duty in time of war, national emergency, or as U.S. national security requires. In addition to its federal mission, the Army National Guard has its state mission to provide an organized, trained, and equipped force to protect life and property, and to preserve peace, order, and public safety under state authority. In recent years, the Army National Guard has assumed an increasing role in supporting drug enforcement operations.

Faced with a Total Army mission that is increasing, while the resources to support it are decreasing, the Army's senior leaders are looking to the RC to provide the flexibility that will make it possible to stretch the Total Army just a little further.

Joining the Team

As you approach the end of your active duty in the Army you should consider joining one of the Army's Reserve components (RC)—the Army National Guard or Army Reserve. The RC face extremely difficult training challenges in preparing their soldiers to accomplish their wartime missions. These challenges include less than 40 days per year available for individual and unit training, widely dispersed units, and the lengthy process necessary to develop competent leaders. Bringing your active duty training and experience into an RC unit could be a rewarding experience.

What if you are a first-term enlistee approaching the end of your active-duty enlistment? In addition to having earned the gratitude and respect of your country, community, family, and friends for serving honorably, you have also gained skills experience, leadership ability, and the pride that comes from doing an important job well. These are achievements that you don't want to lose simply because full-time soldiering isn't for you.

In the Army Reserve, you can sharpen your skills and keep up with the latest equipment and technology in your field. If you plan to find a civilian job related to your Army skill, Reserve training is especially beneficial and could help you advance in your new career.

If you want to branch out into another skill, Army Reserve training could be a welcome change of pace and a chance to prepare for a good job in a different field. Under the Prior Service Training (PST) Program, veterans like you may be eligible for additional active-duty training in a new MOS, with assignment to a unit where your specialty is needed.

Because Army Reservists serve part-time, you can easily fit Reserve membership into your schedule if you decide to further your education at a vocational school, community college, or four-year college or university. As the high cost of school-related expenses continues to rise, it would be good to know that you could count on regular Army Reserve pay to meet those expenses. As an Army Reservist, you are eligible for a

Fig. 16.1. A Wisconsin National Guardsman is instructed in the use of a Soviet RPG-7 antitank rocket launcher during REFORGER '86, Germany

number of educational programs that could help you pay for higher education. You might want to look into them.

As an Army Reservist, you are also entitled to several important benefits that can make your dollars go a lot further. These benefits include selective post exchange (PX) and commissary shopping, unlimited access to movies on military installations (at about half the price of admission to public theaters), and low-cost life insurance.

Earning Army Pay and Benefits as a Civilian

If you are not interested in full-time active duty, you may be eligible to join the Army's RC and start earning benefits that can last you a lifetime. Here is what a young man or woman who joins the RC can look forward to in return for part-time

Army service that minimizes disruption to your job or education:

- Good pay
- Skill training
- Money for college
- Discount shopping at Army facilities
- Retirement benefits
- Service to country and community

These benefits are discussed in greater detail in various chapters of this handbook.

Serving in the Army Reserve or Army National Guard can give you a tremendous feeling of pride in yourself as you play an integral role in keeping America strong and free. Your local Army recruiter can give you current information on the RC program. Make your visit soon!

What You Will Be Doing

You can not have to be a veteran to join one of the Reserve Components. Let's say you are fresh out of high school and want to join the Army Reserve. The process is fairly easy. To begin, you need to find out about specific Army Reserve units located within a reasonable distance from where you live, either at home or away at college. Talk with one of the unit career counselors to see how you can fit into the unit. In cooperation with the counselor determine which Military Occupational Specialties (MOS) are available in those units and pick the one for which you are qualified and in which you would like to train. There are many Career Management Fields open to Army Reservists and more than 250 specialties to choose from.

You will begin Basic Combat Training (BCT) soon after you enlist in the Army Reserve. You will travel at government expense to one of the Army's training centers for your BCT. It is the same training that is given to active-duty Army enlistees and lasts eight weeks (see Chapter 3).

After you complete BCT, you will attend Advanced Individual Training (AIT). Most AIT courses last about 8 to 12 weeks. During your AIT, you will receive intense, comprehensive classroom and hands-on training in the skill you selected and qualified for. You will receive the same training as your active-duty counterparts.

When you complete your AIT, you are ready to become a contributing member of your Army Reserve unit. This will require you to attend unit training assemblies (drills) with your

Fig. 16.2. Field religious service for a Massachusetts National Guard unit on maneuvers in Germany

unit one weekend per month and practicing your MOS as a vital member of your team. Pay for weekend drill is equal to one day of active duty pay. Because each weekend consists of 4 drills, a reservist receives 4 days' pay for a typical weekend of training. During the summer, you will accompany your unit for two weeks of annual active duty training at an Army installation, where your unit will interact with other units. The 1995 Reserve pay chart is in Appendix D.

There are many opportunities for you as an Army Reservist. Check them out!

Don't Lose Your Investment

You may think retirement is a long way off, but it has a way of slipping up on you. If you start thinking about it now, you will have a nice nest egg when the time comes for you to retire. As an Army Reservist, you could receive extra financial security with regular monthly checks after the age of 60. To qualify, you need 20 years of service, based on points accrued during both active-duty and Reserve participation. After retirement, upon reaching age 62, you and your family would have unlimited access to PX and commissary shopping and may be eligible for medical and dental care at a military installation.

As a citizen-soldier in the Army Reserve, you could get all this for attending monthly meetings and two weeks of annual training.

III. The Army Team

17. Branches, Arms, and Services

Tradition

Armies have long organized their soldiers and units by the type of function they perform. Originally, the various groups were identified by different armor, uniforms, insignia, or weapons. Initially these were few and simple, such as heavy and light footmen, horsemen, slingers, etc., but over the centuries armies became larger; weapons, equipment, and tactics became more complex. The types of functions performed by soldiers likewise became more complex and involved more than actual fighting. The efficient providing of supplies and the administration to an army became essential elements of success. This all required the creation of different functional groups.

The Army uses the general term "branch" or "branch of service" to identify its functional groups. Each branch has a different insignia that is worn by its soldiers, usually on the collars and lapels of their uniforms. In addition, each branch has a traditional color associated with it. This is a tradition from the days when colors on a soldier's uniform, such as red stripes on the trousers of artillerymen, reflected their branch. Some formal uniforms of the Army still retain the use of these colors. For some ceremonies and occasions, soldiers will still wear a scarf of their branch color. Table 17.1 describes the branch colors and scarves.

While there may be some who question the continued utility of the branch concept in modern times, using it aids in the personnel management of soldiers. Even more important for soldiers, belonging to a particular branch is a source of intense pride and spirit.

Types of Branches

The Army classifies its branches as either "basic" or "special." Basic branches are those in which a soldier can enlist directly. Special branches require additional training and testing before acceptance. In addition to branches, the Army has several other unique functional areas for which soldiers who are assigned to them wear collar/lapel insignia similar to that of a branch. These are: The Inspector General, Army General Staff, The Sergeant Major of the Army, National Guard Bureau, Staff Specialists, Warrant Officers, Public Affairs, Psychological Operations, and Civil Affairs.

The matter of branch names is complicated, and involves a lot of tradition. Many of the branches, such as Infantry, Engineer, Signal, Ordnance, etc., have traditional names adopted from European armies. Others, like Air Defense Artillery and Special Forces, are more modern. Branch names are also used to identify the types of units trained in the principle functions of that branch, armor and aviation for example.

Several branches have the word "corps" in their titles, such as Transportation Corps and Ordnance Corps. These are simply the traditional names dating back to when the branch was founded. Another example, the Army Medical Department, reflects the period the Army was organized into departments. There are six medical branches, all of which have the word "corps" in their title. Each of these branches has its own insignia based on the Medical Department insignia.

Branch Functions

The Army has four general categories or types of duties that branches or units perform—"combat," "combat support," "combat service support," and "administration." The last two are frequently combined when discussing responsibilities. Most branches perform only one type of function, but some branches have responsibilities so diverse they perform in more than one category. The Corps of Engineers is a good example. Its soldiers perform combat, combat support, and combat service support, as well as civilian engineering functions.

Branches or units that engage in actual combat against an enemy force are called "combat arms" (CA). These are Infantry, Armor, Field Artillery, Air Defense Artillery, some Aviation units, some types of Engineer units, and Special Forces. The branches or units that provide support directly to the combat arms, and which may join them for combat operations are called "combat support arms" (CS). These are some Aviation

TABLE 17.1. Branch of Service—Colors and Scarves

Branch	*Color*	*Scarf*
Adjutant General	Dark blue and scarlet	Dark blue
Air Defense Artillery	Scarlet	Scarlet
Armor	Yellow	Yellow
Army Medical Specialist Corps	Maroon and white	Maroon
Army Nurse Corps	Maroon and white	Maroon
Aviation	Ultramarine blue and golden orange	Ultramarine blue
Branch Immaterial	Teal blue and white	Teal blue
Cavalry	Yellow	Yellow
Chaplains	Black	Black
Chemical Corps	Cobalt blue and golden yellow	Cobalt blue
Civil Affairs, USAR	Purple and white	Purple
Corps of Engineers	Scarlet and white	Scarlet
Dental Corps	Maroon and white	Maroon
Field Artillery	Scarlet	Scarlet
Finance Corps	Silver gray and golden yellow	Silver gray
Infantry	Light blue	Infantry blue
Inspector General	Dark and light blue	Dark blue
Judge Advocate General Corps	Dark blue and white	Dark blue
Medical Corps	Maroon and white	Maroon
Medical Service Corps	Maroon and white	Maroon
Military Intelligence	Oriental blue and silver gray	Oriental blue
Military Police Corps	Green and yellow	Green
National Guard Bureau	Dark blue	Dark blue
Ordnance Corps	Crimson and yellow	Crimson
Quartermaster Corps	Buff	Buff
Signal Corps	Orange and white	Orange
Special Forces	Jungle green	Jungle green
Staff Specialist, USAR	Green	Green
Transportation Corps	Brick red and golden yellow	Brick red
Veterinary Corps	Maroon and white	Maroon
Warrant Officers	Brown	None

units, Chemical Corps, Corps of Engineers, Signal Corps, Military Police Corps, Military Intelligence, Civil Affairs, and Psychological Operations.

The branches or units that provide combat service support (CSS) and administrative support to the Army as a whole are called "services." These are Adjutant General's Corps, some

TABLE 17.2. **Branches, Arms, and Services**

	Branches			*Arms*		*Services*
Name	*Basic*	*Special*	*Functional areas*	*Combat*	*CS*	*CSS/Admin*
Adjutant General's Corps	X					X
Air Defense Artillery	X			X		
Armor	X			X		
Army Nurse Corps		X				X
Aviation	X			X	X	X
Chaplains Corps		X				X
Chemical Corps	X				X	
Civil Affairs	X[1]		X[1]		X	
Corps of Engineers	X			X	X	X
Dental Corps		X				X
Field Artillery	X			X		
Finance Corps	X					X
Infantry	X			X		
Judge Advocate General's Corps		X				X
Medical Corps		X				X
Medical Specialist Corps	X					
Medical Service Corps	X					X
Military Intelligence	X				X	
Military Police Corps	X			X	X	X
Ordnance Corps	X					X
Psychological Operations			X[2]		X	
Public Affairs			X[3]			
Quartermaster Corps	X					X
Signal Corps	X				X	X
Special Forces	X			X		

TABLE 17.2. Branches, Arms, and Services (continued)

Name	Branches: Basic	Branches: Special	Functional areas	Arms: Combat	Arms: CS	Services: CSS/Admin
Transportation Corps	X					X
Veterinary Corps		X				X

Notes:

1. Civil Affairs is a Reserve Component Branch, and a functional area for Regular Army soldiers assigned to active Civil Affairs units.
2. Enlisted soldiers serving in PSYOP positions may wear that insignia.
3. Enlisted soldiers serving in Public Affairs positions may wear that insignia.

Aviation units, Corps of Engineers, Chaplain Corps, Finance Corps, Judge Advocate General's Corps, Ordnance Corps, Transportation Corps, Public Affairs, Military Police Corps, Medical Corps, Medical Service Corps, Army Nurse Corps, Veterinary Corps, Dental Corps, and Army Medical Specialist Corps.

Table 17.2 provides a simple layout of this complex situation. A brief description of the branches and their insignia is in Appendix F.

18. Combat Arms

Infantry

The largest combat branch of the Army trained and equipped to fight on foot is the infantry—the ground-gaining force of the Army. In a general sense, the infantry is the reason for everything else in the Army. As an infantryman, you will live with challenge. As a modern combat soldier, you are as close as you will come to one-on-one combat. So you have to be tougher, smarter, and faster than the enemy.

You will move on foot, by armored personnel carrier (APC), by helicopter, or even assault boat. Sometimes you will move silently at night in small groups; at other times you will charge, shouting a battle cry. In the infantry your training is the best and your weapons the finest in the world.

In the infantry, you must master the greatest challenge of all—yourself. If you can prove yourself in the infantry, you can prove yourself anywhere. Then you can look back over your shoulder and shout the proud slogan of the infantry that has echoed throughout the years, "Follow me!"

Infantrymen can belong to several types of infantry units—light, airborne, air assault, ranger, or mechanized. Each infantryman is trained in his own special skills and he belongs to a unit specifically designed to perform certain types of missions. All infantrymen, however, no matter what their type of unit, share the common mission to close with and destroy the enemy. The distinctions between the different types of infantry are best understood by reading the discussion concerning types of units in Chapter 21.

Infantry training, to include Airborne and Ranger training, is conducted at Fort Benning, Georgia, which has been the "Home of the Infantry" since 1918. Infantrymen are trained in the use of weapons and mines; armored personnel carrier op-

Fig. 18.1. The U.S. Army Infantry School, Fort Benning, Georgia

erations; individual and squad tactics; patrolling; first aid; map reading; communications; and nuclear, biological, and chemical warfare defense.

Armor

The armor branch is the Army's mounted combat arm and consists of armor and armored cavalry units. Armor means tank, and as a gunner, loader, or driver, you will get to know your tank as you know your own mind. Your skill and courage as a tanker will turn your rumbling giant into a fearful fighting machine. Make it move, feint, throw its deadly punch, and then bring it home without a mark on it. That's the challenge of armor and a big one at that. Big enough to test the best, you have to be willing to make a commitment to teamwork. That is what armor is all about.

The armored cavalry is the direct successor to the horse cavalry and performs many of its traditional missions—security, ground reconnaissance, and active combat. Cavalry units can force an enemy unit into terrain where friendly armor can at-

Fig. 18.2. Infantrymen exit an M-2 Bradley fighting vehicle.

tack. Armored cavalry units use the Bradley Cavalry Fighting Vehicle (CFV) to perform their security and reconnaissance missions.

The size and configuration of armored cavalry units may vary considerably. A cavalry squadron (a battalion-size force) may or may not have tanks and/or helicopters. Brigade-size cavalry units are still referred to as "regiments," a reminder of the days when regiments of Army soldiers swept across the plains of the western frontier on horseback.

Soldiers are trained for mounted combat at the Armor Center at Fort Knox, Kentucky. Hands-on training is emphasized, and new techniques, including laser firing, are employed during tactical exercises.

Field Artillery

The field artillery uses its awesome firepower to support the other combat arms, especially the infantry, on the battlefield. It can neutralize enemy artillery, fire on enemy tanks or infan-

Fig. 18.3. A U.S. Army Ranger

trymen, and protect friendly soldiers when they are in a defensive position. The challenge for the field artillery is teamwork and precision. Light artillery guns, airlifted by helicopters or towed by vehicles, and heavy guns and rockets, which move into position on tracked vehicles, are all tools of today's artillery.

To support the other combat arms, the field artillery firing process begins with the command, "Fire mission." Computers plot the direction, distance and trajectory to a target. The gun crew responds to the information by slamming a shell into the breech of the gun. Range and direction are set by the cannoneers. Gun crews step back and fire. The earth shakes and thunder rolls from the muzzle of the gun. The shell screams to the target. Range corrections come back from forward observers on the ground or in spotter aircraft. The process is repeated. The gun fires again: Direct hit on a target miles away that the gunner may never see. Technical skill and teamwork have successfully completed another fire mission. This is the field artillery, one of the most powerful elements of the battlefield.

Artillery units vary in size and configuration. The Field Artillery Training Center at Fort Sill, Oklahoma, annually trains

Fig. 18.4. M1A1 Abrams tank

Fig. 18.5. A 155mm M-109A1 self-propelled howitzer on the move

Fig. 18.6. Chaparral forward-area air-defense missile system

approximately 26,000 recruits in artillery-related Military Occupational Specialties.

Air-Defense Artillery

Air-defense artillery units defend Army ground forces against attack by enemy aircraft. To accomplish this mission, they employ rapid-fire antiaircraft guns, several surface-to-air missile systems, including the shoulder-fired Stinger, the Chaparral, the Hawk, and the Patriot.

Soldiers in air-defense artillery are trained to a fine edge of technical proficiency. Radar operations and maintenance, communications, gunnery, missiles, fire control, and tracking are some of the skills they master. Skilled, patient, responsible, and watchful, air-defense soldiers watch the skies for enemy threats in the green glow of the radar scope. Their watch never falters as they stand ready around the clock. A great deal of satisfaction comes from being in the air-defense artillery.

Air-defense training is conducted at Fort Bliss, Texas. About 8,000 soldiers are trained there annually. A small percentage of them are females, who are trained in support services.

Aviation

Army aircraft play vital and diverse parts in modern warfare, so they fill combat, reconnaissance, and transport roles. Attack

Fig. 18.7. A two-man Stinger missile team scans the horizon for incoming aircraft.

helicopters, such as the AH-64 Apache, provide excellent strike and maneuver power, particularly when they work in conjunction with infantry, armor, and cavalry units. Fast, agile scout helicopters spot enemy positions and take aerial photographs. Small surveillance airplanes provide intelligence and communications to combat units.

Utility helicopters, such as the UH-60A Blackhawk, are transportation vehicles. They move troops and equipment in and out of battle areas quickly. They are also used as ambulances and command centers.

About 2,000 personnel (approximately 10 percent women) are trained at Fort Rucker, Alabama, in aviation-related occupational specialties, including flying, aviation mechanics, air traffic control, and flight operations. To win the wings of an Army pilot, a soldier must complete flight school at Fort Rucker, one of the most demanding and personally rewarding training programs the Army offers.

Corps of Engineers

Engineer units play an important combat role. Building roads, bridges, gun emplacements, and airfields, often under enemy

Fig. 18.8. A UH-60 Blackhawk helicopter, one of Army aviation's many assets

fire, Army engineers pave the way for advancing infantry, armor, and artillery units. They harass the enemy with strategically placed minefields, man-made obstacles, and the precision destruction of bridge spans. Equally skilled with tools and weapons, the engineers are a vital part of the combat team.

Expert in the use of camouflage, hand and power tools, and explosives, the engineer finds no task is too hard, no challenge too great. In the tradition of America's pioneers, he works with his weapons close at hand and is always ready to drop his tools and grab a rifle if he or his work is threatened. Engineer equipment, such as cranes, tractors, and dump trucks, is often delivered to combat engineers by aircraft and is sometimes parachuted into the battle area. Engineer units also have floating bridges, inflatable assault boats, and rafts.

The engineer works side by side with men like himself, overcoming obstacles and solving problems. This is the challenge of the engineer.

As noted earlier, the Corps of Engineers is both a branch and a service. It is one of the most diverse branches in the Army. Its combat engineers are out in front with the rest of the combat units, while its many other types of engineers provide com-

Fig. 18.9. Engineers build a mobile assault bridge over the Aller River, Germany.

bat support, combat service support, as well as topographic (mapping), civil engineering, and many other specialized types of support to the Army.

More than 40,000 personnel are trained annually at Fort Leonard Wood, Missouri, in various combat engineer occupational roles, such as combat engineers, bridge crew members, plumbers, electricians, construction workers, vehicle and equipment operators, and mechanics.

Special Forces

The members of the Army Special Forces (SF) are better known as "Green Berets" for the distinctive beret that sets them apart from the rest of the Army. Special Forces membership demands a tremendous amount of inventiveness and self-reliance. As the name implies, Special Forces deal with special combat situations that you can't always find in a textbook. The primary mission is counterinsurgency and unconventional warfare operations. Special Forces are also used in the areas of foreign, internal defense and nation building. As advisory groups, they help nations build and train their armed forces.

Fig. 18.10. A Special Forces soldier

Special Forces training is the most extensive and the most demanding physically and mentally of any in the Army. It includes training in jungle, desert, and arctic environments, and foreign languages.

Special Forces soldiers usually are organized into small teams of different sizes, the most common being the "A" Team. You have to be a resolute, resourceful, and resilient soldier to earn your place on a Special Forces "A" Team. Each man on the team is a highly skilled specialist in communications, operations, intelligence, weapons, demolitions, or medicine. Each "A" team member is also cross-trained in another area to double his usefulness. Special Forces soldiers undergo their initial training at Fort Bragg, North Carolina.

If you are looking for excitement, Special Forces has got it, but if you don't think you can handle the challenge, don't even attempt it. Only the best wear the proud emblem of the Special Forces, the Green Beret.

19. Combat Support

All six branches discussed in this chapter are both basic branches and arms of the Army and are referred to as combat support. They provide direct operational assistance to the combat arms in accomplishing the Army's combat mission (see table 17.2).

Signal Corps

One of the basic branches of the Army, soldiers of the Signal Corps receive their training at Fort Gordon, Georgia. The Signal Corps is both an arm and a service that provides the communications and electronics expertise necessary to support the Army's mission. The Signal Corps is assigned to plan, develop, organize, install, operate, and maintain communications and electronics systems and equipment for the Army, other armed services, Department of Defense, and other government agencies.

Military Police Corps

Another one of the basic branches of the Army, the Military Police (MP) Corps is a combat support arm and a service since it performs combat, combat support, and combat service-support missions.

Soldiers and units in the Military Police Corps provide the expertise and means to control tactical rear areas of responsibility. They conduct operations directed toward the protection of prisoners of war, civilian internees, detainees, and other victims of war; police internal defense operations; crime prevention and investigation; circulation control of vehicles and personnel; physical security operations; operation of Army confinement and correctional training facilities; and industrial defense activities.

Fig. 19.1. Inside a communications van, a soldier attaches a cable to a TD-204 multiplexer.

In order to perform their missions successfully, military policemen must possess a comprehensive knowledge of both modern police procedures and military operations and tactics. They receive their training at Fort McClellan, Alabama.

Military Intelligence

The scope of activities associated with the Military Intelligence (MI) branch is quite large, encompassing intelligence, counterintelligence, cryptologic and signal intelligence, and security. Frequently working directly for senior commanders, MI soldiers conduct order of battle analysis, interrogations, aerial surveillance, imagery interpretation, and provide support for all related planning, organization, training, and operations.

Trained at Fort Huachuca, Arizona, the primary duties of soldiers assigned to the Military Intelligence branch are the collection, analysis, production, and dissemination of intelligence. To accomplish this mission, it is essential that the soldiers assigned to this branch be highly trained in their specialty and possess extensive knowledge of military strategy

Fig. 19.2. Military police prepare to use a radar detector.

and tactics. Frequently, training in a foreign language is also necessary.

Chemical Corps

After its experience with gas warfare in World War I, the Army formed the ancestor of the Chemical Corps in 1918. The Chemical Corps is one of the basic branches of the Army. With the refinements by potential enemies in weapons of nuclear, biological, and chemical nature, the role of the Chemical Corps has become critical. This branch provides the Army and the nation with expertise in nuclear, biological, and chemical (NBC) defense and in the planning and conduct of chemical combat support operations. This field of activity encompasses planning, organization, training, operation, development, intelligence, supply, and maintenance related to these special types of weapons. Chemical Corps training is given at Fort McClellan, Alabama.

Fig. 19.3. Space collection specialists train at Army Intelligence School.

Civil Affairs

The Civil Affairs (CA) Branch is a U.S. Army Reserve branch. With one exception, a Regular Army battalion at Fort Bragg, North Carolina, all of the Civil Affairs units are in the Reserve Component. The unit at Fort Bragg is filled with active duty soldiers assigned from other branches. The existence of Civil Affairs is a recognition by the Army that most military operations take place in areas inhabited to some degree by civilians. The civil-military nature of operations today such as Bosnia, Somalia, and Haiti make Civil Affairs a critical part of every Army deployment. In addition, the military commander has some responsibility for what happens to civilians and their property in his area of operations.

The job of Civil Affairs is to provide the interface between the Army and the civilian population. This may require everything from temporary governing of civilian areas to handling of refugees fleeing the conflict zone. The branch is composed of specialists in law, culture, language, art and archives, refugee control, and other skills necessary to support the commander. The origins of Civil Affairs in the Army go back at least to the Mexican War, when the Army found that it had to secure and to some degree administer large areas of former enemy territory. This experience was repeated after the Civil War in the South, and then after almost every war since in which the Army has been involved.

Civil Affairs soldiers frequently are highly educated and trained in a foreign language. They are an integral part of the Army's special operations capabilities.

Psychological Operations

This functional area, frequently called a branch, is for enlisted soldiers only. Officers are assigned from other branches to serve in Psychological Operations (PSYOP) jobs. PSYOP units are included in the Army's special operations community. The soldiers working in this field conduct operations to give selected information to foreign audiences using various printed, voice, and other types of media. The purpose is to create or reinforce attitudes and behavior favorable to the U.S. commander's objectives. There is only one active Psychological Operations unit, which is located at Fort Bragg. Other units are in the Army Reserve Components.

20. Combat Support Services and Administration

The branches discussed in this chapter are concerned with providing combat service support and/or administrative support to the Army. They are classified as either basic or special branches and are identified accordingly in this chapter. The special branches make up the various corps of the Army Medical Department. Another special branch, the Staff Specialist Corps, exists only in the Army Reserve, and if mobilized its members would be absorbed by other branches.

The functions and duties of the combat service-support branches are very diversified and there is not space here to discuss each in detail. Rather, a broad description of the scope of their activities will be presented to acquaint you with the many available opportunities in the Army. Specific questions regarding these and the other branches presented in earlier chapters should be directed to your local Army recruiter.

Adjutant General's Corps

The Adjutant General's Corps is a basic branch of the Army. Its primary concern is with personnel and administrative matters. The scope of its activities includes personnel management, casualty and prisoner of war reporting, strength accounting, headquarters internal-communication control and services, postal services, publication services, forms control, records, administration, Army band, and recreation.

In order to accomplish assigned branch functions and duties, soldiers who work in the Adjutant General's Corps must be familiar with military organizations and operations. Members of the Adjutant General's Corps receive their training at Fort Benjamin Harrison, Indiana.

Fig. 20.1. Army Medical Department personnel often minister to civilians in an area of operations—Honduras, 1988.

The Army Medical Department

Medical Corps

The Medical Corps is one of the six officer special branches of the Medical Department. It is composed entirely of fully qualified physicians who are responsible for the medical care of sick and injured soldiers and their families. There are forty areas of medical specialization designed to provide medical care in peacetime and to prepare for health support in time of war.

Dental Corps

The Dental Corps is a special branch of officers who are accredited dentists. They have the mission of ensuring every soldier is in the best oral health and ready to deploy without becoming an unnecessary dental casualty. They perform the functions of restoring and preserving oral health of soldiers and their families. They perform their duties in eleven general fields of dentistry and also assist in the medical management of casualties.

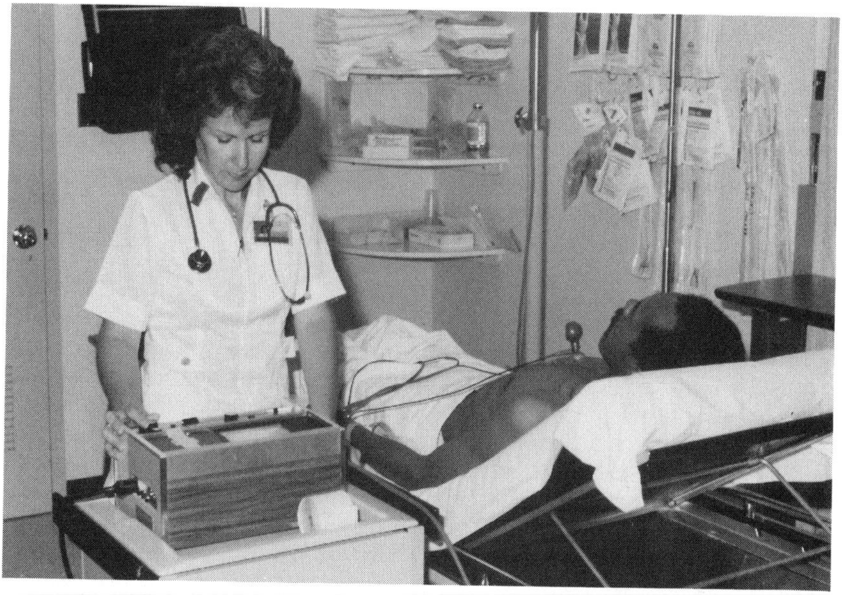

Fig. 20.2. An emergency medical technician performs an electrocardiogram (EKG).

Veterinary Corps

The Veterinary Corps is an officer special branch made up of qualified doctors of veterinary medicine. They perform the services necessary to prevent human illness from food or animal sources, maintaining the health of animals, insuring the quality of materials used in Army food, and conducting biomedical research. They work in many related fields such as community health, preventive medicine and teaching.

Army Medical Specialist Corps

This is another of the officer special branches of the Medical Department. It is organized into four distinct sections: Occupational Therapy, Physical Therapy, Physician's Assistant, and Dietetics. These officers conduct and supervise programs in their areas of qualification, and insure the highest standards are maintained to enhance the health of soldiers. They promote health and readiness programs, conduct research and studies and conduct educational and skill improvement programs for the Army community.

Army Nurse Corps

The male and female officers who comprise the Army Nurse Corps special branch provide the nursing care and services essential to the Army. The nine areas of nursing specialization cover all aspects of nursing care, community health, nursing administration and education that support the medical and health needs of soldiers and their families.

Medical Service Corps

The Medical Service Corps officers belong to a special branch that provides unique administrative, field medical, technical, scientific, and clinical services to the Army. They perform a variety of duties in the areas of health services, laboratory sciences, preventive medicine sciences, behavioral sciences, pharmacy, and air-medical evacuation.

Chaplains

The Chaplains branch is a special branch of the Army. Its officers are clergymen, from recognized denominational groups, who have volunteered to perform their ministry in the Army. They provide spiritual, religious, and moral leadership to the Army community and are assisted by enlisted assistants. The Chaplains' School is located at Fort Monmouth, New Jersey.

Finance Corps

The Finance Corps is one of the basic branches of the Army. It is a service that develops and administers the Army's financial management systems. The scope of activities associated with this corps includes both military and civilian pay and allowances, and disbursing operations and financial management necessary to support the Army's mission. Soldiers receive their Finance Corps training at Fort Benjamin Harrison, Indiana.

In addition to providing all types of pay service to the military and civilian members of the Army, the Finance Corps provides military accounting for appropriated funds. It also provides specialists in developing, implementing, and analyzing financial procedures and related information systems for the Army.

Fig. 20.3. An interior view of the Main Post Chapel, Fort Bragg, North Carolina

Ordnance Corps

The Ordnance Corps is the branch concerned with matériel support in general and with ground mobility and firepower in particular. Its scope of activity includes major participation in maintenance, ammunition service, and repair parts support. It also engages in the research, development, test evaluation, production, and integrated systems management for ground vehicles, weapons systems, missile systems, and conventional and nuclear ammunition.

Soldiers in the Ordnance Corps undergo training at the Aberdeen Proving Grounds, Maryland.

Judge Advocate General's Corps

The soldiers in the Judge Advocate General's (JAG) Corps are the members of a special branch that provides the Army with its experts on both military and civilian law. The officers of the

Fig. 20.4. Unloading military ammunition from a rail car at an ordnance depot

Fig. 20.5. Learning the proper procedures for a pipeline linkup

branch are all lawyers, and their primary function is to give the Army's soldiers total legal service.

The JAG school for Army lawyers, judges, and legal workers is located in Charlottesville, Virginia.

Quartermaster Corps

The Quartermaster (QM) Corps is one of the basic branches of the Army and is also one of the services of the Army. It is involved primarily in the logistical support of military operations. The corps' primary function is to procure, supply, and manage Army matériel and to provide logistical service support to the Army at all echelons. Fort Lee, Virginia, is the home of the Quartermaster School.

Transportation Corps

The Transportation Corps (TC) is one of the Army's basic branches and one of the services of the Army. The primary function of this corps is to move personnel and matériel on land and sea to accomplish the assigned mission of the Army. Support is also provided for other armed services and government agencies. Transportation Corps training, which includes tactical wheeled vehicle, rail, terminal, and waterborne equipment, is given at Fort Eustis, Virginia.

21. Types of Units

"The steady operations of war against a regular and disciplined army can only be successfully conducted by a force of the similar kind."
Alexander Hamilton

The Army has many types of units. Each unit, no matter what type, utilizes soldiers and elements from other Army branches and integrates them into a smoothly functioning team. Units themselves are task-organized and cross-attached to perform particular missions. This chapter focuses on the types of tactical and special operations units in the Army. The majority of soldiers serve in these type of units and a description of them and their missions gives the best overview of what Army units do. In no way, however, should this be interpreted to mean that other types of units, or units performing nontactical missions are less important. All units fill a vital and necessary part on the total Army team. An Army division, no matter what type, contains one or more of almost every type of Army unit. Because of the continuing Army restructuring, the specific units mentioned may change in the future. It should also be kept in mind that traditional unit designations, such as cavalry or airborne, that units may still carry, may no longer describe their current type of organization.

Tactical Units

Infantry

There are five types of infantry units: light, airborne, air assault, ranger, and mechanized. The soldiers of each have their own special skills and their units are specifically designed to perform particular missions. In most cases the greatest differences among them are in the amount of equipment they have and the method of transportation they use to enter combat. Regardless of the type of transportation, however, infantry units are an essential element of combat power on the battlefield. With the exception of ranger units, all of these types of units are found in the Army's active and reserve components.

Light Infantry: Light infantry units can operate in almost every type of terrain and weather. They are readily deployable due to their light equipment and may be among the first forces employed against an enemy. They are well armed and prefer to operate at night or during periods of limited visibility, especially in areas of restrictive terrain. They are particularly well suited for use in urban areas (towns and cities), and to infiltrate enemy lines and move into the enemy's rear areas. Their means of tactical mobility includes the use of helicopter and tactical airlift. There are several light infantry units such as the 10th Mountain Division (Light) and the 25th Infantry Division (Light).

Airborne Infantry: Airborne infantry units, or paratroopers, have the greatest capability for long range rapid movement of large forces. These units move by aircraft to conduct parachute or air landing assaults behind enemy lines to seize and secure key objectives. They are usually combined-arms units and, once on the ground, they have similar capabilities and firepower as other infantry units except for heavy armor. The major active Army airborne unit is the 82d Airborne Division. There are also several other separate battalion-size airborne infantry units.

Air Assault Infantry: Modern technology has created a new type of infantry unit, the air assault infantry. These units have great mobility through the use of helicopters and other Army aircraft. They are trained for a broad range of military operations, and possess a significant antiarmor capability. This together with their easy and quick deployability make them among the first to be sent against heavy enemy forces during contingency operations. These units train and fight with air assault artillery and attack and transport aviation. This gives them the capability to move deep into the enemy's rear to seize important targets, cut lines of communication, block enemy movement, or occupy critical terrain. The Army's air assault unit is the 101st Airborne Division (Air Assault).

Ranger: Ranger units are used for the conduct of special missions in support of conventional operations and independently when conventional infantry cannot be used. Ranger units are quickly transportable by aircraft or helicopters, and they are trained to enter the battle area by every possible means including parachute, air assault, and water craft. The 75th Ranger

Regiment with its three battalions is the active Army's only ranger infantry unit.

Mechanized Infantry: Mechanized infantry units are mounted in infantry fighting vehicles, but the soldiers are prepared to dismount and fight if necessary. Mechanized infantry units have the same mobility as armor forces, but less firepower and protection. They fight together with armor as a team, adding fast, protected mobility, lethal vehicle-mounted weapons, and foot infantry skills to the shock and striking power of armor forces. The Army has more mechanized infantry units than any other type. Major units include the 1st Infantry Division (Mech.), the 4th Infantry Division (Mech.) and the 3d Infantry Division (Mech.).

Armor

There are two types of armor units: heavy and light. In heavy armor units the tank is the primary weapon. It provides those units with heavy firepower, protection from enemy fire, and rapid mobility. Armor units can destroy enemy armor and infantry units, break through defenses, exploit a successful attack by striking deep into the enemy, and pursue fleeing enemy units. Armor units can also blunt enemy attacks and launch counterattacks. Light armor units use lightly armored vehicles in order to be more easily deployable. These armor units can operate in a wide range of conditions, providing security, reconnaissance, and antiarmor capability. They can also conduct standard armor operations in coordination with other arms. Light armor battalions are organic to the airborne and light infantry divisions. The Army's heavy armor units include the 1st Cavalry Division and 1st Armored Division.

Cavalry

The basic missions of cavalry units are reconnaissance, security, and economy of force. They seek out the enemy, develop a situation and give the commander time to react. There are both air and ground cavalry units. They have the same missions, but because of their mobility, the air cavalry units can cover a much greater area in a shorter period of time. During security operations, the air cavalry reconnoiters, screens forward and to the flanks, and acts as a rapid reaction force. All cavalry units have an air capability. Cavalry units in the Army include the 2d and 3d Armored Cavalry Regiments, and the units organic to the infantry and armored divisions.

Army Aviation

The different types of helicopters and aircraft in the Army provide the commander with exceptional firepower, agility, and rapid reaction capability to close with and defeat the enemy. Attack helicopters are capable of moving at high speed over terrain that restricts ground movement and attacking close or deep against the enemy. They can be used to tip the balance of battle when ground forces are decisively engaged. Scout helicopters provide a reconnaissance and security capability. They can be used to detect and identify enemy forces, providing critical current information to the commander. Utility aircraft provide airmobile and air assault transport for infantry and antiarmor units. These forces gain greatly increased mobility and can be placed at key locations quickly around the battlefield by their aviation support units. In addition, utility aircraft can provide other support such as airlifting artillery, carrying supplies and reinforcements, and evacuating wounded. Some of the Army aviation units are the 6th Cavalry (Air Combat) Brigade, 1st Aviation Brigade (Air Assault), and 18th Aviation Brigade (Airborne).

Field Artillery

Field artillery (FA) units are the commander's principal source of fire support on the battlefield. They provide fire support with cannon, rocket, and missile systems, in addition to integrating all the fire support available to the commander. Field artillery units can suppress or destroy enemy forces, attack enemy artillery and mortar positions, and deliver scatterable mines to isolate or block enemy forces. They are as mobile as the maneuver force they support, permitting them to provide continuous fire in support of the commander's operations. Field artillery units include the 212th Field Artillery Brigade, 75th Field Artillery Brigade, and 41st Field Artillery Brigade, plus the field artillery battalions assigned to the Army's divisions.

Air Defense Artillery

Air defense artillery (ADA) units protect friendly forces from air and missile attack in the forward as well as in the rear areas. They also work together with other services to provide joint service protection. In the forward battle area, divisional ADA units are used to protect the maneuver units, while in the corps areas, ADA brigades use high-to-medium-altitude air defense missile units to provide protection. In addition to defending against air and missile attack, ADA units are a significant contributor of intelligence information to the commander on the enemy's air strength. They also hinder the enemy's information gathering by limiting his ability to use aerial reconnaissance and command and control aircraft. Among the Army's ADA units are the 32d Air Defense Brigade, 108th Air Defense Artillery Brigade, and the 31st Air Defense Artillery Brigade.

Engineer

Engineer units operate as integral members of the combined arms team across the battlefield and throughout a theater of operations. In the forward combat zone, the engineers conduct breaching and crossing of obstacles, assisting the assault on fortified positions, and emplacing obstacles. They advise the commander on the effective use of terrain, and construct, improve, and maintain roads, bridges, airfields, and other facilities. When required, engineer units are prepared to fight as infantry. There are also many nontactical engineer units providing general construction work and harbor and waterway improvements. Tactical engineer units include the 20th Engineer Brigade and 130th Engineer Brigade, in addition to the engineer units assigned to the Army's divisions.

Military Intelligence

Military intelligence (MI) units use signal intercepts, imagery, counterintelligence, and human intelligence sources to provide the commander with information concerning enemy capabilities and intentions. They also direct electronic warfare against enemy command and control systems, identify targets for attack, and assess battle damage inflicted on the enemy. Maneuver units of battalion size and larger have MI soldiers to provide the immediate tactical intelligence collection and interpretation needed by the commander. The 504th and 525th Military Intelligence Brigades are two examples of MI units that provide tactical intelligence support to Army corps commanders.

Special Operations Forces

The Army has five types of units that conduct special operations: Special Forces, Rangers, Army Special Operations Aviation, Psychological Operations, and Civil Affairs. Special operations units conduct five principal missions: unconventional warfare, direct actions, special reconnaissance, foreign internal defense, and counterterrorism. These type units are used to combat insurgencies, conduct contingency operations, and perform peace support operations. In peacetime they participate in foreign internal defense efforts, humanitarian and civic assistance programs, and demonstrating U.S. presence in troubled areas.

Special Forces

Special Forces units are organized and trained to conduct special operations. These include deep penetration missions to interdict enemy lines of communications, destroy enemy facilities, collect intelligence, assist in recovery of personnel, train and equip resistance forces, and conduct subversion and sabotage against enemy targets. Active Army Special Forces are composed of the 1st Special Forces and its five elements, the 1st, 3d, 5th, 7th, and 10th Special Forces Groups.

Ranger

Ranger units are also a type of infantry unit and were discussed previously.

Army Special Operations Aviation

These units are specialized aviation units dedicated to conducting special operations missions. They provide a mix of short-, medium-, and long-range lift and light attack capabilities. They can also support special reconnaissance and direct-action missions. The 160th Special Operations Aviation Regiment (Airborne) is the Army's unit for this type activity.

Psychological Operations

Psychological Operations (PSYOP) units are employed to influence the attitudes and behaviors of foreign audiences so they will act in a manner favorable to the plans of the commander.

These units use the latest techniques in audio-visual, print, radio, TV, and other media to support the military objectives. The Army has one of this type unit on active duty, the 4th Psychological Operations Group (Airborne). Other PSYOP units are in the Reserve Components.

Civil Affairs

Civil Affairs (CA) units are employed to enhance relationships between military forces, and civilian authorities and population in areas of military operations. These units are trained to reduce civilian interference and to gain popular understanding, support, and compliance with measures necessary for accomplishment of the mission. Depending on the situation, they may also engage in the temporary operation of military government. While the majority of CA units are in the Army Reserve, the 96th Civil Affairs Battalion (Airborne) provides active duty support.

Supporting Units

In addition to tactical units a commander has many other units to assist in the accomplishment of the mission. These units provide combat support and combat service support critical to success in battle or in the performance of operations in other than war situations. A significant part of the Army's support structure resides in the Reserve Components. All of the Army's heavy helicopter units, chemical brigades, water supply, and rail battalions are in the ANG or Reserve, as are thirty-six of thirty-seven civil affairs units, and more than three fourths of the hospital units and medical support units. All support units, finance, legal, health service support, military police, personnel, maintenance, ammunition, public affairs, signal, field services, and transportation units are indispensable to military operations.

Each element of America's Army team is an important piece of the overall effort. Units are task-organized and employed according to the mission and the situation. They integrate their capabilities to ensure victory across the entire range of military operations while providing the maximum protection and care to American soldiers.

22. Organization of Units

Different levels of command within the Army perform different tactical and operational functions. These functions vary based on a number of factors to include the type of unit, the nature of the conflict, and the number of Army troops committed to the conflict. This chapter provides a general description of Army formations from squad-size units to corps. The combat unit structure is used as a model because it is the most basic and easiest structure to understand and it is the type of organization that a new soldier will first encounter in BCT.

Other types of units use variations of this structure. Some, for example, use a weapons system crew as the most basic element—in armor units the tank crew; in the artillery the gun crew. The number of soldiers in the different squads and crews may vary, but whatever the size, these small elements are the heart of the soldier's world. Above the squad/crew level, unit structures become more standardized. Whatever the size, however, there is always a headquarters element, and two or more elements that perform the basic mission of the unit. A support element may or may not be included. This same pattern continues to the largest units in the Army.

Companies/Batteries/Troops

Company-size units consist of two or more platoons, usually of the same type, with a headquarters and, in some cases, a limited capacity for self-support. Companies are the basic elements of all battalions. They are also assigned as separate units of brigades and larger organizations.

All close combat companies can fight together or by separate platoons. In infantry, armor, and attack helicopter battalions, companies normally fight as integral units. Cavalry troops and attack helicopter companies fight more frequently with their platoons in separate zones, sectors, or areas.

TABLE 22.1. Army Organizations and Leaders

Squad	*Platoon*	*Company*	*Battalion*
• Leader is usually a staff sergeant. • Smallest unit in Army organization. • Size varies depending on type: Infantry—9 men Armor—4 men Engineer—10 men • Three or 4 squads make a *platoon*.	• Leader is usually a lieutenant. • Size varies: Infantry—40 men Armor—4 tanks, 16 men • Three or 4 platoons make a *company*.	• Commander is a captain. • Usually 150 to 200 men. • Artillery unit of this size is called a *battery*. • Armored Cavalry or Air Cavalry is called a *troop*. • Basic tactical element of the maneuver battalion or Cavalry Squadron. • Normally 5 companies make a *battalion*.	• Commanded by a lieutenant colonel. • Tactically and administratively self-sufficient. • Armored Cavalry and Air Cavalry equivalents called *squadrons*. • Two or more combat battalions make up a *brigade*.

Brigade	*Division*
• Commanded by a colonel. • May be employed on independent or semi-independent operations. • Combat, combat support, or combat service-support elements may be attached to perform specific missions. • Normally 3 combat brigades make up a *division*.	• Commanded by a major general. • Fully structured division has own brigade-size artillery, aviation, combat support, and service elements. • Two or more divisions make up a *corps* commanded by a lieutenant general.

22-2: Rifle Squad

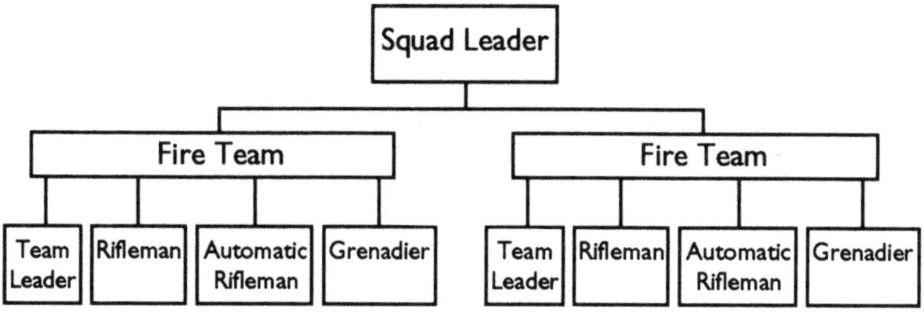

22-3: Infantry Rifle Platoon Organization

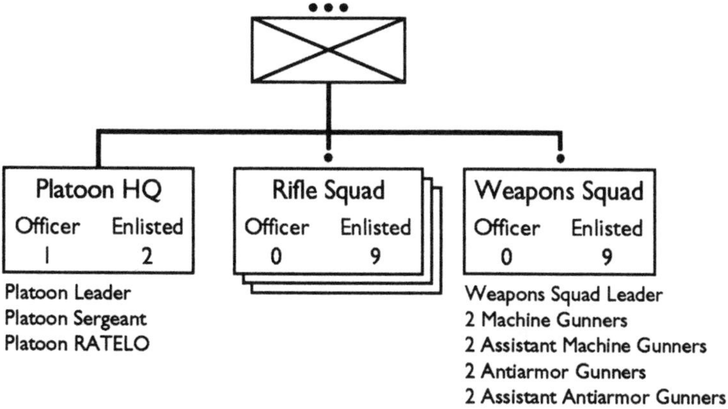

22-4: Rifle Company
Infantry Battalion (Mechanized)

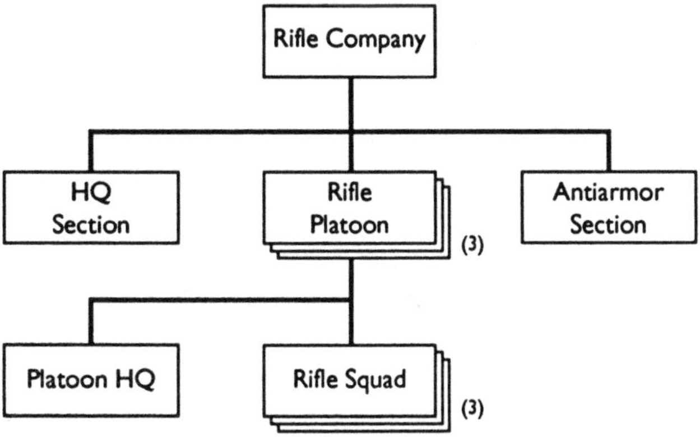

Close combat company-size units are capable of fighting without additional reinforcements. They may, however, be reinforced with maneuver platoons of the same or different types (infantry or armor normally) and with engineer squads or platoons to form teams.

Company teams are formed when forces are tailored for a particular mission. Such tailoring matches forces to missions with greater precision but often disrupts teamwork within the company. Company teams should, therefore, be formed only after careful consideration. They should also train together before they are committed, whenever possible.

Field artillery (FA) batteries are the basic firing units of the artillery. Batteries are organized with a firing battery (normally six artillery pieces), a headquarters, and limited support sections. The battery may fire and move together or by sections. Normally, batteries fight as part of their battalion. Occasionally, they are attached to other batteries or FA battalions. Multiple-launch rocket batteries will often operate independently, and armored cavalry squadrons have their own howitzer batteries.

Air-defense artillery (ADA) batteries operate as the fighting elements of ADA battalions or, if they are short-range air-defense (SHORAD) batteries, they will be attached to maneuver brigades or battalions. Separate SHORAD batteries exist in separate brigade-size organizations.

Combat engineer companies control three or four engineer platoons. They may be employed by their own battalion in a variety of tasks, or they may support maneuver brigades or battalions. Separate brigades and regiments usually have an assigned combat engineer company.

Most other combat support (CS) and combat service-support (CSS) units are formed as companies. Such companies vary widely in size, employment, and assignment.

Battalions/Squadrons

Battalions and cavalry squadrons consist of two or more company-size units and a headquarters. Most battalions are organized by branch, arm, or service. Those battalions that can move against an enemy are called "maneuver" battalions. Squadrons are always considered to be maneuver units. The headquarters company gives them the ability to perform some administrative and logistic services. Typically, battalions have three to five companies in addition to their headquarters.

Combat arms battalions/squadrons are designed to perform single tactical missions as part of a brigade's tactical operations.

Battalions attack, defend, delay, or move to assume new missions. Air and ground cavalry squadrons also perform reconnaissance and security missions. FA battalions fire in support of any of these missions.

Maneuver battalions can be reinforced with additional combat and CS companies to form task forces for special missions. *FA battalions* can be reinforced with batteries of any kind to form artillery task forces.

Engineer, ADA, and signal battalions assigned to or supporting divisions routinely operate throughout the division area of operations. Their commanders also perform the additional duties of division special staff officers.

CS and CSS battalions vary widely in type and organization. They may be separate divisional or nondivisional battalions, but, in any case, they normally perform functional services for a larger supported unit within that unit's area of operations. All battalions are capable of at least limited, short-term self-defense.

Brigades/Regiments/Groups

Brigade-size units control two or more battalions. Their capabilities for self-support and independent action vary considerably with the type of brigade.

Maneuver brigades are the major combat units of all divisions. They can also be organized as separate units. They can employ any combination of maneuver battalions, and they are normally supported by FA battalions, by aviation units, and by smaller combat, CS, and CSS units. While separate brigades and regiments have a fixed organization, division commanders can adjust and change the composition of their brigades as frequently as necessary.

22-5: Infantry Battalion (Mechanized)

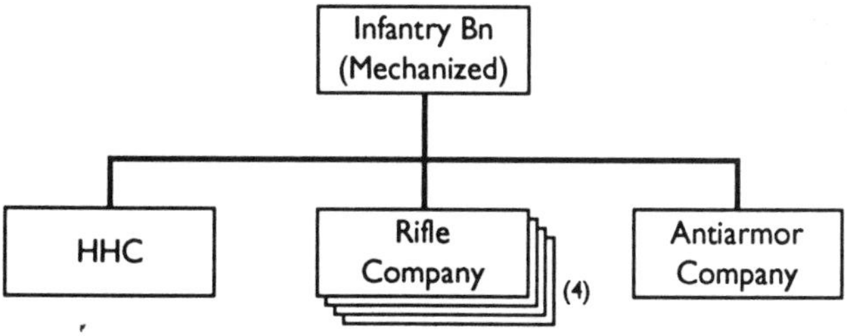

Brigades combine the efforts of their battalions and companies to fight engagements and to perform major tactical tasks in division battles. Their chief tactical responsibility is synchronizing the plans and actions of their subordinate units to accomplish a task for the division or corps.

Separate brigades of infantry, armor, FA, ADA, engineer, or aviation and armored cavalry regiments can be used to reinforce corps or divisions. They can be shifted from unit to unit to tailor forces for combat. Separate brigades and regiments are usually employed as units when attached to divisions or corps.

Other combat, CS, and CSS brigades and groups are organized to control nondivisional units for corps and larger units. Engineer, ADA, signal, aviation, MP, and transportation brigades are typical of such units. They may also be the building blocks of large unit-support structures, such as corps, and of CS commands, such as engineer commands. Divisions are supported by their own brigade-size support command of mixed CSS battalions and companies.

Divisions

Divisions have a fixed organization of combined-arms, usually 8 to 11 maneuver battalions, 3 to 4 FA battalions, and other combat, CS, and CSS units. Capable of performing any tactical mission and designed to be largely self-sustaining, divisions are the basic units of maneuver at the tactical level. Infantry, armor, mechanized infantry, airborne, and air-assault divisions are currently in the Army force structure.

Divisions possess great flexibility. They tailor their own brigades and attached forces for specific combat missions. Their CS and CSS battalions and separate companies may be attached to, or placed in support of, brigades for a particular mission. Divisions perform major tactical operations for the corps (the next echelon of command above division) and can conduct sustained battles and engagements.

Divisions are organized with varying numbers and types of maneuver battalions. The basic organizations are alike, however, and include the following:

- a division headquarters, headquarters (HQ) company, and three brigade HQ companies, which provide command and control (C^2) for units assigned or attached to the division;
- infantry, mechanized, and tank battalions to destroy the enemy and to seize and hold terrain;
- an air cavalry squadron for reconnaissance, security, and economy-of-force operations;

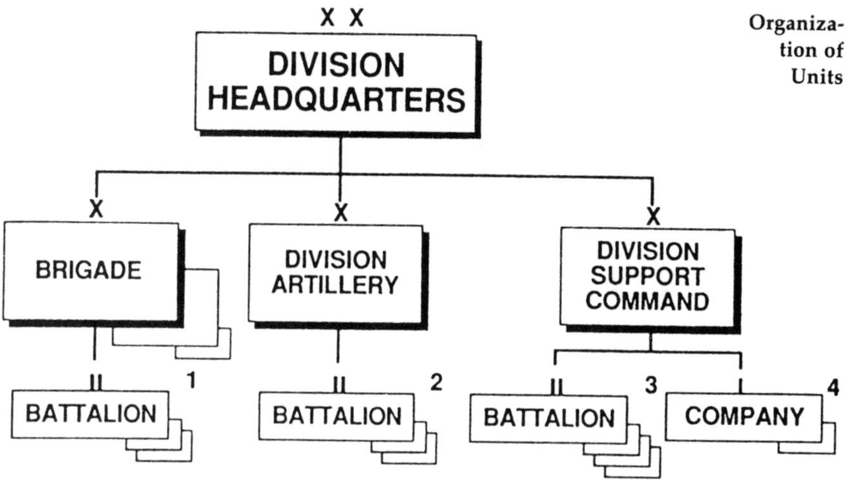

1. Either Infantry, Mechanized, or Tank.
2. Light, Medium, or Heavy.
3. Engineer, Signal, Combat Aviation, and Air Defense.
4. Military Police, Nuclear, Biological, and Chemical Defense.

Fig. 22.6.

- a division artillery consisting of a mix of light, medium, and heavy artillery battalions to provide indirect fire support, a target-acquisition battery to assist in target acquisition, and an HQ battery for C^2;
- an air-defense artillery battalion to help protect the division from air attacks;
- an engineer battalion for combat engineer support;
- a signal battalion to provide communications throughout the division;
- a combat electronic-warfare intelligence battalion, which collects, processes, and disseminates intelligence;
- a nuclear, biological, and chemical (NBC) defense company to provide for decontamination and to reconnoiter areas to be contaminated;
- a military police company to provide traffic control, security for enemy prisoners of war, and assistance in area security in the division's rear;
- a combat aviation battalion to provide C^2 aircraft to the division, attack helicopter support, and air transport with a single-lift capability of two rifle companies; and
- a division support command to provide combat services support to all units assigned to the division.

Corps

Corps are the Army's largest tactical units, the organizations with which higher commanders conduct maneuver at the operational level. Corps are tailored for the theater and mission for which they are deployed. Once tailored, however, they contain all the combat, CS, and CSS capabilities required to sustain operations for a long time.

Corps plan and conduct major operations and battles. They synchronize tactical activities including the maneuver of their divisions, the fires of their artillery units and supporting aerial forces, and the actions of their CS and CSS units. While corps normally fight as part of a larger land force, they may also be employed alone, either as an independent ground force or as the land component of a joint task force.

Corps may be assigned divisions of any type required by the theater and the mission. They possess support commands and are assigned combat and combat support organizations based on their needs for a specific operation.

23. The Fighting Force: Present and Future

The Army's Divisions

As this is written, the Army is in the difficult process of restructuring itself to a smaller force. From a 1992 level of fourteen active Regular and ten Army National Guard (ANG) divisions, America's Army will be reduced to a force of only eight active divisions and six ANG divisions. Plans are under study to determine exactly how many of what type division to retain and the best role for the Reserve components. The information provided in this chapter as to the number and designation of the active and reserve units may therefore be changed by the time you read it. However, as uncertain as the future is, it will still be of value to you to know something of the major units you will hear about, or to which you may even be assigned.

This chapter provides a brief history of each of the fourteen Regular Army divisions on active duty in late 1993. Also shown are the division shoulder sleeve insignia, campaigns, and division-level decorations. Many other awards and decorations have been won by the brigades and battalions within the divisions as well as by individual soldiers. A complete list of those is available from the U.S. Army Center of Military History. The divisions are presented in the order of their constitution.

Whatever the level of strength or mix of type units, the active force will be primarily composed of the divisions listed here. In the case of the 6th Infantry Division, the division headquarters has been inactivated and only one brigade remains; however, the information on the division itself is provided as it is a very senior unit.

1st Infantry Division (Mech.)
Germany

History

With the nickname "The Big Red One," the 1st Infantry Division is the oldest Regular Army division. It was organized on 8 June 1917. While in France during World War I, a division soldier clipped a piece of red cloth in the form of a "1" from the cap of a dead enemy soldier and pinned it to his sleeve, thus creating the first of the division's shoulder sleeve insignia and its nickname. In World War II, after service in North Africa and Sicily, the division stormed ashore on Omaha Beach in Normandy, enduring some of the most difficult fighting. The division has fought in every major national conflict since its creation except the Korean War. Most recently, during Operation Desert Storm, it helped lead the penetration of the Iraqi defenses and the consequent destruction of the Republican Guard. Its units are some of the oldest in the Army. One brigade will be at Fort Riley, Kansas.

Campaigns

World War I
Montdidier-Noyon
Aisne-Marne
St. Mihiel
Meuse-Argonne
Lorraine 1917
Lorraine 1918
Picardy 1918

World War II
Algeria—French Morocco (with arrowhead)
Tunisia
Sicily (with arrowhead)
Normandy (with arrowhead)
Northern France
Rhineland
Ardennes-Alsace
Central Europe

Vietnam
Defense
Counteroffensive
Counteroffensive, Phase II
Counteroffensive, Phase III
Tet Counteroffensive
Counteroffensive, Phase IV
Counteroffensive, Phase V
Counteroffensive, Phase VI
Tet 69/Counteroffensive
Summer–Fall 1969
Winter–Spring 1970

Southwest Asia (Desert Storm)
Defense of Saudi Arabia
Liberation and Defense of Kuwait

Decorations

World War II
French Croix de Guerre with Palm—Kasserine
French Croix de Guerre with Palm—Normandy
French Croix de Guerre, Fourragère
Cited in Belgian Army Order of the Day—Mons
Cited in Belgian Army Order of the Day—Eupen-Malmédy
Belgian Fourragère 1940

Vietnam
Meritorious Unit Commendation (Army)—Vietnam 1968
Republic of Vietnam Cross of Gallantry with Palm—1965–1968
Republic of Vietnam Civil Action Honor Medal, 1st Class

Southwest Asia
Meritorious Unit Commendation

82d Airborne Division
Fort Bragg, NC

History

The 82d Airborne Division was organized 25 August 1917 as an infantry division, and as such took part in three campaigns of World War I. Because its soldiers came from all over the country, the division selected the nickname "All American." This is reflected also by the "AA" in the center of its shoulder sleeve insignia. After World War I, the division became part of the Army Reserves. In March 1942, the division was recalled into active military service and the following August was reorganized as an airborne division and renamed 82d Airborne Division. During World War II it served in Sicily and Italy before participating in the Normandy and Nijmegen–Arnham assaults. The division has also participated in the Dominican Republic, Panama, and Southwest Asia campaigns. One of its brigades served in Vietnam. Stationed at Fort Bragg, the 82d Airborne Division is the Army's only active airborne division.

Campaigns

World War I
St. Mihiel
Meuse-Argonne
Lorraine 1918

World War II
Sicily
Naples-Foggia

Normandy (with arrowhead)
Rhineland (with arrowhead)
Ardennes-Alsace
Central Europe

Armed Forces Expeditions
Grenada 1983

Southwest Asia (Desert Storm)
Defense of Saudi Arabia
Liberation and Defense of Kuwait

Decorations

World War II
Presidential Unit Citation (Army)—Ste.-Mère-Église
French Croix de Guerre with Palm—Ste.-Mère-Église
French Croix de Guerre with Palm—Cotênin
Belgian Fourragère 1940
Cited in Belgian Army Order of the Day—Ardennes
Cited in Belgian Army Order of the Day—Belgium and Germany
Military Order of William, Knight 4th Class—Nijmegen
Netherlands Orange Lanyard

2d Infantry Division South Korea

History

Organized in France in 1918, the "Indianhead" Division was initially composed of both Regular Army and Marine Corps regiments. The division participated in World War I in France, and adopted its distinctively American star and Indianhead shoulder sleeve insignia there. It is the only division in which all of its units are authorized to wear the shoulder cord (fourragère) of the French Croix de Guerre. After the war, the division was reorganized to an all-Army unit. Between the world wars it tested new organizational concepts, including the "triangular" structure using three rather than four regiments. In World War II, the division fought in Europe across France, Belgium, and Germany. In 1950 it fought again in Korea. It is one of only two divisions awarded the Presidential Unit Citation for its Korean service. After a tour at Fort Benning where it helped test the new air assault concept, the division returned to Korea in 1965, where it remains on guard today. One brigade will be stationed at Fort Lewis, Washington.

Campaigns

World War I
Aisne
Aisne-Marne
St. Mihiel
Meuse-Argonne
Ile de France 1918
Lorraine 1918

World War II
Normandy
Northern France
Rhineland
Ardennes-Alsace
Central Europe

Korean War
UN Defensive
UN Offensive
CCF Intervention
First UN Counteroffensive
CCF Spring Offensive
UN Summer-Fall Offensive
Second Korean Winter
Korea, Summer–Fall 1952
Third, Korean Winter
Korea, Summer 1953

Decorations

World War I
French Croix de Guerre with Palm—Aisne-Marne
French Croix de Guerre with Palm—Meuse-Argonne
French Croix de Guerre Fourragère

World War II
Cited in Belgian Army Order of the Day—Ardennes
Cited in Belgian Army Order of the Day—Elsenborn Crest
Belgian Fourragère 1940

Korea
Presidential Unit Citation (Army)—Hongchon
Republic of Korea Presidential Unit Citation—Naktong River
Republic of Korea Presidential Unit Citation—Korea

3d Infantry Division (Mech.)
Fort Stewart, GA

History

The 3d Infantry Division was organized in November 1917, and deployed to France in March 1918. The following July, it held fast against massive German assaults trying to cross the Marne River, earning the division the nickname "The Marne Division." After the war the division was sent to Fort Lewis where it spent the years until World War II. In 1943 the division assaulted into North Africa and then fought in Sicily, Italy and Southern France, taking part in four amphibious assaults. One of its most famous members was Audie Murphy. The division returned to the United States after the war, but was sent to Europe for the third time in 1958. One of its brigades took part in Operation Desert Storm. The division's shoulder sleeve insignia shows three white lines, which represent the three major operations in which it participated in World War I. The division is currently structured as a mechanized unit.

Campaigns

World War I
Aisne
Champagne-Marne
Aisne-Marne
St. Mihiel
Meuse-Argonne
Champagne 1918

World War II
Algeria–French Morocco (with arrowhead)
Tunisia
Sicily (with arrowhead)
Naples-Foggia
Anzio (with arrowhead)
Rome-Arno
Southern France (with arrowhead)
Rhineland
Ardennes-Alsace
Central Europe

Korean War
CCF Intervention
First UN Counteroffensive
CCF Spring Offensive
UN Summer–Fall Offensive
Second Korean Winter
Korea, Summer–Fall 1952
Third Korean Winter
Korea, Summer 1953

Decorations

World War II
Presidential Unit Citation (Army)—Colmar
French Croix de Guerre with Palm—Colmar
French Croix de Guerre Fourragère

Korea
Republic of Korea Presidential Unit Citation—Uijongbu Corridor
Republic of Korea Presidential Unit Citation—Iron Triangle
Bravery Gold Medal of Greece—Korea

6th Infantry Division (Light) Inactive

History

The 6th Division was organized in November 1917, and moved to France the following year. It participated in two World War I campaigns and had so many long marches that it became informally known as the "Sightseeing Sixth." The six points of its star-shaped insignia refer to the division's designation. After World War I the division was inactivated, but was recalled to active duty at Fort Lewis in 1939. During World War II the division was committed to the Pacific and took part in a number of bloody battles in the Philippines and New Guinea. After the war the division was inactivated again. Other than two short periods during the 1950s and late 1960s, the division remained inactive until 1986 when it was activated in Alaska. As a part of the Army's recent reductions, the division headquarters was inactivated again in 1994.

Campaigns

World War I
Meuse-Argonne
Alsace 1918

World War II
New Guinea (with arrowhead)
Luzon (with arrowhead)

Decorations

World War II
Philippine Presidential Unit Citation—October 1944–July 1945

4th Infantry Division (Mech.)
Fort Hood, TX

History

The 4th Infantry Division was organized in December 1917 and trained with the British in France for the first months of its deployment to Europe. The division adopted an insignia composed of four ivy leaves arranged in a cross. The four leaves and the ivy, a play on the Roman numeral for four (IV) refer to the unit's designation. The division was in the thick of the fighting during World War I, receiving credit for six campaigns. Inactivated after the war, the division was recalled to active service in 1940 at Fort Lewis as a motorized unit. Reorganized as an infantry division, the 4th landed at Utah Beach on D-Day, with one of former President Teddy Roosevelt's sons as an assistant division commander. The 4th then fought its way inland and fought through Europe. A patrol of the division claimed the honor of being the first Americans into Germany. After the war the division was inactivated for sixteen months, then reactivated at Fort Ord. Although it was not sent to Korea, the division saw extensive action in Vietnam. It is organized as one of the Army's mechanized divisions. One brigade will be at Fort Carson, Colorado.

Campaigns

World War I
Aisne-Marne
St. Mihiel
Meuse-Argonne
Champagne 1918
Lorraine 1918

World War II
Normandy (with arrowhead)
Northern France
Rhineland
Ardennes-Alsace
Central Europe

Vietnam
Counteroffensive, Phase II
Counteroffensive, Phase III
Tet Counteroffensive
Counteroffensive, Phase IV
Counteroffensive, Phase V
Counteroffensive, Phase VI
Tet 69/Counteroffensive
Summer–Fall 1969
Winter–Spring 1970
Sanctuary Counteroffensive
Counteroffensive, Phase VII

Decorations

World War II
Cited in Belgian Army Order of the Day—Belgium
Cited in Belgian Army Order of the Day—Ardennes
Belgian Fourragère 1940

Vietnam
Republic of Vietnam Cross of Gallantry with Palm 1966–1969
Republic of Vietnam Cross of Gallantry with Palm 1969–1970
Republic of Vietnam Civil Action Honor Medal, 1st Class, 1966–69

7th Infantry Division (Light)
Inactive

History

Organized in January 1918, the 7th Infantry Division saw service in the Lorraine sector of France. The soldiers of the 7th adopted the hourglass symbol used to mark their equipment and as their shoulder insignia, using the colors of red and black. The two black triangles resemble two figure "7"s, one of them upside down. After the war the 7th was inactive almost twenty years, returning in 1940. The division retook the only U.S. territory captured by the Japanese in World War II, in the Aleutian Islands off the coast of Alaska, and then joined the Marines on Guadalcanal. Its soldiers later stormed ashore on Kwajalein Island—again with the Marines—and helped retake the Philippines. Its toughest battle came when the 7th invaded Okinawa and fought a fanatical Japanese defense. After the war the division was sent to Korea to assist guarding the 38th Parallel border. The division moved to Japan in 1948, but only two years later it returned to Korea where it remained for twenty-one years. The division adopted its Korean War code name "Bayonet" as its nickname. Inactivated in 1971, the division was reactivated as a light division in 1974 and participated in the Panama operation. The division headquarters has been inactivated.

Campaigns

World War I
Lorraine 1918

World War II
Aleutian Islands
Eastern Mandates

Leyte
Ryukyus

Korean War
UN Defensive
UN Offensive
CCF Intervention
First UN Counteroffensive
CCF Spring Offensive
UN Summer–Fall Offensive
Second Korean Winter
Korea, Summer–Fall 1952
Third Korean Winter
Korea, Summer 1953

Armed Forces Expeditions
Panama 1989–1990

Decorations

World War II
Philippine Presidential Unit Citation—17 October 1944–4 July 1945

Korea
Republic of Korea Presidential Unit Citation—Inchon
Republic of Korea Presidential Unit Citation—Korea 1950–1953
Republic of Korea Presidential Unit Citation—Korea 1945–1948; 1953–1971

101st Airborne Division (Air Assault)
Fort Campbell, KY

History

The division began to organize in November 1918 for service in France, but was halted one month later because of the end of World War I. In 1921, the division was finally organized with its headquarters in Wisconsin. In commemoration of the famous Civil War "Iron Brigade" that had a number of regiments from that state, and the equally famous bald eagle "Old Abe" that had been a brigade mascot, the division adopted the bald eagle for its shoulder insignia. In August 1942, the division was selected to convert to an airborne division, and in that structure went on to participate in four campaigns in Europe. The division made combat jumps into Normandy and later into Holland, winning many honors. One of its most famous exploits was the defense of the Belgian town of Bastogne during the surprise German offensive in the winter of 1944. The division was inactivated fifteen months after the war, but was reactivated in 1954. It later served with great distinction as an airmobile division in the Vietnam War. After the war it was reorganized to be the Army's only air assault division. Most recently the division took part in the Southwest Asia campaigns, striking deep into Iraqi territory.

Campaigns

World War II
Normandy (with arrowhead)
Rhineland (with arrowhead)

Ardennes-Alsace
Central Europe

Vietnam
Counteroffensive, Phase III
Tet Counteroffensive
Counteroffensive, Phase IV
Counteroffensive, Phase V
Counteroffensive, Phase VI
Tet 69/Counteroffensive
Summer–Fall 1969
Winter–Spring 1970
Sanctuary Counteroffensive
Counteroffensive, Phase VII
Consolidation I
Consolidation II

Southwest Asia (Desert Storm)
Defense of Saudi Arabia
Liberation and Defense of Kuwait

Decorations

World War II
Presidential Unit Citation (Army)—Normandy
Presidential Unit Citation (Army)—Bastogne
French Croix de Guerre with Palm—Normandy
Belgian Croix de Guerre 1940 with Palm—Bastogne
Cited in Belgian Army Order of the Day—Bastogne
Cited in Belgian Army Order of the Day—France and Belgium
Belgian Fourragère 1940
Netherlands Orange Lanyard

Vietnam
Republic of Vietnam Cross of Gallantry with Palm—Vietnam 1966–1969
Republic of Vietnam Cross of Gallantry with Palm—Vietnam 1971
Republic of Vietnam Civil Action Honor Medal, 1st Class

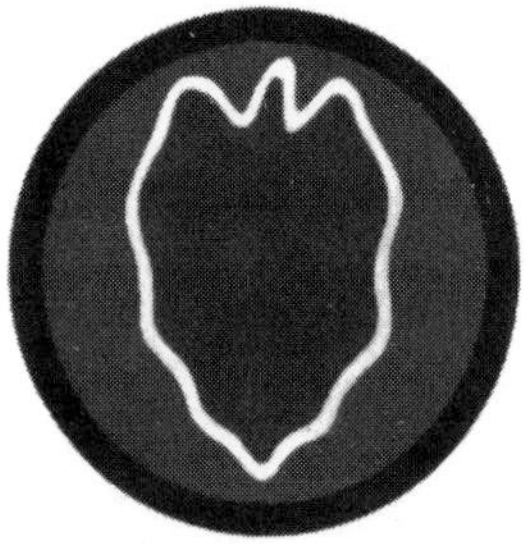

24th Infantry Division (Mech.) Inactive

History

The 24th Infantry Division was first organized at Schofield Barracks, Hawaii in March 1921 as the Hawaiian Division. Its insignia of a green tropical taro leaf was chosen to reflect the association with Hawaii. Reorganized in 1940, the division sent some of its elements to form the 25th Infantry Division. The 24th Division was deployed to Australia in 1943, and went on to fight through four campaigns in the Pacific, earning the nickname "Victory" division. After the war the division was stationed in Japan as part of the occupation forces. In 1950 the 24th was the first division sent to face the North Korean invasion of South Korea. It earned a Presidential Unit Citation for its heroic service there. In 1958 the division was transferred to Germany where it remained until inactivated in 1969. Reactivated in 1975, the 24th Infantry Division was converted to a mechanized division, and as such was a leading participant in the defeat of the Iraqi Army in Southwest Asia.

Campaigns

World War II
Central Pacific
New Guinea (with arrowhead)
Leyte (with arrowhead)
Luzon
Southern Philippines (with arrowhead)

Korean War
UN Defensive
UN Offensive

CCF Intervention
First UN Counteroffensive
CCF Spring Offensive
UN Summer–Fall Offensive
Second Korean Winter
Korea, Summer 1953

Southwest Asia (Desert Storm)
Defense of Saudi Arabia
Liberation and Defense of Kuwait

Decorations

World War II
Philippine Presidential Unit Citation—17 October 1944–4 July 1945

Korea
Presidential Unit Citation (Army)—Defense of Korea
Republic of Korea Presidential Unit Citation—Pyongtaek
Republic of Korea Presidential Unit Citation—Korea

1st Cavalry Division
Fort Hood, TX

History

The 1st Cavalry Division was organized in September 1921, at Fort Bliss, Texas, to provide security along the U.S. southern border. Its units served along the border until World War II. The wife of a division commander designed the division insignia, combining the horse, a stylized scaling ladder, and the bold cavalry yellow color to make the largest shoulder insignia in the Army. In 1943 the division gave up its horses and reorganized as an infantry division, retaining its traditional cavalry name and units. It fought in the Pacific through four campaigns, liberating Manila and freeing American prisoners of war. It was the first division into Tokyo, and remained on occupation duty there until 1950. One of the first units into Korea, the division faced hard fighting. The division returned to Japan in 1951. It stayed there until 1957 when its troopers were sent to the Korean DMZ for guard duty along the truce line. In 1965 the division returned to the U.S. to become the first airmobile division in history. The 1st Cav was sent to Vietnam that same year, and remained there until 1972. "The First Team" is the only division awarded both the Presidential Unit Citation and the Valorous Unit Citation for its actions. After Vietnam, the division went to Fort Hood, where it was restructured as an armored division. With Iraq's invasion of Kuwait, the division moved to Southwest Asia where it served in two campaigns.

Campaigns

World War II
New Guinea
Bismarck Archipelago
Leyte (with arrowhead)
Luzon

Korean War
UN Defensive
UN Offensive
CCF Intervention
First UN Counteroffensive
CCF Spring Offensive
UN Summer–Fall Offensive
Second Korean Winter

Vietnam
Defense
Counteroffensive
Counteroffensive, Phase II
Counteroffensive, Phase III
Tet Counteroffensive

Counteroffensive, Phase IV
Counteroffensive, Phase V
Counteroffensive, Phase VI
Tet 69/Counteroffensive
Summer–Fall 1969
Winter–Spring 1970
Sanctuary Counteroffensive
Counteroffensive, Phase VII

Southwest Asia (Desert Storm)
Defense of Saudi Arabia
Liberation and Defense of Kuwait

Decorations

World War II
Philippine Presidential Unit Citation—17 October 1944–4 July 1945

Korea
Republic of Korea Presidential Unit Citation—Waegwan–Teagu
Bravery Gold Medal of Greece—Korea

Vietnam
Presidential Unit Citation (Army)—Pleiku
Valorous Unit Award—Fish Hook
Republic of Vietnam Cross of Gallantry with Palm—Vietnam 1965–1969
Republic of Vietnam Cross of Gallantry with Palm—Vietnam 1969–1970
Republic of Vietnam Cross of Gallantry with Palm—Vietnam 1970–1971
Republic of Vietnam Civil Action Honor Medal, 1st Class, 1969–1970

1st Armored Division
Germany

History

Originally organized in March 1932 as the 7th Mechanized Cavalry Brigade, the unit was reorganized and expanded into the 1st Armored Division in 1940. The division landed and fought in North Africa and then served in all five of the Italian campaigns. While in Italy the division's soldiers began to refer to it as "Old Ironsides," and the division formally adopted that as its nickname. The insignia is the standard armored division triangle design with the colors of the three branches of its main units—yellow for cavalry/armor, blue for infantry, and red for artillery. The division number "1" is placed over a crossed tank tread, gun, and lightning bolt, which symbolize mobility, power and speed. The division's nickname is on a tab across the bottom of the insignia. After World War II the division was inactivated, and then recalled in 1951 to bolster the Army's strength during the Korean War. In 1970 Old Ironsides moved to Germany, where it stood vigilant against Soviet aggression for twenty years. In the fall of 1990, the division deployed with U.S. forces to Southwest Asia where it helped crush Iraqi forces. Its mission completed, it returned to Germany.

Campaigns

World War II
Tunisia
Naples-Foggia
Rome-Arno
Anzio
North Apennines
Po Valley

Southwest Asia (Desert Storm)
Defense of Saudi Arabia
Liberation and Defense of Kuwait

Decorations

None

25th Infantry Division (Light)
Schofield Barracks, HI

History

Organized in 1940 from elements formerly assigned to the Hawaiian Division, the 25th Infantry Division first saw combat when Pearl Harbor was attacked on 7 December 1941. The division insignia reflects its Hawaiian and 24th Division origins, using a taro leaf design. A lightning bolt was added to represent the suddenness and power with which the division operates. While fighting on Guadalcanal, the division adopted the nickname "Tropical Lightning." From there the division fought in the jungles of the Northern Solomon Islands and Philippines. After World War II the division served on occupation duty in Japan until the start of the Korean War. It fought in all ten campaigns of that war before returning to Hawaii in 1954. When combat troops were sent to Vietnam, the 25th was among them, serving from 1966 to 1970, when the division again returned to Hawaii. In the mid-1980s it was reorganized as a light infantry division.

Campaigns

World War II
Central Pacific
Guadalcanal
Northern Solomons
Luzon

Korean War
UN Defensive
UN Offensive
CCF Intervention

Decorations

World War II
Philippine Presidential Unit Citation—17 October–4 July 1945

Korea
Republic of Korea Presidential Unit Citation—Masan–Chinju
Republic of Korea Presidential Unit Citation—Munsan-ni

Vietnam
Meritorious Unit Commendation (Army)—Vietnam 1969
Republic of Vietnam Cross of Gallantry with Palm—Vietnam 1966–1968
Republic of Vietnam Cross of Gallantry with Palm—Vietnam 1968–1970
Republic of Vietnam Civil Action Honor Medal, 1st Class, 1966–1970

10th Mountain Division (Light)
Fort Drum, NY

History

The 10th Mountain Division was organized at Camp Hale, Colorado, in July 1943 as the 10th Light Division. In November 1944, the designation was changed to 10th Mountain Division with the intent to make better use of soldiers trained especially for winter warfare. It deployed to Italy and fought there in two campaigns, breaking the Germans loose from their last mountain defensive line. The dark blue insignia of the division bears two red bayonets crossed in an "X" to form the Roman numeral for 10. The blue color and bayonets symbolize the infantry. Over the insignia is a blue tab that says "Mountain." When the division returned to the U.S. in 1945, it was inactivated. In 1948 the division returned to duty for ten years as the 10th Infantry Division, then was inactivated again until 1985. In that year the division was reactivated as a light division with its old title of 10th Mountain Division. Several of its units were deployed to Somalia in 1993, where they assisted the UN distribution of food and establishment of security. "Mountaineer" soldiers of the division engaged in a number of serious firefights with local militia during their UN assignment. In September 1994, units of the 10th deployed to Haiti for peacekeeping duties.

Campaigns

World War II
North Appennines
Po Valley

Decorations

Somalia
Joint Meritorious Unit Award, 5 December 1992–4 May 1993

2d Armored Division
Inactive

History

The 2d Armored Division was activated 15 July 1940 at Fort Benning, Georgia. It was one of the spearhead divisions into North Africa, and fought the Germans in the Tunisian desert alongside its sister armored division, the 1st. It then fought through Sicily. Its nickname, "Hell on Wheels," was borne out when it landed in France and blasted its way across France, Holland, and into Germany. It helped stop the German offensive in the Belgian Ardennes during the Battle of the Bulge and led the counterattack on the northern flank. Racing across Germany, the 2d Armored was the first American unit to reach the Elbe River, where it linked up with Soviet forces. It was also the first American armored unit into Berlin. Following the war the division remained in Europe until returning to Fort Hood in 1958. Its 1st or "Tiger" Brigade deployed back to Europe in 1975. The brigade remained there until 1990 when it was sent to Southwest Asia to serve as a brigade of the 1st Cavalry Division. On arrival, however, it was detached and sent to provide heavy armor support to the Marines units attacking along the coastal area of Kuwait. After the Gulf War, the brigade came home to the 2d Armored at Fort Hood, where it is now stationed. The division insignia is the standard armored division tricolored triangle, with the number "2" over the track, and its nickname "Hell on Wheels" on a tab across the bottom of the insignia.

Campaigns

World War II
Algeria-French Morocco (with arrowhead)
Sicily (with arrowhead)
Normandy
Northern France
Rhineland
Ardennes–Alsace
Central Europe

Decorations

World War II
Cited in Belgian Army Order of the Day—Belgium
Cited in Belgian Army Order of the Day—Ardennes
Belgian Fourragère 1940

The Future Force

The size and composition of America's Army for the future is an issue of serious ongoing debate. The threat of a massive Soviet led Warsaw Pact attack in Europe faded with the breakup of the Soviet Union, and the dissolution of the pact. Yet threats to U.S. security and interests from other potential adversaries and international requests for American military assistance continue. The Persian Gulf, Somalia, Bosnia, and Haiti are the crisis points today; there will be others in the future. Not everyone agrees on the best-size Army to answer the future calls for help. There is the ever-present demand for less military spending so that more money can be provided for other national problems.

The Army began 1995 with thirteen active divisions, two of which had only one brigade. Three of those thirteen divisions will inactivate in the near future. The size of the Reserve Components is also going to be reduced. The Army will have ten active divisions and a total active strength of about 500,000 soldiers by 1996. The RC strength would also be reduced.

Wherever possible, the Army is returning its divisions to a full strength of three active brigades. Previously, many divisions had only two active brigades with Reserve Component brigades designated to be the third brigade. The decision to reconsider the role of the RC brigades came after careful analysis of the Gulf War experience, and the recognition that these units needed extra training time before being committed into combat. Under one Army plan the RC brigades would continue to be associated with specific active divisions to serve as a fourth or "round-up" brigade.

Whatever the plan the Army follows, there will always be room for highly motivated soldiers seeking to serve their country. America's Army will remain true to its mission of defending the American people.

IV. Weapons and Equipment

24. Selected U.S. Army Weapons

The past success and survival of the American soldier has been the result of many factors—not the least of which have been the finest weapons and equipment in the world. These are the best science and American industry can provide. Today the Army is continuing its weapons-modernization program, which started in the late 1970s. Adjusted for budget changes, the present restructuring is expected to continue well into the 1990s.

Modernization is a continuous process by which the Army develops and fields war-fighting capabilities needed to deter war and, if necessary, to fight and win. It is more than just developing and fielding advanced weapons systems and equipment and establishing production, mobilization, and sustainment bases. Equally important are developing and implementing modern doctrine, tactics, weapon design, leader development, and training programs. Maintaining the lethality of the Army through a disciplined, modernization effort will become increasingly important as the Army gets smaller and the proliferation of sophisticated weapon systems continues around the world.

The challenge facing the Army now is to ensure that modernization of America's Army (the active and reserve components) is, in fact, continuous. It must be in order to maintain the lethality of the force. The Army must carefully decide which requirements call for new weapons systems and which can be met by adaptations in tactics or weapon design, reinforced by aggressive training.

Selected Army Weapons

The following presents some information on a selection of the most common weapons that new soldiers will see and with which they will probably become most familiar, especially in one of the combat arms. The weapons are categorized by the type of combat in which they are used. These weapons are available now to the American soldier. Some future weapon developments are discussed in Chapter 26.

Close-Combat Weaponry

Close-combat involves the use of direct combat power at close range—weapon to weapon, soldier to soldier. The weapons employed in this type of fighting include individual and crew-served infantry weapons, tanks used by armor battalions, fighting vehicle systems and armored personnel carriers used by mechanized infantry.

M-16A1/A2 Rifle

The most basic individual weapon is the soldier's rifle. Every soldier learns how to fire and care for the M-16 rifle (figure 24.1). The most current model, the M-16A2, is the Army's primary combat rifle. This is an improved version of the older M-16 and M-16A1. It has been redesigned with a slightly heavier barrel, improved muzzle compensator, and new selector switch. It is a lightweight, air-cooled, gas-operated, low-recoil rifle that fires either single shot, or a three-round burst, as determined by a selector switch. It weighs only 8.9 pounds, and has a 30-round magazine. It fires a NATO standard 5.56mm round, the same round used by the Squad Automatic Weapon, and has a maximum effective range of 460 meters. This is the maximum range at which a weapon is most accurate, although it will shoot much farther. The M-16 series rifles that do not have the M-203 Grenade Launcher can be fitted with a bayonet.

M-203 Grenade Launcher

The M-203 is a 40mm single-shot launcher mounted under the barrel of an M-16A1 or A2 rifle. It replaced the M-79 grenade launcher, which was a separate weapon used during the Vietnam War. The barrel of the M-203 is aluminum and rifled to provide spin stabilization to the grenade projectile. The launcher fires a single 40mm projectile of various types—explosive grenade, buckshot, tear gas, illuminating, colored smoke, and others. The trigger for the launcher is located just forward of the rifle magazine. The launcher uses two sets of sights, one on the top of the special modified rifle handguard, and one on the side of the rifle's carrying handle. The launcher unloaded adds 3 pounds to the weight of the rifle, and the projectile another half pound. The maximum effective range

Fig. 24.1. Soldiers of the 82d Airborne Division armed with M-16A2 rifles during an exercise in Honduras.

against area targets is 350 meters, and against point targets such as a fighting position about 200 meters. This weapon is carried by the two grenadiers in the rifle squad.

M-4 Carbine

The M-4 carbine is essentially a shorter, lighter version of the M-16 rifle. It is intended for use by armor personnel as a replacement for the M-3 .45 caliber "grease gun," and by selected individuals such as vehicle drivers who need a short automatic weapon. It will replace some M-16A2 rifles and pistols in a unit. The M-4 fires the same 5.56mm round as the M-16A2.

M-9 Pistol

The M-9 is a relatively new pistol (figure 24.2), made by Beretta USA, which replaces the .45 caliber and .38 caliber pistols previously used by the Army. It is a semiautomatic double-action pistol that fires a 9mm round. The M-9 uses a 15-round magazine and weighs only 2.6 pounds loaded. The maximum effective range of the pistol is 50 meters, and it is intended for use by soldiers who are not normally issued a rifle, and others who have a need for close-in self-defense.

Hand Grenades

The Army uses a variety of hand grenades. The most common types are the high-explosive fragmentation grenades, and grenades used for signaling. In addition there are grenades with

Fig. 24.2. M-9 pistol

riot-control agents such as tear gas, and incendiary grenades used to start very intense fires, for example to destroy enemy equipment. The grenades come in distinctive shapes and with their own special color markings to tell them apart. The M-67 fragmentation grenade is used primarily against enemy personnel, and is shaped like a baseball with the fuse and handle attached at the top. It is olive-drab (OD) with yellow markings. Smoke grenades used for signaling and obscuring movement are shaped like soft-drink cans, again with the fuse and handle at the top. These type grenades are OD or light green with the color of the smoke shown on the top. A third type of grenade uses white phosphorous (WP) to make dense white smoke, but it also produces enemy casualties from the pieces of burning white phosphorous thrown off at the same time.

Mines

While mines are not considered a true individual weapon, the types most soldiers will encounter will be emplaced and removed by individual soldiers. The most common are the antipersonnel mines—the M-14 (Toe Popper), M-16A1 (Bouncing Betty), M-18A1 (Claymore), and the M-21 Antitank mine. While these mines are similar in several ways such as methods of arming and disarming, each of them also has its own specific characteristics and uses to defend positions, block avenues of enemy approach, or deny the enemy the use of terrain.

Fig. 24.3. M-249 squad automatic weapon (SAW)

M-249 Squad Automatic Weapon (SAW)

The M-249 SAW (figure 24.3) provides the infantry squad with a lightweight, one-man-portable fully automatic weapon capable of providing a large volume of effective fire. It fires the same 5.56mm round as the M-16A2 and M-4, and has a mounted plastic magazine with a capacity of 200 linked rounds. The SAW will also accept single rounds. The gunner normally carries two additional loaded magazines in pouches. The SAW can fire at a rate of 750 rounds per minute with a maximum range of 3,600 meters and an effective range of 800 meters. It is normally fired from its folding bipod, but it can also be mounted on a tripod. The overall length of the SAW is 39.4 inches and it weighs 15.6 pounds. Two of these weapons are assigned to each infantry squad.

MK-19-3 Automatic Grenade Launcher

The MK-19-3 is an automatic grenade launcher that fires the same 40mm grenade as the M-203, but in a rapid-fire manner similar to a machine gun. The rate of fire is 325–375 rounds per minute. It is designed to provide accurate, intense fire against enemy personnel and lightly armored vehicles. It has a maximum effective range of 1,600 meters against point targets and 2,200 meters against area targets. The MK-19-3 is a primary weapon for combat and combat support units, and may be mounted on wheeled and tracked vehicles (figure 24.4).

Fig. 24.4. MK-19-3 automatic grenade launcher

Crew-Served Automatic Weapons

M-60 Machine Gun

The M-60 (figure 24.5) is a 7.62mm belt-fed, air-cooled, gas-operated machine gun normally operated by a crew of two—a gunner and assistant gunner. It weighs 23 pounds, is 43.5 inches long, and can be mounted on a bipod, tripod, or vehicle pedestal. It has a maximum rate of fire of 550–650 rounds per minute, with a sustained rate of fire of 125 rounds per minute. The M-60 has an effective range of 1,100 meters using the tripod, and a maximum range of 3,725 meters. It fires three types of combat ammunition—ball, tracer, and armor-piercing—from a metal-link belt. The M-60 has several models for use as either a ground or vehicle-mounted weapon.

Caliber .50 Machine Gun

The caliber .50 machine gun is one of the oldest and most dependable weapons still in the Army inventory (figure 24.6). There are several variations of the weapon, and it can be used as a ground or wheeled and tracked vehicle weapon, effective against personnel, lightly armored vehicles, or aircraft. It has a rate of fire of up to 450 rounds per minute, but only 40 rounds per minute for sustained firing due to heat buildup. Mounted on a tripod, it is very accurate, with an effective range of 1,800 meters against area targets. It is a heavy

Fig. 24.5. M-60 machine gun mounted on an M-113 armored personnel carrier (APC)

Fig. 24.6. M-2 .50 caliber machine gun mounted on an APC

weapon, weighing 84 pounds without tripod, and fires four types of ammunition from a linked belt. These types are ball, tracer, armor-piercing, and armor-piercing incendiary.

Antitank and Special Weapons

M-72A2 Light Antitank Weapon (LAW)

This is a shoulder-fired, short-range antitank weapon. The LAW consists of a 66mm high explosive antitank (HEAT) rocket in a disposable fiberglass and aluminum launcher tube. It weighs only 4.7 pounds and is 22 inches long (35 inches extended for firing). The LAW has a maximum range of 1,000 meters, and can penetrate 12 inches of armor out to a range of 200 meters, making it very useful against enemy armor and bunkers. The weapon is carried, aimed, and fired by a single soldier.

M-136 Lightweight Multipurpose Weapon (AT-4)

This Swedish-produced weapon was intended to replace the LAW. It is not a rocket launcher, but a one-shot disposable recoilless gun that fires an 84mm projectile. Because it uses a unique combustion system, it has very little recoil and the barrel can be constructed out of glass-reinforced plastic and aluminum, saving weight. It is a one-soldier weapon, with a maximum range of 2,100 meters and is capable of penetrating 17 inches of armor plate. The round is stabilized in flight by six fins and uses a shaped charge that produces enhanced effects when it strikes armor. It weighs 14.8 pounds and is 40 inches in length. The sights of the M-136 are similar to those of the M-16A2, and easy for a soldier to use.

M-47 Dragon Medium Antitank Weapon

The Dragon is a wire-guided missile system, man-portable and shoulder-fired (figure 24.7). The launcher rests on a bipod and the soldier's shoulder. The optical tracker part of the system is reusable, but the launcher is disposable after firing the missile. The tracker is used to direct the missile using electronic signals sent through the guidance wire to the missile. The total weight of the system is 68.5 pounds, and it has a length of 44 inches. The maximum range is 1,000 meters.

TOW Antiarmor Weapons System

The name "TOW" stands for Tube-Launched, Optically Tracked, Wire Command-Link Guided. It is a long-range heavy antiarmor missile system designed to destroy enemy armor and field fortifications (figure 24.8). It requires a crew of three,

Fig. 24.7. M-47 Dragon deployed in Korea

and may be used as either a ground weapon or mounted on a vehicle. The system consists of several parts including a missile-guidance set, a tube launcher, optical sight, tripod, and missile. Weight of the system without the missile is 280 pounds. It also has a thermal sight for use at night or in reduced visibility. Guidance commands from the gunner are transmitted to the missile by the guidance wire. The missile has a maximum range of 3,750 meters. There are several versions: The latest model of missile, the TOW can defeat all known enemy armor.

M-202A1 Multishot Rocket Launcher (Flash)

The Flash is a lightweight man-portable rocket launcher containing four 66mm rockets. It is fired by one soldier from the shoulder. A single rocket can be fired, or all four rockets at a rate of one per second. The weapon can then be reloaded using a clip of four more rockets. The rockets use a bursting incendiary warhead that explodes with a brilliant flash. It has a range for area targets of 750 meters and point targets of 200 meters. Loaded, the Flash weighs 26.6 pounds, and its length extended for firing is 35 inches.

Fig. 24.8. Ground-configured TOW being fired

M-3 RAAWS (Ranger Antiarmor-Antipersonnel Weapons System)
The Army's Ranger battalions are equipped with the RAAWS to replace the old 90mm recoilless rifle. It is particularly desirable because of the ease with which it is carried in airborne operations. The RAAWS fires four different types of 84mm rounds, which weigh only 7 pounds each. The weight of the weapon itself is only 22 pounds and it is 42.6 inches long.

Armored Fighting Vehicles

M1A1/A2 Abrams Main Battle Tank
Designed for armor battles in Europe, the M1A1 Abrams tank is the Army's primary ground-combat weapon system for closing with and destroying enemy forces by employing shock action, mobility, and firepower (figure 24.9). The M1A1 is used, in conjunction with other ground and air systems, under all battlefield conditions. Operated by a four-man crew, it has

Fig. 24.9. M1A1 Abrams main battle tank

special armor and a fire-detection and suppression system. It was extremely effective in Operation Desert Storm.

The M1A1 has a 120mm smooth-bore cannon that is able to hit tank-sized targets at ranges beyond 3,000 meters. Added to the already proven combination of thermal sight, laser rangefinder, and full stabilization, its NBC microclimatic cooling system makes the M1A1 able to operate under all climate and light conditions as well as in an active chemical environment. Its 1,500-horsepower turbine engine and improved suspension provide superior handling and maneuverability, thus decreasing the tank's exposure to direct and indirect fire. The M1A1 weighs 67 tons (combat loaded) and has a top speed of 41 miles per hour (mph). In addition to its 120mm cannon, the M1A1 also is equipped with one .50 caliber machine gun and two 7.62mm machine guns. An improved M1A2 tank is under development.

M-2/M-3 Bradley Fighting Vehicle Systems (FVS)
The M-2 allows for mounted combat and provides the infantry with a means to protect tanks and consolidate gains in the offensive (figure 24.10). It is designed for a nine-man infantry squad, including the two-man turret for the commander and gunner. The main armament is the 25mm "chain gun." Both armor-piercing discarding sabot (APDS) and high-explosive

Fig. 24.10. M-2 Bradley fighting vehicle

(HE) ammunition are available. A 7.62mm coaxial machine gun is mounted to the right of the 25mm main gun. A Tube-Launched Optically Tracked Wire-Guided (TOW) antitank guided-missile launcher, housed in an armored rectangular box, is hinged to the left side of the turret. It is folded flat against the turret for traveling and then raised. The fire-control system features an integrated day/night sight incorporating a thermal-imaging infrared device. The firing port weapons are modified 5.56mm M-16A1 rifles, mounted in the rotating ball firing ports. The M-2 has a top road speed of 42 mph and a cruising range of 300 miles. An upgraded version, the M-2A1, has NBC protection and the improved TOW 2A missile system.

An armored cavalry scout version of the FVS, the M-3 is used for screening, reconnaissance, and security missions. It is externally similar to the M-2 and has the same armament and automotive performance. Also, both the M-3 and the M-2 provide day and night thermal-sight capability for the commander and gunner and image-intensification night-vision capability for the driver.

The major differences between the two vehicles are the arrangements of the crew compartment and the internal stowage, with the M-3 designed to accommodate a five-man cavalry squad and their weapons. The M-3 carries twice as many stowed rounds for the 25mm main gun (1,200) as the M-2, has different seating arrangements, and does not have firing ports.

M-113 Armored Personnel Carrier

The M-113 was designed to transport troops, equipment, and cargo during combat. The current M-113A2 is being replaced by the M-2/M-3 FVS; however, the M-113 will continue to be upgraded for use as a mortar carrier, command post, medical-evacuation carrier, and maintenance support vehicle beyond the year 2000. The M-113A2 weighs 12.5 tons and carries 11 men at a road speed of 42 mph and a cross-country speed of 19 mph. It has an 11-horsepower engine and features a .50 caliber machine gun.

Armed Helicopters

AH-64A Apache

The Apache is the Army's primary attack helicopter (figure 24.11). It is a fast-reacting, airborne antitank weapon. In wartime, the Apache is dispatched to locate, engage, and destroy enemy armor forces and a wide variety of other targets during day, night, and bad weather. Crew-station armor plating and a blast-fragment shield can prevent the two-man crew from being incapacitated from high-explosive incendiary rounds.

The Target Acquisition Designation Sight (TADS) and Pilot Night Vision Sensor (PNVS) are the keys to the Apache's day, night, and adverse-weather capability. They allow the two-man crew to employ the Hellfire laser-guided missile system, 70mm (2.75-inch) aerial rocket, and the 30mm cannon with unprecedented accuracy and range.

The Apache's mission weight is 14,445 pounds. Maximum level-flight speed is 184 mph (158 knots), with a service ceiling of 20,000 feet. The self-deployment range is more than 1,000 nautical miles. Mission endurance is 2.5 hours when carrying eight Hellfire antitank missiles, 38 Hydra 2.75-inch rockets, and 1,200 rounds of 30mm cannon ammunition at a speed of 146 knots.

The Apache has proven to be a critically important element of the Army's combined arms team. It complements other weapon systems on the battlefield, with its high survivability, mobility, and lethal firepower. Deployed in 1985, the Apache is supported in the field by the Cobra.

AH-1S Cobra

The Cobra is an attack helicopter with the primary missions of anti-armor, armed escort, and reconnaissance (figure 24.12). Armed with various weapon systems, the AH-1S provides a highly mobile aerial platform that can fire on targets immediately, taking advantage of the element of surprise. Planned air-

Fig. 24.11. AH-64A Apache

craft and weapons subsystems improvements will enhance the Cobra's capabilities.

Performance includes maximum sea-level speed of 171 knots, normal cruise speed of 123 knots, maximum range of 362 nautical miles, and maximum endurance of 2.6 hours. The Cobra weighs 10,000 pounds, carries a crew of two, and features eight TOW missiles and 76 2.75-inch rockets.

The Army's Cobra Fleet Life Extension (C-FLEX) program provides improvements that will keep the Cobra in service for the foreseeable future. Reduced requirements in the active Army, however, will release the AH-1 aircraft to fill National Guard shortages.

OH-58D Kiowa

The Kiowa Warrior is the Army's current armed scout helicopter. It conducts armed reconnaissance, light attack, and multipurpose light helicopter missions such as troop and cargo lift and medical evacuations (figure 24.13). The Kiowa has a rapid-development kit that permits it to be operational and in flight within 15 minutes of off-loading from a C-130 aircraft. It cruises at a maximum speed of 118 mph, and can carry various combinations of Stinger air-to-air missiles, .50-caliber machineguns, 2.75 Hydra rockets, and Hellfire missiles. Mounted on the top of the rotor mast is a sighting system that incorporates

Fig. 24.12. AH-1S Cobra

Fig. 24.13. OH-58D Kiowa (*courtesy of Bell Helicopter/Textron*)

thermal imaging, a low light television, and a laser range finder. The navigation system permits precision location of targets for other weapons systems to engage while maintaining a safe stand-off range. There is also an unarmed version of the helicopter. The Kiowa is replacing the older OH58A/C and AH-1 Cobra in light forces.

Indirect Fire-Support Weapons Systems

Indirect fire–support weapons provide firepower against targets out of the line of sight of the gunners, and usually at a greater distance from the enemy than direct-fire weapons. They rely on target information from intelligence or forward observers who can provide information to adjust the impact of the projectiles. Infantry and armor units have a limited capability to provide their own indirect fire support through the use of their mortars. However, the majority of indirect-fire support is provided by artillery units armed with cannons and rockets. Presented here are some of the Army's indirect-fire weapons to give an idea of the variety available to support the soldier. Note that the following list is not all-inclusive nor is there space to discuss the many types of ammunition used by indirect fire weapons.

Multiple-Launch Rocket System (MLRS) The MLRS is a free-flight artillery rocket system that greatly improves the conventional indirect-fire capability of the Army (figure 24.14). The MLRS uses a 12-round launcher mounted on a modified M-2 Bradley Fighting Vehicle. It is capable of firing its rockets, which are 13 feet long and 9 inches in diameter, either one at a time or in rapid ripples to ranges beyond 40 kilometers. One launcher salvo's explosive power is approximately equivalent to that of a battalion of 155mm tube artillery.

The primary missions of MLRS are counterfire and suppressing enemy air defenses. The MLRS employs "shoot-and-scoot" tactics to limit vulnerability to counterbattery fire. In addition to carrying a large number of the M-77 miniwarheads, the MLRS can deliver an antitank (AT2) scatterable mine warhead, each of which dispenses 28 AT mines. The MLRS has the potential for delivering other warheads, including "smart" munitions.

The MLRS launcher is being updated to fire the Army Tactical Missile System (TACMS) against tactical missile sites and other priority targets.

Army Tactical Missile System (TACMS) The TACMS is a long-range missile weapon that operates day or night in nearly

Fig. 24.14. A multiple-launch rocket system (MLRS) in firing position

all weather. It can be transported by air and can effectively engage high-priority targets farther away than cannons and rockets can reach. The system is used to attack tactical surface-to-surface missile sites; air-defense systems; logistics elements: command, control, and communications (C^3) complexes; and second-echelon maneuver units arrayed in depth throughout the corps' area of influence (a geographic area where the commander can influence the operation by maneuvering his forces or applying fire support systems under his command or control).

The Army TACMS is a ground-launched, conventional, surface-to-surface, semiguided ballistic missile with an Anti-Personnel/Anti-Material (APAM) warhead. It is fired from the modified M-270 MLRS launcher. The TACMS utilizes the same targeting systems, engagement systems, and command and control systems as the MLRS.

Artillery Howitzers

The Army's artillery cannons, or howitzers, fall into two general categories: those that are towed by another vehicle, and those that are mounted on their own vehicle and are self-propelled. The active Army uses two calibers or sizes of howitzer, the 155mm and the 105mm. The 155mm guns are of both the self-propelled (SP) and towed type, while the 105mm is now only of the towed type. Some Reserve Component units may also have the self-propelled M110A2 eight-inch howitzer; however, this system has been phased out of the active force.

155mm Howitzers

The latest model of the 155mm SP howitzer is the M-109A6 Paladin. It carries a crew of six and weighs 32 tons. Its primary armament is the M-284 155mm cannon, while the secondary armament is a flexible .50 caliber machine gun mounted in a turret hatch. Maximum ranges for the projectiles, based on different charges, vary from 14,600 meters to 23,500 meters. The maximum rate of fire is four rounds per minute for three minutes. The sustained rates of fire vary with the types of charges fired.

The M-198 155mm towed howitzer is a helicopter-transportable, medium towed howitzer (figure 24.15). A successor to the M-114A1, the M-198 provides significant improvements in lethality, range, reliability, availability, emplacement, and movement. At 15,750 pounds, it is light enough to be lifted by the CH-47 helicopter. It can also be towed across country by the M-939-series five-ton truck. The cannon will fire a rocket-assist projectile to a range of 30 kilometers. Less than five minutes are needed to set up the howitzer for firing or to move. The maximum rate of fire is four rounds per minute for the first three minutes and two rounds per minute for sustained rate of fire.

105mm Howitzers

The M119A1 105mm howitzer is a lightweight towed cannon that provides improved direct-support artillery capabilities to the Army's light forces. The crew is seven men. The cannon fires all conventional 105mm ammunition, plus the new rocket-assisted rounds and the Dual Purpose Improved munitions being developed. The range of the gun, depending on the type of round fired, varies from 14 to 19 kilometers. It weighs only 4,000 pounds and is easily transportable by the Blackhawk helicopter. On the ground it is normally towed by the HMMWV.

Air-Defense Weapons

Air-defense weapons are ground-firing systems used to detect and engage enemy aircraft. They protect all ground-force ele-

Fig. 24.15. Checking the fire control of an M-198 155mm howitzer

ments, including troop formations, depots, lines of communication, air bases, and key command and control facilities.

Chaparral

The Chaparral forward-area, air-defense missile system is a mobile, heat-seeking missile system that is effective against high-performance aircraft at low altitude and against helicopters, either moving or stationary (figure 24.16). The Chaparral launcher is mounted on a tracked vehicle and carries four ready missiles on launch rails and eight additional missiles in storage compartments. The supersonic missile is 9.5-feet long and carries a high-explosive fragmentation warhead.

The Chaparral will remain in the Army inventory for some time because of an extensive improvement program. A forward-looking, infrared (FLIR) night sight—a target-acquisition device—has been added to the system. The FLIR gives the gunner day, night, and some adverse-weather acquisition capability at significant ranges, thus extending the useful performance envelope.

Patriot

The Patriot is the Army's new medium- and high-altitude ground-to-air missile system (figure 24.17). It provides the pri-

Fig. 24.16. Chaparral forward-area air-defense missile system

mary air defense of the field Army and defends vital military bases. The mobile, all-weather Patriot features a high kill probability, fast reaction time, and multiple target engagement capability. The system is designed to operate in an intense countermeasures environment.

The Patriot uses command guidance through midcourse, with terminal guidance provided by a concept called "track-via-missile." It works like this: As the missile nears its target, it informs the ground-based radar of its location in relation to the target. Ground-based computers then direct the missile on a path to ensure a kill. The supersonic missile employs a conventional warhead.

Hawk

The Hawk is a medium-range, surface-to-air guided missile designed to defend against low- to medium-altitude aircraft. It is a mobile, all-weather system that utilizes pulse and continuous-wave radars and proportional navigation guidance combined with semiactive terminal homing (figure 24.18). The missile's two-stage, solid-propellant motor endows it with

Fig. 24.17. **Patriot ground-to-air missile system**

supersonic speed, and the high-explosive, proximity-fused warhead needs only to pass near the target to destroy it.

Improvements have been made to all major elements of the Hawk system to increase performance and reliability. These include solid-state electronics, a larger warhead, improved motor propellant, and an information coordination center to provide automatic data processing and to prioritize targets.

M-163A2 and M-167A2 Vulcan

The M-163A2 self-propelled (SP) Vulcan air-defense system (VADS) is a lightweight, lightly armored 20mm gun system on a full-tracked vehicle, designed to provide air-defense coverage against the low-altitude air threat in the forward combat area (figure 24.19). The Vulcan may also be used in the ground role against stationary or moving targets such as personnel, trucks, and lightly armored vehicles.

Fig. 24.18. Hawk missile launcher prepared for firing

The Vulcan is highly mobile, capable of high-speed operation on improved roads, cross-country travel over rough terrain, and amphibious operation on streams and small lakes. The system can be transported by cargo aircraft. It is also capable of delivering selected rates of fire of 1,000 or 3,000 rounds per minute. The M-163A2 SP carries 1,000 ready rounds in a linkless feed system.

The M-167A2 VADS, a towed version, can be moved at high speed over improved roads, as well as rough terrain, and can ford streams. The M-167A2 has essentially the same missions as the SP Vulcan: its cannon characteristics, fire-control system, and modes of operation are the same. Aside from the trailer mounting, the primary difference in the two systems is that the towed Vulcan uses a linked feed system holding 500 rounds of ready-to-fire ammunition.

Stinger

The shoulder-fired Stinger provides effective, short-range air defense for Army ground personnel against low-level, fixed-wing aircraft and helicopters (figure 24.20). The 35-pound supersonic fire-and-forget Stinger features quick-reaction acquisition and tracking and the ability to engage aircraft ap-

Fig. 24.19. M-163A2 Vulcan system mounted on an M-113 APC

Fig. 24.20. Stinger ground-to-air missile launcher

proaching from any direction, including head-on. The missile's speed, range, maneuverability, flight tracking, and countermeasures rejection have made the individual combat air defender using the Stinger the equal of most sophisticated aircraft.

Three variants are in the Army inventory: basic Stinger, Stinger POST (passive optical seeker technique), and Stinger-RMP (reprogrammable microprocessor). All operate in a similar fashion, are fielded as certified rounds in a disposable, sealed launch tube, and require no field testing or maintenance.

Avenger

The Avenger is an air defense system that integrates all the functions necessary to perform day/night and adverse weather target detection, acquisition, tracking, and engagement. It uses eight ready-to-fire launchers containing Stinger missiles and a .50 caliber machine gun, all of which are mounted on a modified HMMWV. The system is designed to counter low-flying, high-speed, fixed-wing aircraft and helicopters. It is manned by a crew of two and can engage aircraft either from a stationary position or while moving.

25. Support Systems

The soldiers of America's Army are fully supported in the performance of their missions by a modern and highly efficient support system that provides every thing necessary for life in the garrison or success on the battlefield. This system includes vehicles and equipment that can operate in all environments—land, sea, and air. It can quickly transport soldiers, give them their location anywhere in the world to within a few feet, provide ammunition to the front lines under fire, detect enemy movement and locations miles behind enemy lines, provide food and pure water, detect toxic agents, provide secure communications around the world, and, if required, evacuate and treat wounded soldiers with the best medical care possible.

It comes as a surprise to many soldiers to discover that the Army has its own navy, small but vital, operated by the Transportation Corps. The purpose of these ships and amphibious craft is to provide responsive over-the-beach support to Army units. The Army's soldier-sailors work together with the U.S. Navy and Marine Corps to insure that U.S. forces have the best support in the world.

To describe in detail all of the types and capabilities of the Army's support equipment would take many books. This chapter presents only a small selection of the types of support equipment that a new soldier may see or hear about. It is intended only as a sample to show the extent of the support behind the soldier on the battlefield wherever it may be, and to illustrate the variety of the many non-combat Army career fields and assignments available to soldiers today.

Transportation

Family of Medium Tactical Vehicles (FMTV) Wherever possible the Army attempts to use the same basic vehicle chassis to perform several types of missions. Modifications are made to the vehicle as necessary, but many of the basic parts are the

Fig. 25.1. FMTV truck

same, saving money and simplifying the repair procedures. When this is done the similar vehicles are called a "family." The Army's new tactical transportation vehicles are just such a family. The family consists of a light medium (2½-ton) capacity truck (LMTV) and a heavy medium (5-ton) capacity vehicle (HMTV) that use the same chassis. The LMTV comes in van and cargo models, while the HMTV has cargo, tractor, wrecker, and dump truck models. These vehicles are able to operate worldwide on roads, trails, and overland. See figure 25.1.

M939 Series 5-Ton Trucks A 240 HP diesel-powered, 6x6 wheel-drive tactical vehicle, this series of trucks provides general cargo support and unit mobility. The basic M939 has a cargo-carrying capacity of 5 tons and can also tow a load of 21,000 pounds. The wheels are equipped with a unique central tire-inflation system that permits the driver to change the tire inflation to best meet the conditions of the terrain. This greatly enhances the ability of the truck to travel cross-country. The M939 truck series has six models: cargo truck, dump truck, tractor, wrecker, van, and long–wheel base cargo carrier.

Heavy Expanded Mobility Tactical Truck (HEMTT) The HEMTT family of vehicles are the Army's current heavy cargo and utility vehicles. The cargo version can carry 10 tons at a

Fig. 25.2. HEMTT truck

speed of 55 mph. The vehicles use a 8x8 wheel drive and can ford water up to a depth of 48 inches. The 445 HP diesel engine has a fully automatic transmission and is capable of climbing a 60-degree slope. The family has five different models—a light cargo vehicle with crane, a 2,500-gallon fuel tanker, a tractor, a wrecker, and a heavy cargo carrier with handling crane. Used in Operation Desert Storm, the HEMTT vehicles proved they can operate in all types of weather and over all types of terrain. See figure 25.2.

Palletized Loading System (PLS) The Palletized Loading system (PLS) is based on a 16½-ton capacity truck that uses a 10x10 wheel-drive system to provide mobility, and a 16½-ton cargo trailer, providing a total of 35 tons capacity. PLS has an integral cargo-handling system for self-loading and unloading, and the trailer can use several methods of cargo carrying. The PLS vehicles supporting field artillery units also have a cargo-handling crane.

Light Amphibious Resupply Craft (LARC-LX) The LARC is one element of the Army's equipment for providing over-the-shore logistics support. The vehicle is a wheeled amphibian, 62 feet long and 27 feet wide. It has four 165 HP diesel engines. The mission of the LARC is to transport from ship to the beach wheeled and tracked vehicles and general cargo. As an amphibian, the LARC is capable of carrying cargo across the beach to inland unloading points, and to help establish logistics sites in areas where ports do not exist.

Logistics Support Vessel (LSV) The LSV is a seagoing ship specifically designed to carry military equipment and supplies in support of troop deployments to underdeveloped areas along coastlines and inland waterways. It is 272 feet long and 60 feet wide with a crew of 30 soldiers. Fully loaded with 2,000 tons of cargo, the LSV can travel at a speed of about 10 mph, and has a range of 5,500 nautical miles. The Army has five LSVs on station.

Engineer and Vehicle Recovery Equipment

M-9 Armored Combat Earthmover (ACE) To provide a capability for a highly mobile armored earthmover for piercing enemy earthworks and providing support in defense operations, the Army developed the M-9 ACE. It is a fully tracked, armored vehicle that has a variety of engineer capabilities including preparation of positions, combat roads, obstacles and ditches, and removal of roadblocks. The M-9 is 20 feet 5 inches long and 8 feet 9 inches high, weighing 18 tons. It is air transportable, can swim at 3 mph, and travel at 30 mph on the road. The engine and compartment for the one-person crew are in the rear of the vehicle, and a dozer blade with scrapper bowl and apron is in the front. The ACE was used to open breaches in the Iraqi defensive works during Operation Desert Storm. See figure 25.3.

M-88A1 Recovery Vehicle Recovery of damaged vehicles and heavy equipment on the battlefield is the job of the M-88A1. It is a fully tracked armored vehicle designed for hoisting, winching, and towing operations on the battlefield, and evacuation of tanks and other tracked combat vehicles such as the M-2/M-3 Bradley, M-60-series tanks, and self-propelled artillery. It is a large vehicle, 27 feet long, over 11 feet wide, and 10 feet high with a weight of 56 tons. The engine is a 12-cylinder, 750 HP diesel with a three-speed transmission and a top speed of 30 mph. An improved M-88 is being developed to handle the M-1A1/2 Abrams tank.

Aviation

UH-60 Blackhawk Helicopter The Blackhawk has replaced the old familiar "Huey" as the Army's primary transport and

Fig. 25.3. M-9 Armored Combat Earthmover (ACE)

Fig. 25.4. UH-60 Blackhawk

general utility helicopter. It has a crew of two pilots and a crew chief and can carry an entire 11-man fully equipped infantry squad. Cruising at 138 mph, the Blackhawk has a range of almost 300 miles, and can carry up to 9,000 pounds externally by sling. It is armed with two 7.62mm door guns. This helicopter is faster than the Huey, can fly in most weather conditions, and has armored or duplicative critical systems that enable it to sustain multiple bullet hits. As an example of its lift capability, the Blackhawk can lift the 105mm howitzer, its 6-man gun crew, and 30 rounds of ammunition at one time. See figure 25.4.

OV-1D Mohawk The Mohawk is a dual-engine, fixed-wing aircraft that is equipped with a side-looking radar surveillance system for locating and reporting enemy locations. It has a crew of two, a speed of about 200 mph, and is unarmed. It is assigned to military intelligence units and can be used for day, night, and near all-weather surveillance of enemy forces. It was used with great success against the Iraqi Army. This system is being phased out over the next several years and will be replaced.

NBC and Smoke Support

M-93 Fox NBC Reconnaissance Vehicle The M-93 Fox is a six-wheeled armored vehicle that provides a fully integrated nuclear, biological, and chemical (NBC) detection, warning, and communication system. It is used to detect, identify, and mark areas of NBC contamination, collect soil samples, and relay the information to commanders. Powered by a 320 HP diesel V8 engine, the Fox has a top speed of 65 mph and a range of 500 miles. The crew of 4—only 3 in the improved model—are protected from NBC contamination by a closed pressurized crew compartment with heating and cooling systems. The improved version has a stand-off detection system, jam-proof communications, and a global positioning system.

M-40 Series Protective Masks The new M-40 series protective masks are designed to protect the soldier's eyes, face, and respiratory system against chemical and biological agents in the field. A design using an improved seal and silicon rubber construction gives greater protection than older masks, while redesigned eyepieces provide improved use of weapons sights and vision devices. The M-40 mask is for the individual soldier and the M-42 is for the combat-vehicle crewman. The M-42 has a microphone and hose-mounted canister that can be connected to a combat vehicles systems. The M-43 is an aircrew protective mask specifically designed for the Apache crew. The eyelenses are made to fit the Apache crew member's helmet-mounted sight. In addition, a blower system provides filtered air to the aviator's face and head, affording additional comfort and protection.

Smoke and Obscurant Generators Smoke and obscurants greatly improve the soldier's ability to survive on the modern battlefield. Smoke grenades fired from combat vehicles produce an instantaneous screen that hampers enemy sensors and weapons guidance systems. Smoke delivered by artillery, mortars, and rockets also decreases the enemy's ability to see. In addition, large area smoke generators are mounted on various vehicles and used to screen friendly troop movements and obscure potential targets such as bridges, depots, and airfields from enemy observation.

Communications

Mobile Subscriber Equipment (MSE) To meet the requirements for a modern tactical communications system capable of handling the quantity and wide variety of types of data needed by America's Army, a family of mobile subscriber equipment (MSE) was developed. MSE provides a secure, automatic, highly mobile, quickly deployable, survivable communications system that answers the Army's needs. It is capable of passing data, fax, and voice messages throughout a division- or corps-size area of operations. Users of the system can enter using either wire or electronic means and their calls are automatically routed to the desired receiver, whether stationary or mobile. Area coverage is achieved through automatic switching and relocating switching terminals to provide continual coverage. Commanders and staff are able to retain the same telephone number no matter what their location.

Military Satellite Communications (MILSATCOM) The Army has the responsibility for all Department of Defense (DOD) satellite communications ground equipment, including the Navy fleet/Air Force system; DOD satellite communications system; and the future military strategic/tactical relay (MILSTAR) system. To support contingency and special operations forces, the Army is obtaining new terminals and related equipment. To improve tactical communications the Army is modifying its satellite terminals to provide communications security and anti-jam features, developing manpack and multi-data terminals.

Medical Support

Deployable Medical Systems (DEPMEDS) DEPMEDS is medical equipment preset into standard packages that is used to equip deployable hospitals. The Army uses seven types of deployable hospitals, ranging from the front-line Mobile Army Surgical Hospital (MASH) to general hospitals in the rear areas. Each hospital has different combinations of the standard module components. The DEPMEDS hospital sets provide the latest medical technology and equipment, medical supplies, and non-medical support equipment, tactical shelters, and climatic control equipment available. Using standard modules improves medical unit mobility. The hospital sets can be deployed under all climatic conditions.

26. Future Developments

"We must remain the best army in the world even as we transform ourselves into the preeminent army of the future."
Gen. Gordon R. Sullivan, 1994

Force XXI

America's Army for the twenty-first century—Force XXI—is being built today. Despite a time of declining budgets and force levels, the researchers and developers of the Army continue to look ahead, continue to search the latest technology for applications to the Army's missions, and continue to refine the weapons and equipment already on hand to insure the soldiers of tomorrow's Army remain the best-trained and -equipped fighting force in the world. The very latest in computer technology, digitalization, simulations, laser and fiber optics, artificial intelligence, medicine, metallurgy, and biotechnology are being used to produce weapons, clothing, food, vehicles, and other equipment and matériel that will be used by American soldiers into the next century. Many of the developments are still in the experimental stage and some may never get into production for many reasons. However, there are a number of new developments planned and now under testing. This chapter presents a selection of these, to give you a feel for the Army of the future—the Army of which you may be a part.

The Soldier Integrated Protective Ensemble (SIPE) The soldier of the future must be prepared to fight, win, and survive in a deadly environment. SIPE is an effort to develop a modular, head-to-toe, individual fighting system for the dismounted infantry soldier. Its purpose is to improve combat effectiveness of the individual soldier while at the same time providing improved protection against the various hazards of the modern battlefield. SIPE integrates technologies and components for clothing, equipment, weapons, communications, night vision, and an individual computer and climate control into one system. One of the primary elements of SIPE is a protective headgear that integrates a visual display, communications, wide-angle night vision, thermal imaging, laser-eye, breathing, and hearing protection. Also included is a protective uniform, body armor, hand and footwear, and web harness to carry equipment. This will provide protection against fragments, flechettes, flame, chemicals, and other hazards. The soldier's individual computer will provide ground position from satellites, communications, map information, and monitoring of the soldier's medical condition. See figure 26.1.

XM8 Armored Gun System (AGS) The Army intends to replace the old M-551A1 Sheridan armored reconnaissance vehicle with a new, more powerful weapon, the XM8 AGS. This is a direct-fire 105mm gun mounted on a tracked armored vehicle. It is lightweight and capable of being dropped from an aircraft in a low-velocity airdrop. Fully combat loaded, it has a range of 288 miles and a top speed of 45 mph. Three levels of armor protection are used so the crew can be protected from enemy fire from small arms to handheld antitank weapons, depending on the situation. It has a crew of three, and uses an automatic loader for the 105mm gun that gives a rate of fire of 12 rounds per minute. Also included are a digital weapons control system, laser range finder, and thermal sights.

Navigational System Timing and Range (NAVSTAR) Global Positioning System (GPS) NAVSTAR GPS is a long name for a system that uses signals from satellites to tell a precise location on the earth or in the air. It can be used for navigation or for finding a stationary location. The Army is developing a lightweight version called PLGR that will be self-contained and handheld. It will be used for determining target locations, and navigation information, and can be used while moving.

RAH-66 Comanche Armed Reconnaissance Helicopter The Comanche is the first helicopter designed from concept for armed reconnaissance. It is intended for air cavalry and attack units, greatly improving the Army's capability for day and night operations in all types of terrain and weather. It has a cruising speed of over 160 mph and a range of more than 1,260 miles. The Comanche has a crew of two and is armed with air-to-ground and air-to-air missiles and a turret-mounted 20mm cannon. It is equipped with a night-vision piloting system, helmet-mounted display, electro-optical target acquisition, and a data modem for exchange of digital information with other weapons systems.

Fig. 26.1. Soldier Integrated Protective Ensemble (SIPE)

Line-of-Sight Antitank (LOSAT) Weapons System The LOSAT is planned for employment in antitank companies of the mechanized infantry battalions. It is intended to place fixing fire on enemy armor, giving friendly forces the chance to rapidly maneuver into the enemy's flanks and rear. The LOSAT will use a kinetic-energy missile-launching system mounted on a Bradley chassis. With a crew of three, the vehicle will be able to keep up with the most modern tanks and infantry fighting vehicles. The kinetic-energy round will give the system a capability to defeat all predicted future armor vehicles.

Longbow Weapons System Longbow is an air-ground radar integrated with the Hellfire missile system capable of use day or night in all weather and battlefield visibility conditions. It will be employed by the Apache and Comanche helicopters.

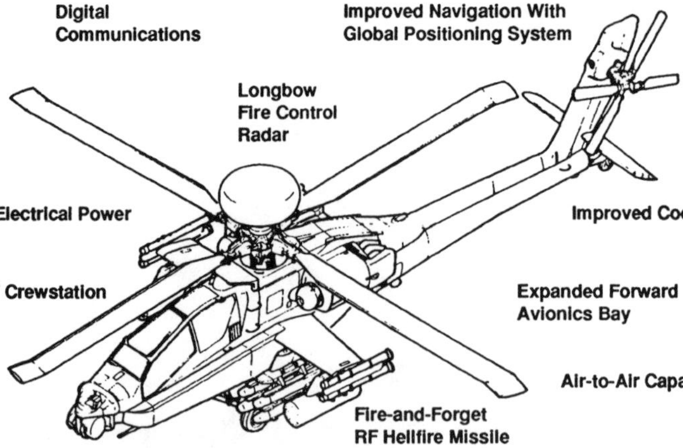

Fig. 26.2. Longbow weapons system

The system includes the radar, which will be mounted on the mast of the helicopters, a radio emitter frequency detector, and the missile system. A central processor will take the target information from the radar and emitter detector, identify the nature of the target, assign a priority when handling multiple targets, and pass the information to the missile. The pilot can then decide to engage the targets much quicker and with less exposure to enemy fire. The system is capable of engaging up to sixteen targets in less than one minute. Digital links to other weapons systems will also permit Longbow to pass the target information to them for engagement. See figure 26.2.

Javelin Antitank Weapons System The Javelin is a man-portable shoulder-fired antitank weapon that provides high lethality against conventional and reactive armor. It is composed of a reusable sighting and launch unit and a missile. Javelin uses an integrated day/night sight and can effectively engage enemy armor in conditions of limited visibility. The sighting system can also be used alone for battlefield surveillance. The system weighs less than 50 pounds and has a maximum range of 2,000 meters. It uses a "fire-and-forget" technology that permits the gunner to fire and immediately take cover without having to keep the target in the sighting device. Special features of the missile include a top-attack capability to hit hidden targets, infrared imaging, target lock-on capability, and no recoil. It can be fired safely from covered fighting positions and enclosures.

V. Sample Soldier Skills

27. Leadership

Equipment and weapons alone do not make a winning army. Every soldier in that army must be the most highly skilled, confident, and motivated soldier on the battlefield. All must be fully trained and competent in their job, and bring their individual competency together with that of fellow soldiers to make a smoothly functioning team. However, the basic building block of that team is still the individual skill of each soldier under the leadership of equally skilled NCOs and officers. This section introduces you to a sample of some very basic skills you must master to be a winning soldier.

Leadership

Effective leadership is the Army's key to success in training and combat. Leadership is the process of influencing others to accomplish the mission by providing

- purpose
- direction
- motivation

Purpose gives soldiers a reason why they should do difficult things under stressful and sometimes dangerous circumstances.

Direction gives soldiers an orientation of tasks to be accomplished based on the priorities set by the leader.

Motivation gives soldiers the will to do everything they are capable of doing to accomplish a mission. It also causes them to use their initiative when they see the need for action.

Leaders

The Army has, as its foundation, competent and confident leaders who are developed through a process consisting of three equally important pillars:

- institutional training (schools), which provides formal education and training;
- operational assignments, both in the Army and in other agencies, to use and build upon what was learned through institutional training; and
- self-development (Army correspondence courses, civilian and self-study programs) to expand your knowledge base.

Leaders in the Army are faced with many challenges. For example, they must develop their soldiers into cohesive teams, take care of their needs, train them under tough, realistic conditions to demanding standards, assess their performance, assist them with their personal and professional growth, and reward them for successes.

Effective Army leaders are flexible in the way they interact with subordinates, using appropriate methods as a subordinate develops or as the situation or mission changes. The manner and approach that a leader takes in leading soldiers will depend on his or her training, education, and experience.

In peacetime, a leader must create the kinds of bonds that will enable soldiers to follow him or her in combat. A soldier's trust and confidence must be won before, rather than after, combat has commenced.

In the Army you will be exposed to a wealth of training material and on-the-job training that will help you develop your leadership skills. Not only will you learn how to lead, but also how to conduct leadership counseling, how to develop soldiers, and the principles of leadership.

Principles of Leadership

The Army has eleven principles of leadership. They are excellent guidelines that were developed many years ago but have stood the test of time both in peacetime and in war. How you measure up to these principles will help you to assess your ability to lead soldiers and your potential to advance to a leadership position in the Army. A brief explanation of each of the eleven principles follows. (A more detailed discussion may be found in FM 22-100.)

- Know Yourself and Seek Self-Improvement.
  To know yourself, you must understand who you are and know what your preferences, strengths, and weaknesses are. Seeking self-improvement means continually developing your strengths and working on overcoming your weaknesses.
- Be Technically and Tactically Proficient.
  You are expected to be proficient in your job and to accom-

plish tasks that are assigned to you. You develop technical and tactical proficiency through a combination of the knowledge you gain while attending formal schooling (institutional training), your day-to-day jobs (operational assignments), professional reading, and personal self-study (self-development).

- Seek Responsibility and Take Responsibility for Your Actions.
  Leading always involves responsibility. When you make mistakes, accept just criticism and take corrective action.
- Make Sound and Timely Decisions.
  You must be able to assess situations rapidly and make sound decisions. Indecisive leaders create hesitancy, loss of confidence, and confusion.
- Set the Example.
  Your soldiers want and need you to be a role model. You must set high, but attainable, standards and be willing to do what you require of your soldiers and to share dangers and hardships with them. Your personal example affects your soldiers more than any amount of instruction or form of discipline.
- Know Your Soldiers and Look out for Their Well-Being.
  You must know and care for your soldiers. It's important that you know what is important to them. If your soldiers trust you, they will never let you down.
- Keep Your Subordinates Informed.
  American soldiers perform best when they know why they are doing something. Keeping your subordinates informed helps them make decisions and execute plans in accordance with your intent, encourages initiative, improves teamwork, and enhances morale.
- Develop a Sense of Responsibility in Your Subordinates.
  Give your subordinates challenges and opportunities you feel they can handle. They will feel a sense of pride and responsibility when they successfully accomplish a task you have given them.
- Ensure the Task Is Understood, Supervised, and Accomplished.
  Your soldiers must understand what you expect from them. They need to know what you want done, what the standard is, and when you want it done. Supervising should let you know if your soldiers understand your orders. In addition, supervision shows your interest in your soldiers and in the mission they are to accomplish.
- Build the Team.
  You must develop a team spirit among your soldiers that motivates them to go willingly and confidently into combat in a

quick transition from peace to war. Your unit becomes a team only when your soldiers trust and respect you and each other as trained professionals and see the importance of their contribution to the unit.

- Employ Your Unit in Accordance with its Capabilities.
  Your unit has capabilities and limitations. As a leader, you are responsible for recognizing both. Your challenge as a leader in the Army is to attain, sustain, and enforce high standards of combat readiness in your unit and to develop and challenge each soldier through tough, realistic training.

28. Guard Duty

Guard Duty

Guard duty is one of the most important duties you will perform in the Army. In peacetime, guards prevent theft of government property, vandalism, and possible acts of terrorist violence. In a combat zone, guards can make the difference between life and death for their fellow soldiers.

You will also spend quite a few hours learning what guard duty is all about—including the composition, purpose, and duties of a guard and the meaning of general and special orders. Field Manual FM 22-6, *Guard Duty,* will help you become familiar with this area of soldiering.

There are two types of guards that you will become familiar with while in the Army—interior and exterior.

Interior Guards

The commander of a military installation establishes an interior guard to protect government property and to enforce specific Army regulations. An interior guard consists of a main guard and special guards.

The main guard is a combination of patrols and fixed guard posts. Special guards are used to protect aircraft, ammunition storage points, supply facilities, and other government property.

Two sets of orders govern a guard who is on duty: general and special. *General orders* outline the basic responsibilities of all guards. *Special orders* are established by the commanding officer and differ from post to post. Special orders might specify, for example, who has access to ammunition storage points and during what hours. They may be posted in the guardhouse or given to you by the soldier you relieve, either orally or in writing, when you report to your post.

General Orders

Three general orders apply to all interior guards. In BCT, you will be required to memorize, understand, and comply with these three orders. You might want to get a head start and memorize them now. General orders are the same no matter where you are stationed in the Army.

1. I will guard everything within the limits of my post and quit my post only when properly relieved.
2. I will obey my special orders and perform all my duties in a military manner.
3. I will report violations of my special orders, emergencies, and anything not covered in my instructions to the commander of the relief.

A brief explanation of these orders may help you better understand them.

General Order Number 1 gives you responsibility for everything that occurs within the limits of your post while you are on duty. You must investigate immediately any unusual or suspicious occurrence on or near your post, provided you do not have to leave your post to do so. You must apprehend all suspicious persons, using only necessary force to overcome resistance. If you should require relief for any purpose, you must contact the commander of the relief for instructions.

General Order Number 2 requires you to become thoroughly familiar with the special orders before you are actually posted. In addition to the special orders connected with your post, you are required to obey and carry out any orders or instructions from the commanding officer, field officer of the day, and officers and noncommissioned officers of the guard. No other persons are authorized to give orders to soldiers on guard duty. You should pass on instructions and special information to your relief when appropriate.

General Order Number 2 also requires you to perform your duties in a military manner, to be courteous to all, and to speak to no one except in the line of duty. You must maintain an erect and soldierly bearing, carrying your weapon as instructed by the commanding officer or commander of the guard. You must salute individuals according to Army regulations. The special orders will tell whether and when to challenge.

General Order Number 3 requires you to report all special order violations and emergencies. In case of a fire on or near your post, you should call, "Fire, post number ——." You should alert the occupants if the fire is in an occupied building and give the alarm or make sure one is given. If possible, extinguish the fire. Help direct firefighting apparatus to the fire. If a disturbance occurs that requires assistance, call, "The guard, post number ——." If the danger is great, fire your weapon into the air three times in rapid succession.

Exterior Guards

This type of guard duty is not as formal and restricted as interior guards. Examples of exterior guards are lookouts, listening posts, outposts, patrols and other guards in field training exercises and in combat zones, and guards posted outside the limits of a military installation.

Exterior guards perform their duties according to special orders and instruction.

29. Drill and Manual of Arms

Drill: Terms and Commands

You will learn drill in basic training and use many of the drill procedures throughout your time in the Army. Field Manual FM 22-5, *Drill and Ceremonies,* will be your primary reference. This chapter is an introduction to Army drill so that it will not be totally strange to you.

Why Drill?

The purpose of drill is to:

- Enable a commander to move a body of soldiers from one place to another in an orderly manner.
- Aid in teaching soldiers discipline by developing habits of precision and response to their leader's orders.
- Provide a means of conducting organized and well-executed ceremonies for the purpose of enhancing soldier morale, and of presenting traditional, interesting parades.
- Provide a means for all soldiers to develop leadership skills from the practice of commanding troops.

The Army defines a drill as a series of movements by which a unit or individuals are moved in an orderly, uniform manner from one formation to another or from one place to another. Units vary in size, but in basic training, you will ordinarily be part of a squad, section, platoon, or company. Figure 29.1 illustrates some drill formations.

Drill Terms

The following are some of the drill terms you will need to know:

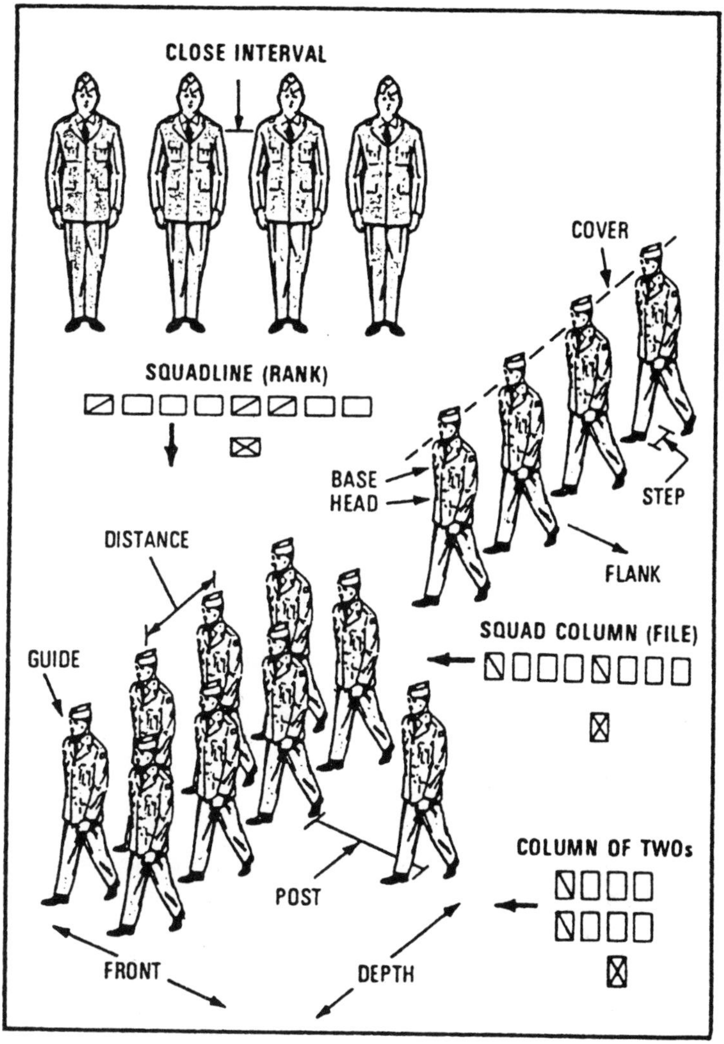

Fig. 29.1. Drill formations

ELEMENT. An individual, squad, section, platoon, company, or larger unit forming a part of the next higher unit.

FORMATION. The arrangement of the unit elements in a prescribed manner, such as a *line* formation in which the elements are side by side and a *column* formation in which the elements are one behind the other. In a platoon column, the members

of each squad are one behind the other with squads abreast of each other.
CADENCE. A uniform rhythm or number of steps or counts per minute.
QUICK TIME. A walk of 120 counts or steps per minute.
DOUBLE TIME. A run of 180 counts or steps per minute.

Drill Commands

Drill commands are oral orders by your commander or leader, usually given in two parts: a preparatory command followed by a command of execution. The *preparatory command* states the movement to be carried out and gets you ready to execute the order. In the command "Forward, march," the preparatory command is "Forward." The *command of execution* tells when the movement is to be carried out. In "Forward, march," the command of execution is "March."

In some commands, the preparatory command and the command of execution are combined, for example, "Fall in," "At ease," and "Rest." These commands are given without inflection and at a uniformly high pitch and loudness comparable to that for a normal command of execution.

To call back or revoke a command or to begin again a movement that was not intended, the command is "As you were." The movement is supposed to stop, and the former position is taken.

Basic Movements and Commands

You will spend many hours in BCT learning drill procedures, facing and marching commands, and movements. Your drill sergeant will instruct you in the specifics of correct body positions, and performance of the drill commands with and without weapons. The following examples are intended only to introduce you to the language and concept of drill and to acquaint you with a few of the commands and movements so that you will have a better appreciation of what they mean and how they are done.

Formations

There are many sizes and types of formations used by the Army. The most basic and common formation is made up of one or more squads of soldiers in lines one behind the other. Normally each squad forms its own line, with its members side by side. The squad lines are positioned one behind the other. Each line of soldiers across the front, in this case a squad, is referred to as a "rank" of the formation. Each line of the soldiers standing one behind another from front to rear is called a "file." The sides of a formation are "flanks," and the directions "left" and "right" are the left and right of the soldiers in the formation. The senior person in the squad is normally the first soldier on the right flank of the squad. In this type formation this soldier acts as the base or "guide" person for the rest of the squad, and for the right flank soldiers of the ranks behind. The other squad members form side by side to the left of the base soldier. If there is more than one squad, they align themselves in the same manner directly behind the soldier in front of them.

Fall In

The command "Fall in" directs soldiers to assemble themselves into an orderly formation facing the commander. Normally soldiers will form side by side in their assigned positions in a squad rank. Soldiers automatically assume the position of attention in the formation and remain silent awaiting further instructions.

Position of Attention

You assume the position of attention on the command "Fall in" or "Squad (Platoon), attention." All movements except rest movements start from this position. When assuming the position of attention, your weight is distributed equally on the heels and balls of your feet with your toes of your opposing feet forming a 45-degree angle. Hold your body and head erect, keep your legs straight without locking your knees, and look straight to the front. Let your arms hang straight but not stiff. Curl your fingers so that the tips of your thumbs are alongside and touching the first joint of your forefingers. Figure 29.2 illustrates the position of attention.

Parade Rest

Parade rest is commanded only from the position of attention. On the command of execution "Rest," move your left foot 10 inches to the left of your right foot. At the same time you move your foot, place your hands at the small of your back, centered on your belt. Keep the fingers of both hands extended and joined, interlocking your thumbs as shown in figure 29.3, so that the palm of your right hand is outward.

Alignment

The Army term for aligning the soldiers in each rank of a formation into a straight line is called "dressing the ranks." Dressing is normally done to the soldier's right, using the first soldier on the right as an alignment guide. On the command

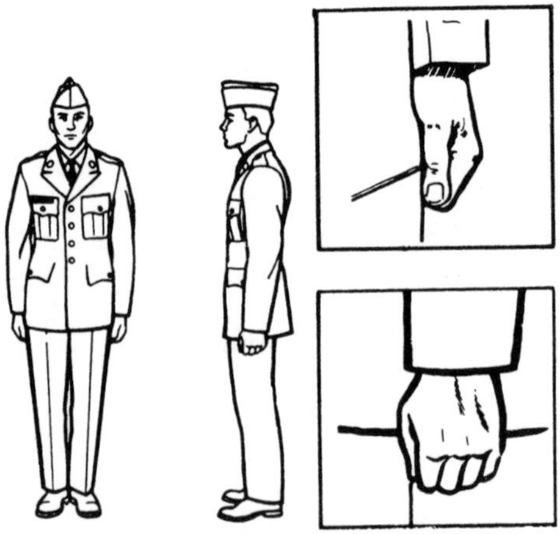

Fig. 29.2. Position of attention

"Dress right, dress!" the first soldier on the right end or "flank" of each rank takes position directly behind the base or guide soldier in the front rank. The rest of the soldiers in each rank look to their right and position themselves in straight alignment with the soldier on their right. The right flank soldier continues to look straight ahead.

Interval

The distance between each soldier in the rank and between ranks is called the "interval." The interval within the rank is achieved at the same time as dressing the rank. Unless otherwise commanded, the normal interval is one arm length. As the soldiers look to their right and dress themselves in response to the command "Dress right, dress!" all except the soldier on the far-left flank of each rank simultaneously raise their left arm to shoulder height in straight line with their body. The soldiers then move to the right until their right shoulder brushes the tips of the extended fingers of the soldier on their right. Soldiers remain looking to the right with their arms extended until ordered "Ready, front!" Soldiers then resume the position of attention. Intervals shorter or greater than an arm's distance can also be ordered by the commands "At close interval" or "At double interval." These directions are given as part of the command to dress. The normal interval between ranks is also about an arm's length. On command this also can be modified.

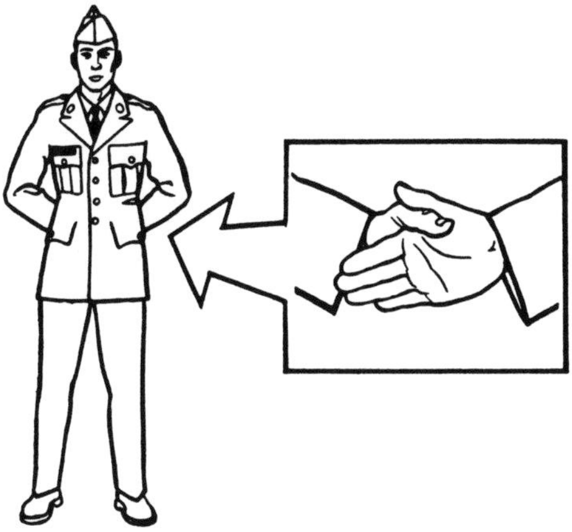

Fig. 29.3. Parade rest

Cover

Because soldiers will have different arm lengths, the alignment from front to rear of the soldiers in each file may not be exactly straight after dressing. This alignment of the soldiers in the files is called "cover." A final adjustment to the position of the soldiers in a formation may be made after the dressing is completed by the command "Cover!" This directs the soldiers in the ranks behind the front rank to align themselves exactly behind the soldier in front of them.

Hand Salute

The hand salute is a simple movement. The command is "Present, arms." When wearing headgear with a visor (with or without glasses), on the command of execution, "Arms," raise the right hand sharply—fingers and thumbs extended and joined, palm facing down—and place the tip of the right forefinger on the visor's rim slightly to the right of the right eye. The outer edge of the hand is slightly canted downward so that neither the back of the hand nor the palm is clearly visible from the front. The hand, wrist and forearm are straight, the elbow inclined slightly forward, and the upper arm horizontal with the shoulder as shown in figure 29.4.

When wearing headgear without a visor (or with no headgear) and not wearing glasses, execute the hand salute in the same manner as previously described, except touch the tip of the right forefinger to the forehead near the right eyebrow and slightly to the right of the right eye.

When the garrison cap, cold weather cap, or beret is worn, the hand salute is to the forehead—except when wearing glasses, when the tip of the fingers should touch the corner of the frame. When the utility cap, camouflage cap, or helmet is worn, the salute is to the visor.

Fig. 29.4. The hand salute

When wearing headgear without a visor (or with no headgear) and wearing glasses, execute the hand salute in the same manner as previously described, except touch the tip of the right forefinger to the glasses where the frame meets the brow.

To end the hand salute, the command is "Order, arms." On the command of execution, "Arms," return the hand sharply to the side, resuming the position of attention.

The hand salute may be executed while marching. When double-timing, a soldier must come to quick time (see below) before saluting. However, when a formation is marching at double time, only the individual in charge assumes quick time and salutes.

Steps and Marching

All steps in marching are variations of 30-inch steps or 15-inch steps. All steps except right step begin with the left foot.

30-Inch Step

The command to march with a 30-inch step from the halt is "Forward, march." When you hear the preparatory command "Forward," shift your weight to the right leg. On the command "March," step forward with your left foot and continue marching with 30-inch steps. Keep your head and eyes looking straight ahead. Swing your arms in a natural motion, without bending your elbows, approximately 9 inches straight forward and 6 inches to the rear of the seams of your trousers or skirt. Keep your fingers curled as in the position of attention.

15-Inch Step (Half Step)

The command for marching with a 15-inch step is "Half step, march." This command may be given from the halt, or it may be given to change a 30-inch step to a 15-inch step.

Halt

To halt while marching, the command "Squad (Platoon), halt" is given as either foot strikes the ground. The movement is executed in two counts. On hearing "halt," you take one more step and then bring your trailing foot alongside your leading foot, resuming the position of attention.

Manual of Arms

Once you have learned the basic drill movements discussed above, you will learn to execute drill movements (the manual

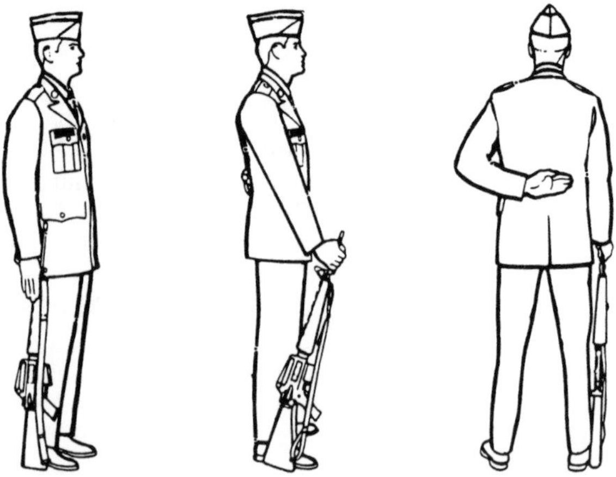

Fig. 29.5. Order arms and parade rest with rifle

of arms) with the M-16 rifle, both at halt and while marching. The manual of arms takes a little time to master, but your drill sergeant will make sure you get it down pat.

Order arms, for example, is the position of attention with the M-16 rifle. The butt of the rifle is on the ground, centered on the right foot, with sights to the rear. You hold the rifle with your right hand. Figure 29.5 illustrates the position of order arms with the M-16 rifle.

Fig. 29.6. Sling arms

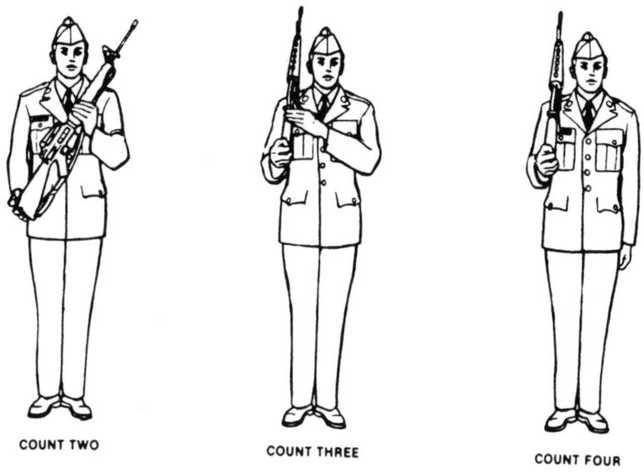

Fig. 29.7. Right shoulder arms

Rest positions with the rifle are done the same as without it, with the following additions:

- On the command "Parade, rest," grasp the barrel with the right hand and thrust the muzzle forward, keeping the right arm straight (figure 29.5).
- Execute "Stand at ease" in the same manner as parade rest with the rifle, except turn your head and eyes toward the commander.
- On the command "At ease" or "Rest," keep the butt of the rifle in place.

Many of the commands in the manual of arms also apply when the rifle is slung over a soldier's shoulder. The manner of performance is slightly different as shown in Figure 29.6. Movements with a rifle also include transferring the weapon from one shoulder (see Figure 29.7) and other elements of the manual of arms that a soldier learns.

You will use the drill procedures you learn in BCT throughout your Army service in daily formations and in military ceremonies, such as parades and reviews, to honor visiting military or civilian dignitaries.

30. Map Reading and Land Navigation

Among the most critical skills that a soldier must master are map reading and land navigation. Your instructors and unit leaders will assist you in learning them. These subjects may seem too complex at first, but with the classroom instruction and actual experience in the field, you will quickly learn them.

This chapter is intended only to introduce these subjects to you and acquaint you with some of the basic concepts in Field Manual FM 21-26, *Map Reading and Land Navigation.* It is not intended to replace the much more detailed instruction you will receive or field manuals that cover these subjects. Let us begin with a brief definition of a map, its purpose, and the types of maps used by soldiers.

Definition and Purpose

Soldiers use maps quite frequently in their work. A map is a graphic representation drawn to scale of a portion of the earth's surface as seen from above. Man-made and natural features are depicted by symbols, lines, colors, and forms. The ideal representation would be realized if every feature of the area being mapped could be shown in its true shape. Obviously, this is impossible. Therefore, to be understandable, features must be represented by signs and symbols.

A map provides information on the existence, location, and the distance between ground features, such as populated places and routes of travel and communication. It also indicates variations in terrain, heights of natural features, and the extent of vegetation cover. Because Army forces are dispersed throughout the world, a great deal of planning is done by using maps.

Security and Care

Even when the markings on a map have been erased, it is possible to determine some of the information that had been written on it. Maps that you use in the Army are documents that must not fall into unauthorized hands. If no longer needed, maps should be turned in to the proper authority.

All maps should be considered as documents requiring special handling. Maps are printed on paper, which requires protection from water, mud, and tearing. Whenever possible, a map should be carried in a waterproof case, in a pocket, or other place where it is handy for use but still protected. Because they have to last a long time, if you have to mark a map, use a pencil. Use light lines so that they can be erased easily without smearing or leaving marks that may later cause confusion.

Scale and Types of Maps

There are several kinds of military maps, each designed to provide specific information. To tell the different kinds of maps apart, soldiers look at two attributes of each map: the scale of the map and the type of map.

Scale

The scale is the relationship between a distance on the map and that distance actually on the ground. This is expressed as a ratio of map distance to ground distance. A small-scale map, for example 1:100,000 (the larger the last number the smaller the scale), has a much larger ground area compressed onto the map than a 1:50,000, and therefore has less detail. The standard scales used for military maps are normally 1:50,000 and 1:75,000. These scales are large enough to clearly show the information most useful to a soldier. The scale is included in the information on the bottom border of the map.

Type

The Army uses several different types of maps. The one used by most soldiers is called a *topographic* map. This type of map portrays the ground as it would be seen from directly above. The differences in terrain features caused by the rise or fall of the earth, such as hills and valleys, are shown by the use of a series of elevation or contour lines on the map. Other features such as streams, forests, towns, and roads, etc., are also

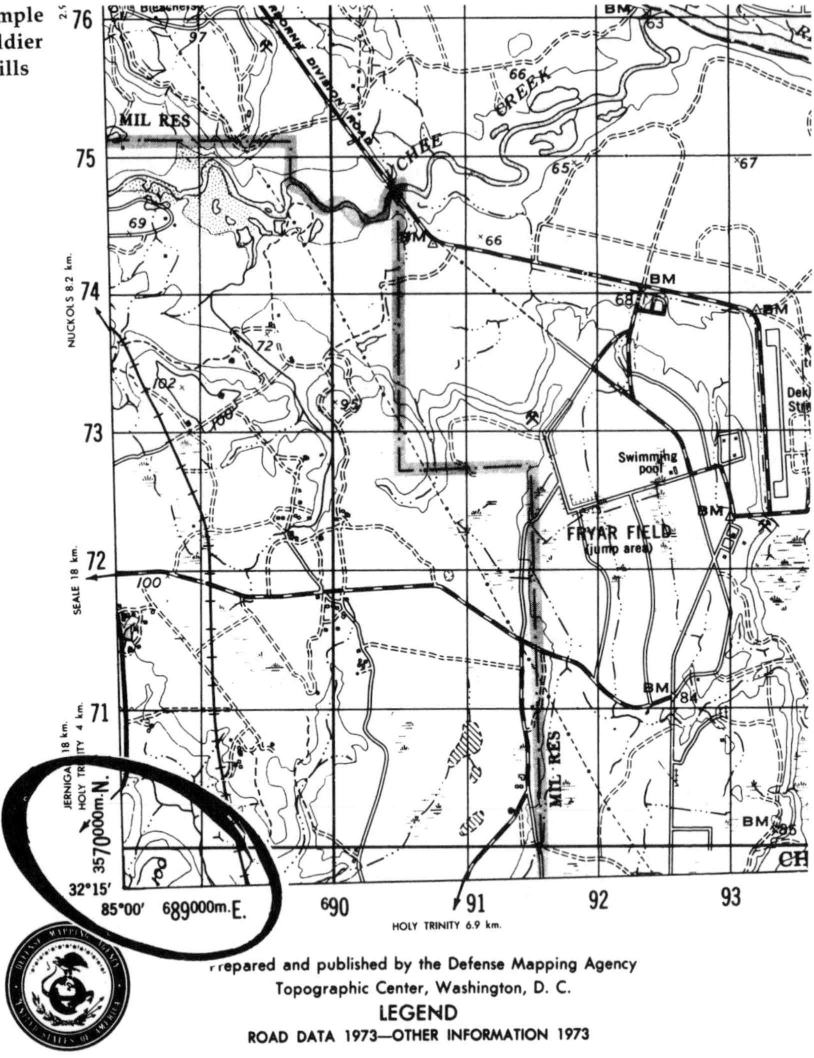

Fig. 30.1. Section of topographic map

shown by various colors and symbols. Figure 30.1 shows a typical topographic map.

Map Symbols and Colors

Soldiers normally are concerned with two types of symbols that can be used on a map. These are the *topographical* symbols that describe natural and man-made features, and *military* symbols that show military activity of some type, such as the location of a unit, fortifications, or weapons. Military symbols may be printed on the map, but are most often temporarily drawn on the map by the user. You will learn more detail on how to read and make symbols during BCT. Examples of topographic and military symbols are shown in figures 30.2 and 30.3.

To make it easier to identify features on a map, the topographical and cultural (man-made) information is usually printed in different colors. These colors may vary from map to map. On a standard large-scale topographical map, the colors used and the features they each represent are as follows:

Black	cultural features, such as buildings and roads
Reddish-Brown	cultural features, all relief features, and elevation, such as contour lines on red-light readable maps
Blue	hydrography, or water features such as lakes, swamps, rivers, and drainage
Green	vegetation with military significance, such as woods, orchards, and vineyards
Brown	all relief features and elevation, such as contours on older edition maps
Red	cultural features—such as populated areas, main roads, and boundaries—on older maps
Other	occasionally used to show special information and are generally indicated in the marginal information

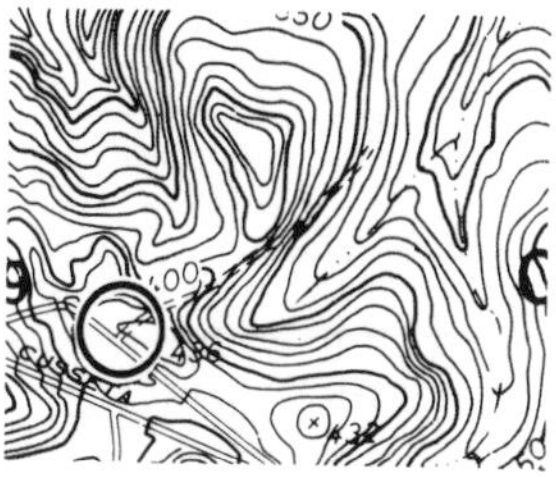

1. ROAD JUNCTION - WHERE ONE ROAD JOINS ANOTHER.

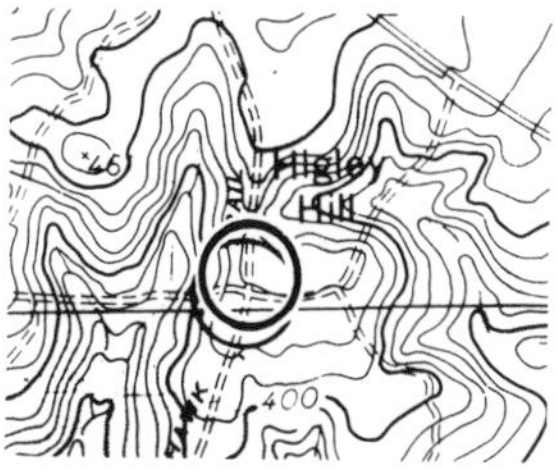

2. ROAD INTERSECTION - WHERE ONE ROAD CROSSES ANOTHER.

Fig. 30.2. Topographic map symbols

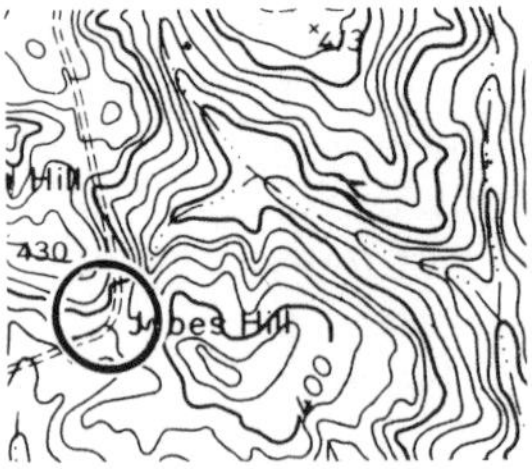

3. CURVE - A BEND IN THE ROAD.

4. DEAD END - WHERE THE ROAD STOPS WITH NO OUTLETS.

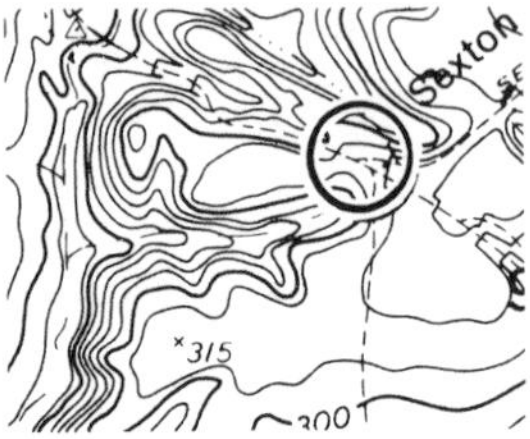

5. TRAIL JUNCTION - WHERE TWO TRAILS JOIN.

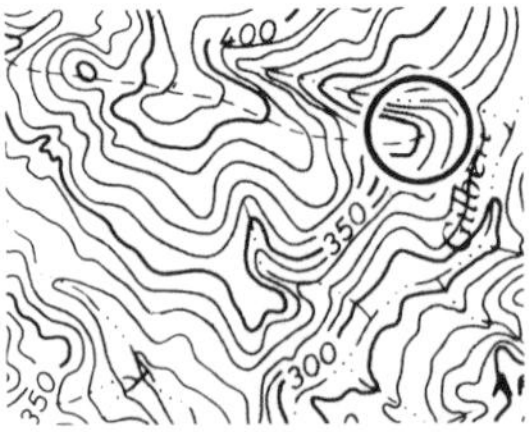

6. TRAIL DEAD END - WHERE THE TRAIL STOPS.

7. TRAIL CURVE

Fig. 30.2. *(continued)*

8. ROAD AND TRAIL JUNCTION - WHERE A ROAD INTERSECTS WITH TWO TRAILS.

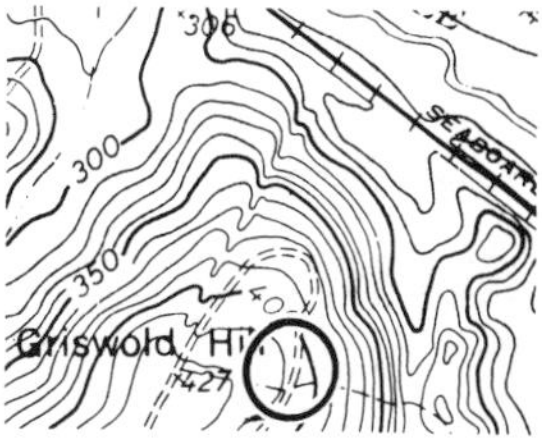

9. ROAD AND TRAIL INTERSECTION - WHERE A ROAD CROSSES A TRAIL.

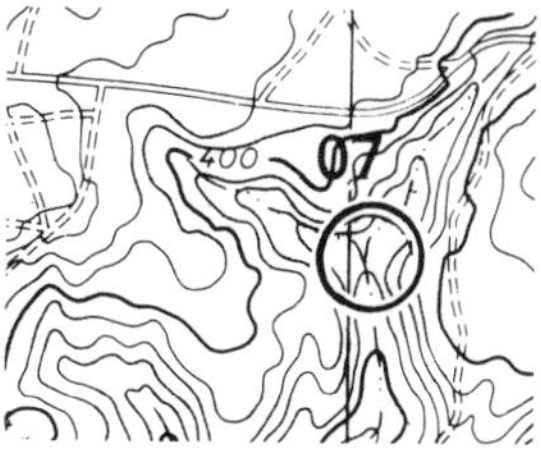

10. INTERMITTENT STREAM JUNCTION

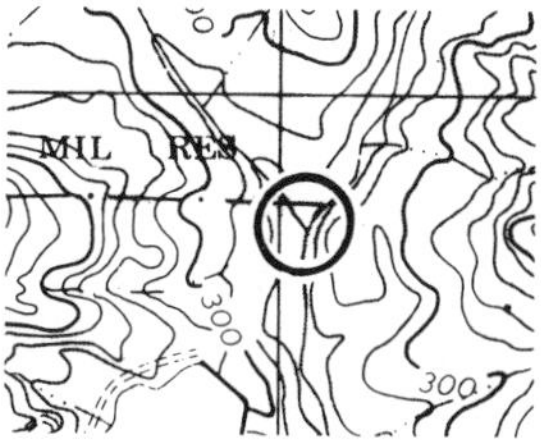

11. STREAM JUNCTION

12. BEND IN STREAM

Fig. 30.2. (*continued*)

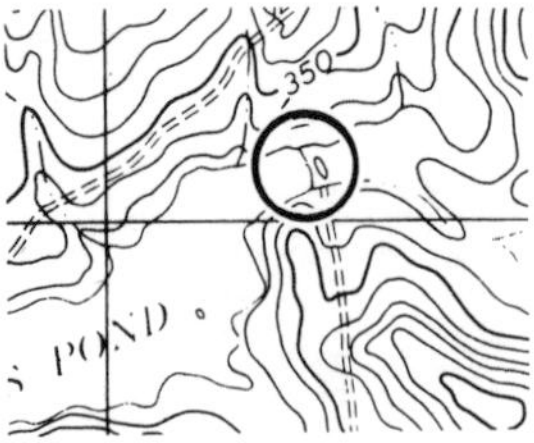

13. POND'S EASTERNMOST POINT

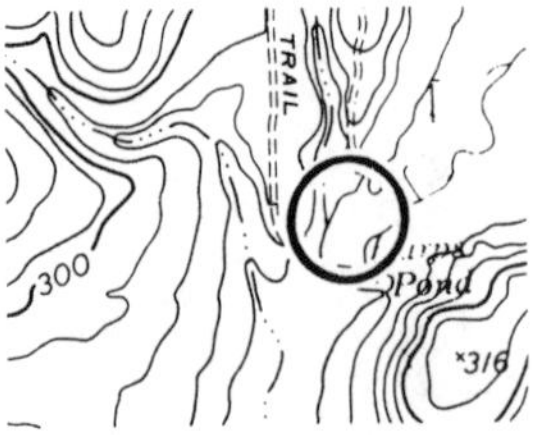

14. POND

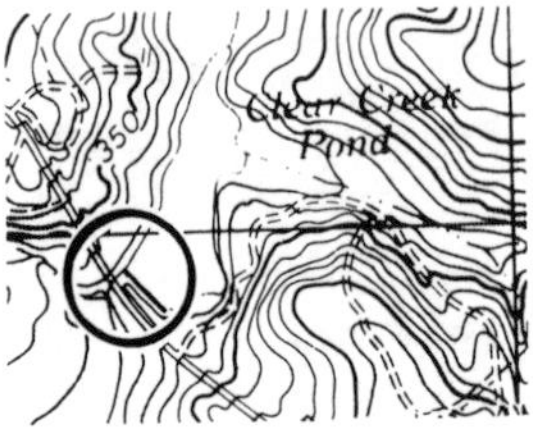

15. OUTLET - WHERE WATER FLOWS OUT OF POND.

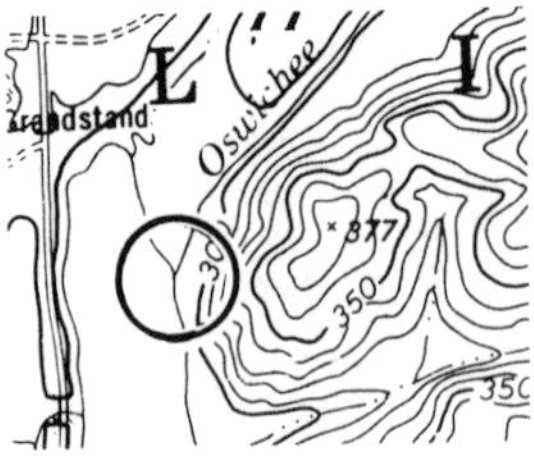

16. INLET - WHERE WATER RUNS INTO A POND.

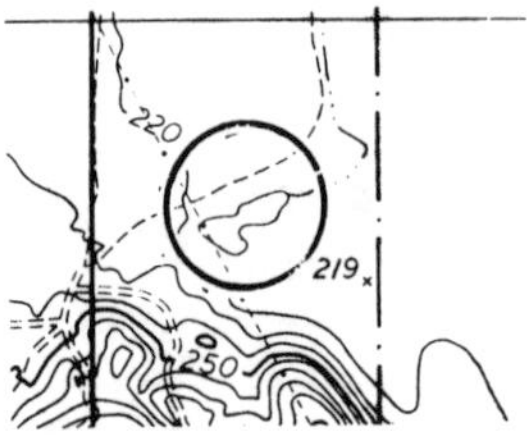

17. MARSHY OR SWAMPY POND

Fig. 30.2. *(continued)*

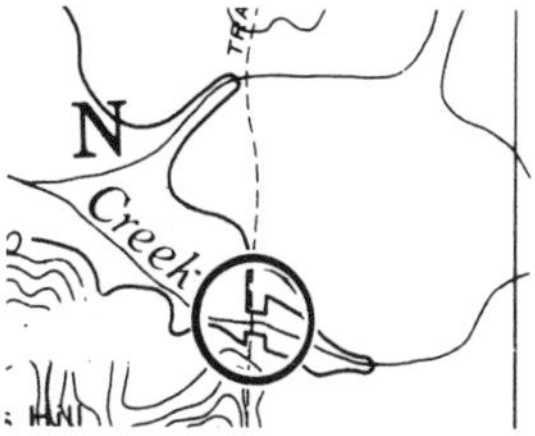

18. TRAIL AND STREAM INTERSECTION – WHERE A TRAIL CROSSES A STREAM (IN MOST CASES, THERE IS NO BRIDGE)

19. ISLAND – LAND SURROUNDED BY WATER.

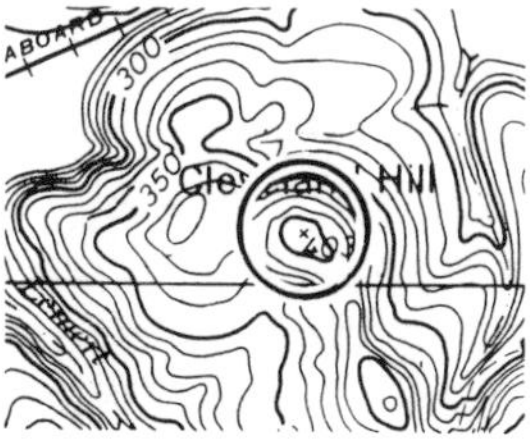

20. HILLTOP – THE HIGHEST ELEVATION OF A LANDMARK.

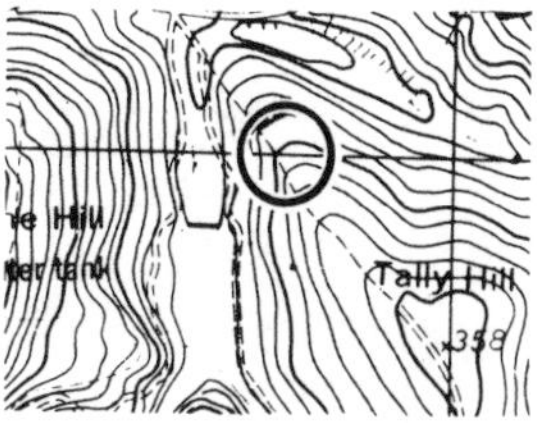

21. RIDGE – THE TRAIL FOLLOWS THE PATH OF A RIDGE.

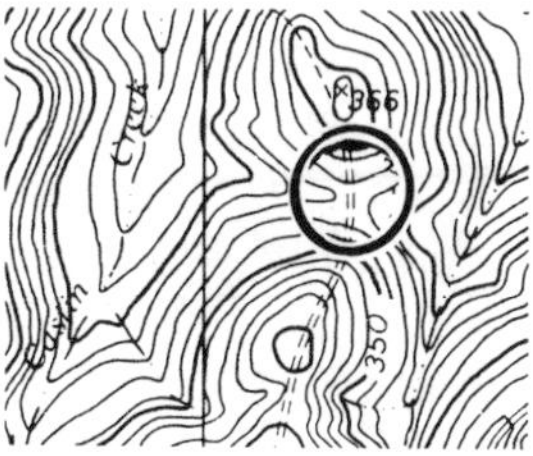

22. SADDLE – THE LOW POINT BETWEEN TWO OR MORE POINTS OF HIGHER GROUND.

Fig. 30.2. *(continued)*

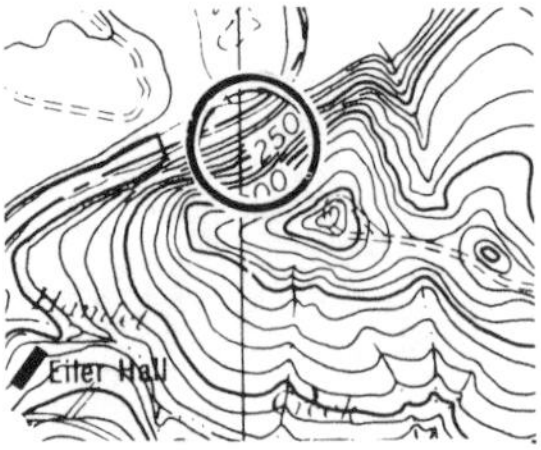

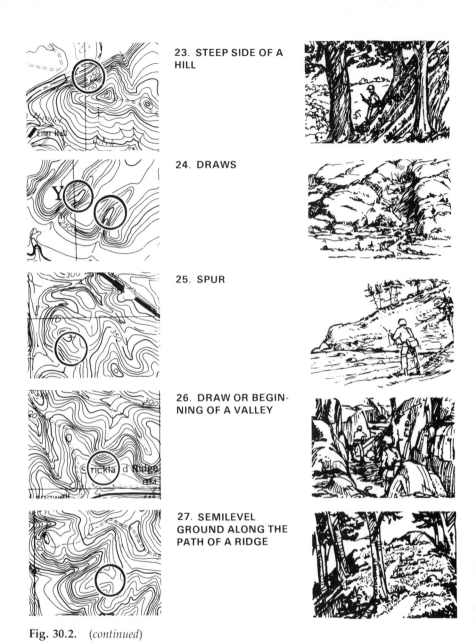

23. STEEP SIDE OF A HILL

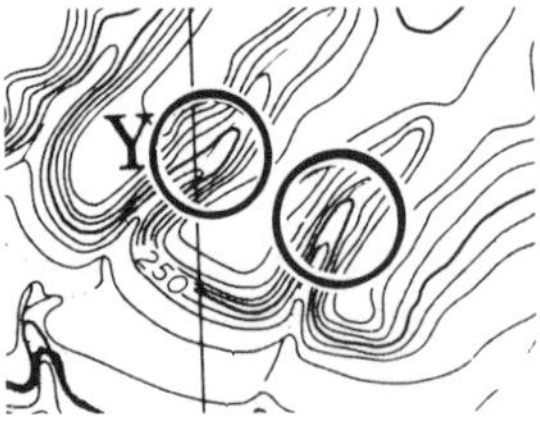

24. DRAWS

25. SPUR

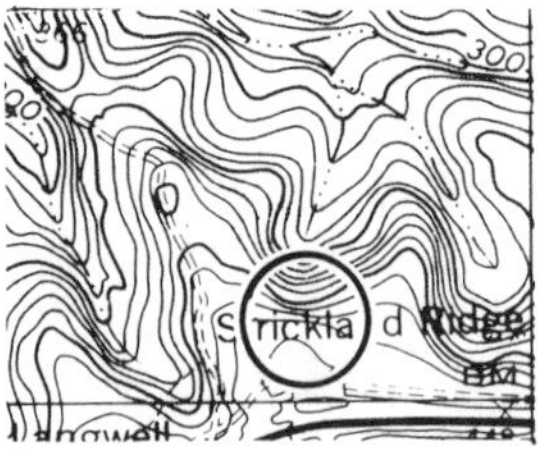

26. DRAW OR BEGINNING OF A VALLEY

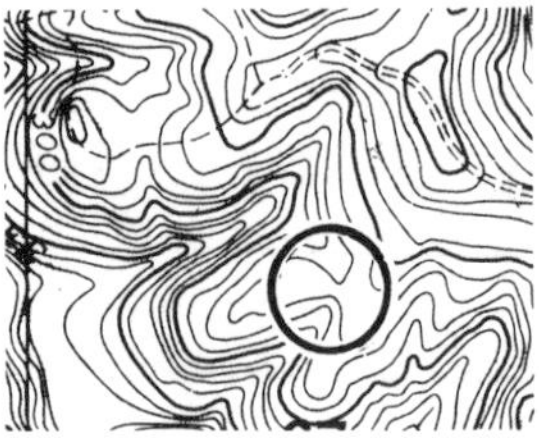

27. SEMILEVEL GROUND ALONG THE PATH OF A RIDGE

Fig. 30.2. *(continued)*

28. JUNCTION OF STREAMS – TWO INTERMITTENT STREAMS JOIN ANOTHER STREAM.

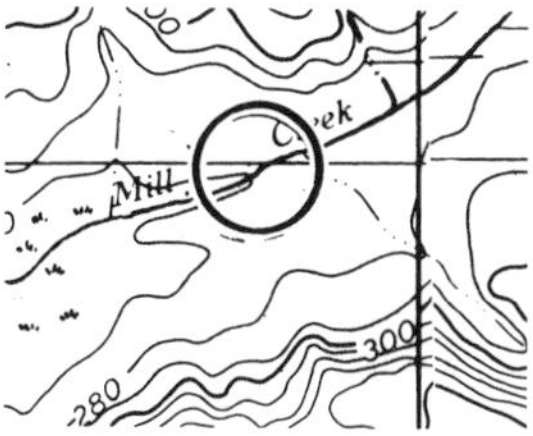

29. VALLEY – IN BOTH DIRECTIONS OF A CREEK.

30. CREEK JUNCTION

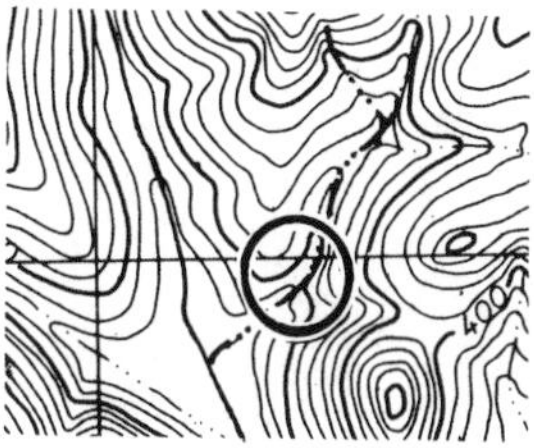

31. DRAW WITH INTERMITTENT STREAM

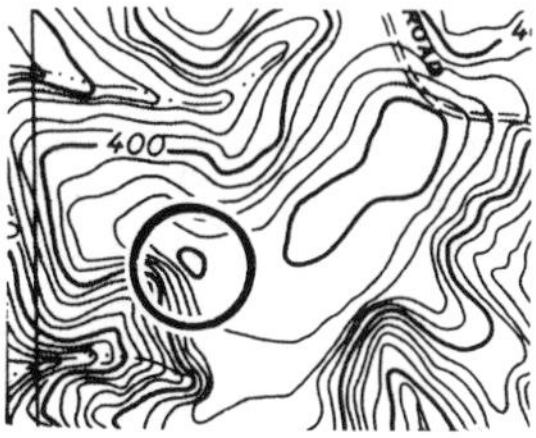

32. HILL TOP

Fig. 30.2. (*continued*)

33. VALLEY

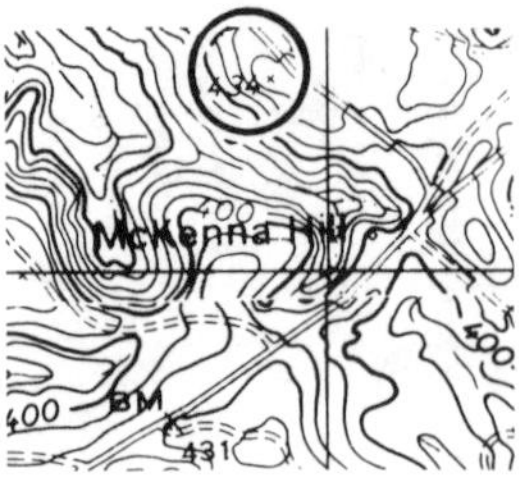

34. SPOT ELEVATION

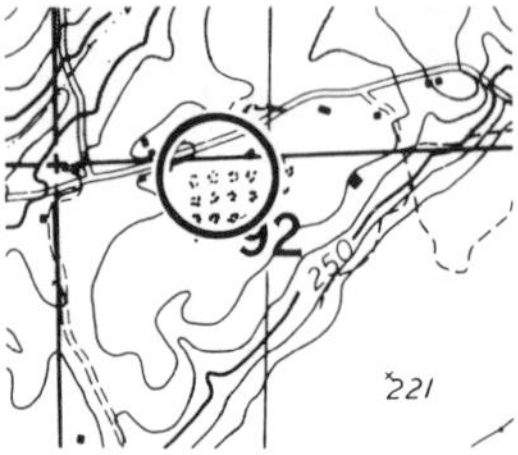

35. ORCHARD

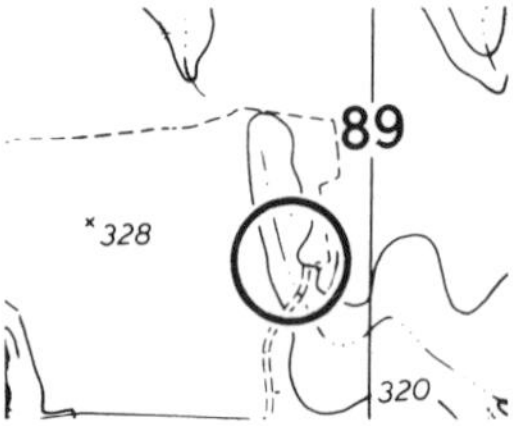

36. MARSH OR SWAMP

37. DEPRESSION

Fig. 30.2. *(continued)*

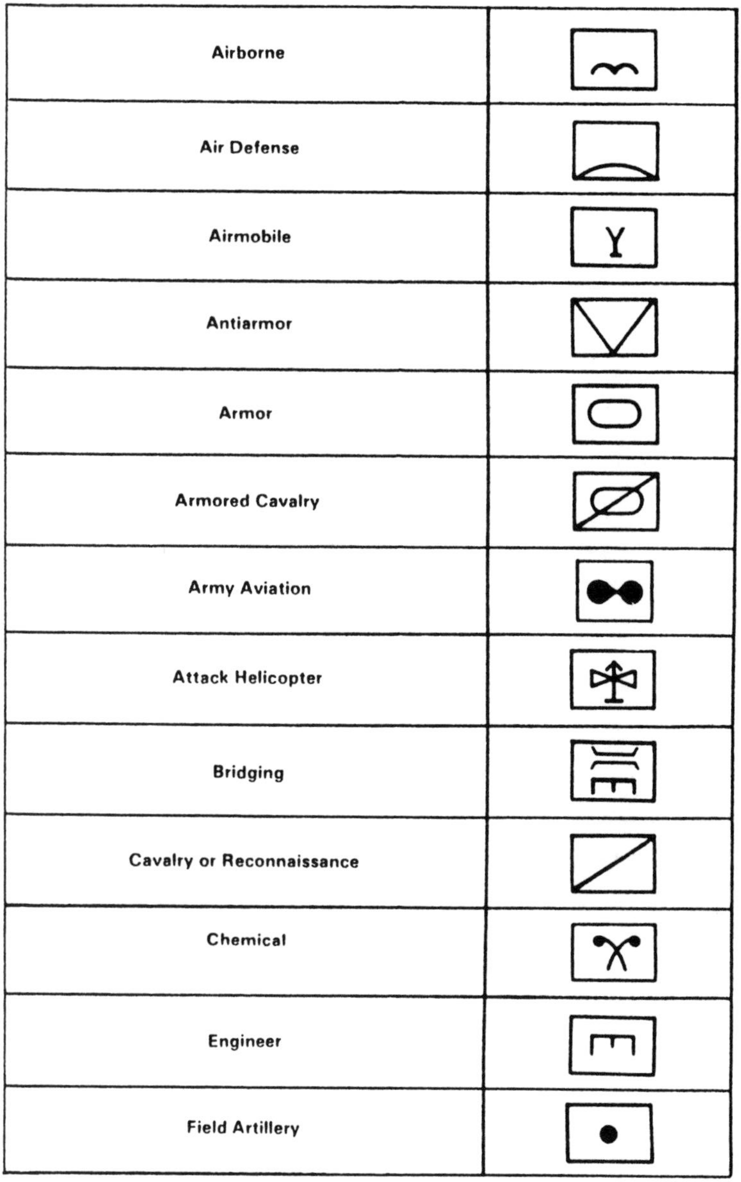
Airborne
Air Defense
Airmobile
Antiarmor
Armor
Armored Cavalry
Army Aviation
Attack Helicopter
Bridging
Cavalry or Reconnaissance
Chemical
Engineer
Field Artillery

Fig. 30.3. Basic unit identification symbols

Infantry	
Light	
Maintenance	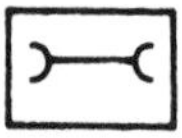
Mechanized	
Medical	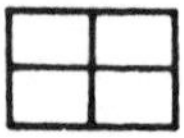
Military Police	
Mountain	
Petroleum Supply	
Quartermaster	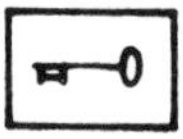
Signal/Communications	
Transportation	

Fig. 30.3. *(continued)*

Grids

Military maps are printed with an overlay of intersecting numbered horizontal and vertical lines called *grid lines.* Depending on the scale of the map, the distance between these lines is equivalent to either 1,000 or 10,000 meters. Grid lines are used as reference points to find locations. The direction North is always toward the top of a military map; this makes the vertical grid lines north-south lines and the horizontal lines east-west lines.

Locations on a map are given as grid coordinates using the grid numbers. To find a location on a map using grid lines, a soldier always follows the principle of reading the numbered grid lines *Right and Up.* That is to say, north-south grid line first and east-west grid line second. From the intersection of the two grid lines determined by the coordinates, the soldier looks at the grid square right and up. Using the further coordinates, again right and up, it is possible to find the desired location. The number of digits in the coordinate determines the degree of precision with which the location can be found on the map—the more digits, the more precise the measurement.

Scale and Distance

Every military map has a scale bar at the bottom that is used to determine distances on the map. You will learn how to read the different scales on the scale bar, and the different techniques for measuring straight-line and curved-line distances.

The distance on most maps is marked in meters. Thus, following is a brief refresher on the metric system:

1 meter contains 100 centimeters (cm).
100 meters is a regular football field plus 10 meters.
1,000 meters are 1 kilometer (km).
10,000 meters are 10 kilometers.

Graphic Bar Scales

A graphic scale is a ruler printed at the bottom of a map. It is used to convert distances on the map to actual ground distances. The graphic scale is divided into two parts. To the right of the zero, the scale is marked in full units of measure (kilometers, statute miles, and nautical miles) and is called the *primary scale.* To the left of the zero, the scale is divided into tenths and is called the *extension scale.* Most maps have three or more graphic scales, each using a different unit of measure. When using the graphic scale, be sure to use the correct scale for the unit of measure desired.

Land Navigation

Reading a map is one thing, putting that knowledge to work by actually moving in the most effective manner across terrain to a desired location is quite another. It is even more difficult if there is no map, only a compass to use. This skill of navigating over land is another critical skill needed by the soldier.

This section introduces you to the basic tool used in land navigation—the lensatic compass. In BCT you will learn the fundamentals of using the compass and your unit leaders will give you further instruction plus a lot of practice once you arrive in your unit.

The Lensatic Compass

There are many types of compasses, but the most common and simplest that soldiers use is the lensatic compass (seen in figure 30.4). It consists of three parts: the cover, the base, and the lens.

Cover The compass cover protects the floating dial. It covers the sighting wire (front sight) and two luminous slots or dots used for night navigation.

Base The body of the compass contains the following movable parts:

a. The *floating dial* is mounted on a pivot so it can rotate freely when the compass is held level. Printed on the dial in luminous figures are an arrow and the letters *E* and *W*. The arrow always points to magnetic north, and the letters fall at east *(E)* 90 and west *(W)* 270 on the dial. There are two

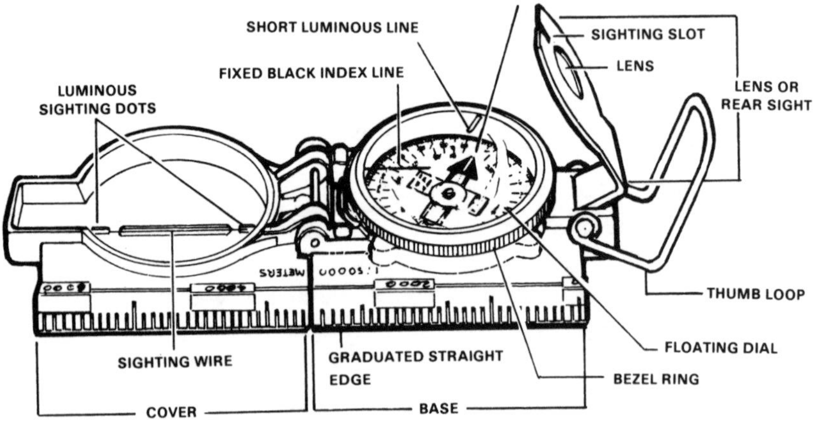

Fig. 30.4. **Lensatic compass**

scales: the outer scale denotes miles and the inner scale (normally in red) denotes degrees.

b. Encasing the floating dial is a glass containing a fixed, black *index line.*

c. The *bezel ring* is a ratchet device that clicks when turned. It contains 120 clicks when rotated fully; each click is equal to 3 degrees. A short luminous line that is used in conjunction with the north-seeking arrow during navigation is contained in the glass face of the bezel ring.

Lens The lens is used to read the dial; it contains the rear-sight slot used in conjunction with the front slot for sighting on objects. The rear sight also serves as a lock and clamps the dial when closed for its protection. The rear sight must be opened more than 45 degrees to allow the dial to float freely.

Handling the Compass

The lensatic compass, like all compasses, is a delicate instrument and should be cared for accordingly. You should inspect your compass when you get it. One of the most important parts to check is the floating dial that contains the magnetic needle. You should also make sure that the sighting wire is straight, that the glass and crystal parts are not broken, that the numbers on the dial are readable, and most important, that the compass does not stick. You should be aware that metal objects and electrical sources can affect the performance of a compass, but nonmagnetic metals and alloys do not affect compass readings. The following are suggested as approximate safe distances that you should maintain to ensure the proper functioning of a compass.

High-tension power lines	55 meters
Field gun, truck, or tank	10 meters
Telegraph or telephone wires and barbed wire	10 meters
Machine gun	2 meters
Helmet or rifle	½ meter

A compass in good working condition is very accurate. However, a compass has to be checked periodically on a known line of direction, such as a surveyed azimuth using a declination station. Compasses off by more than 3 degrees in either direction should not be used.

If traveling with a compass unfolded, make sure the rear sight is fully folded down onto the bezel ring. This will lock the floating dial and prevent vibration, as well as protect the crystal and rear sight from damage.

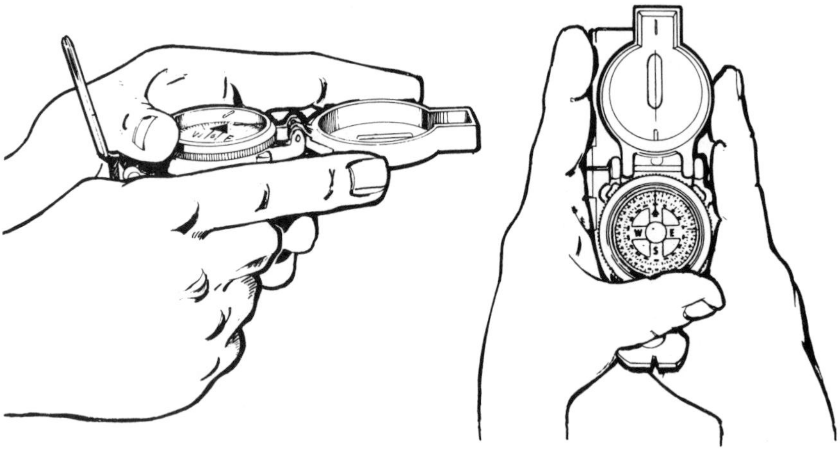

Fig. 30.5. Centerhold technique

Using the Compass

Magnetic azimuths are determined with the lensatic compass. There are several techniques that you will learn to employ the compass. As an introduction to the use of the compass one of the easiest techniques is discussed next.

Using the Centerhold Technique First, open the compass to its fullest so that the cover forms a straightedge with the base (see figure 30.5). Move the lens (rear sight) to the rearmost position, allowing the dial to float freely. Next, place your thumb through the thumb loop, form a steady base with your third and fourth fingers, and extend your index finger along the side of the compass.

Then place the thumb of the other hand between the lens (rear sight) and the bezel ring. Extend the index finger along the free side of the compass and your remaining fingers around the fingers of your other hand. Pull your elbows firmly into your sides. This will place the compass between your chin and your belt.

To measure an azimuth (degrees from North), simply turn your entire body toward the object, pointing the compass cover directly at the object. Once you are pointing at the object, look down and read the azimuth from beneath the fixed, black index line. This method offers the following advantages over sighting techniques:

- It is faster.
- It is easier.

Fig. 30.6. A soldier takes a compass reading.

- It can be used under all visibility conditions.
- It can be used when navigating over any type of terrain.
- It can be used without putting down the rifle; however, the rifle must be slung well back over one shoulder.
- It can be used without removing the helmet or eyeglasses.

31. Communications

Communications is one of the most vital functions necessary for the Army in order to operate on and off the battlefield. The Army has many communication means from the most modern to the most basic. Modern technology has brought many advances using the most sophisticated electronics and scientific techniques. For example, soldiers can set up a small suitcase-size transmitter almost anywhere in the world and dial up or send a fax to a compatible receiver anywhere else in the world, in code. Satellites, lasers, fiber optics, and digital transmission of information are only a few of the Army's communication wonders, and research continues to bring even better technology to the Army.

For most new soldiers, however, the first communications they experience in the Army is far less sophisticated, yet much more important for them than satellite phone systems. These are the tactical means of communication used at the lowest unit levels to pass instructions to the soldier, gather information, and request support. This chapter addresses those types of tactical communications.

Tactical Communication Means

Most soldiers spend their early years in squads, platoons, and companies. Each tactical communication means available to squads, platoons, and companies for training purposes or for combat has different capabilities and should complement one another. If at all possible, there should be a backup means of communicating. The common means available to squads and platoons to communicate are

- Visual communications
- Sound communications
- Messengers
- Wire communications
- Radio

Let's review these seven tactical communication means.

Visual Communication

Visual communications are the simplest and most common means of transmitting messages and instructions at the small unit level. They are used when electrical types of communications are not appropriate or inadequate. However, their use requires that the sender sees the receiver and both use prearranged signals. A soldier learns methods to signal in daylight as well as in darkness. These are taught in IET and by the soldier's unit leaders. Briefly described here are some of the most common methods: hand and arm signals, flags, flashlights or chemical lights, flares, and smoke grenades. There are many other methods and signals that can be used, including special ones for communicating with aircraft or helicopters.

Hand and Arm Signals Among the most basic visual signals are those used by the infantry to direct the combat formations and battle drill for squads and platoons. Here are a few examples.

Flag Signals Flags are issued to armored and mechanized units for visual control purposes and as an alternate means of communication within these units. Each combat vehicle is equipped with a flag set consisting of one red, one yellow, and one green flag. Most units use a single flag to signal the following meanings:

- Red—Danger, or enemy in sight
- Green—All clear, ready, or understood
- Yellow—Disregard previous signal, or vehicle out of action

Each unit establishes its own standard signals that the unit leaders teach the soldiers in the unit. Some of the more common flag signals are shown here.

Pyrotechnics Pyrotechnics are chemical burning devices that produce either smoke or light. When used for communications, prearranged or prescribed signals are developed and used throughout a unit. These signals are based on the color and characteristics of the pyrotechnic device used. Pyrotechnic signals supplement or replace normal means of communication and allow a large number of troops and/or isolated units to be signaled quickly. They can be used to identify friendly units, control maneuver elements, control fire support, mark targets, and report locations. When pyrotechnics are used, the signal and its meaning are included in the command and signal portion of the operation order and in the unit's communications-electronics operating instructions (CEOI).

Raise the arm vertically overhead, palm to the front, and wave in large, horizontal circles.

NOTE: Signal is normally followed by the signaler pointing to the assembly or rally site.

Fig. 31.1. Assembly or rally

Point toward person(s) or unit(s); beckon by holding the arm horizontally to the front, palm up, and motioning toward the body.

Fig. 31.2. Join me, follow me, or come forward

Hold the rifle in the ready position at shoulder level. Point the rifle in the direction of the enemy.

Fig. 31.3. Enemy in sight

Extend the arm at a 45-degree angle from the side, above the horizontal, palm down, and then lower the arm to the side.

Fig. 31.4. Take cover

Extend the arms parallel to the ground.

Fig. 31.5. Line formation

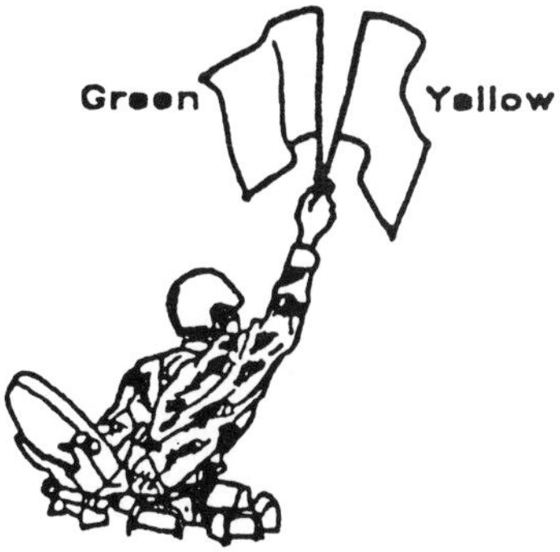

Fig. 31.6. Assemble or close

Fig. 31.7. Dismount and assault

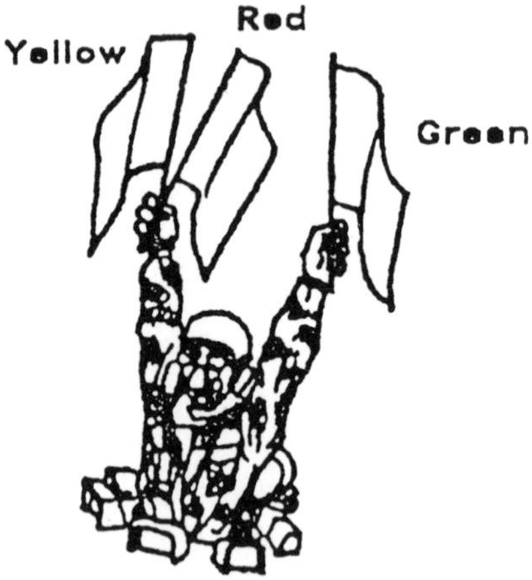

Fig. 31.8. Nuclear, biological, chemical hazard present

Two or three movements upward with the open hand, palm uppermost.

Fig. 31.9. Mount

Extend the arms, make two or three movements up and down, hands open toward ground.

Fig. 31.10. Dismount

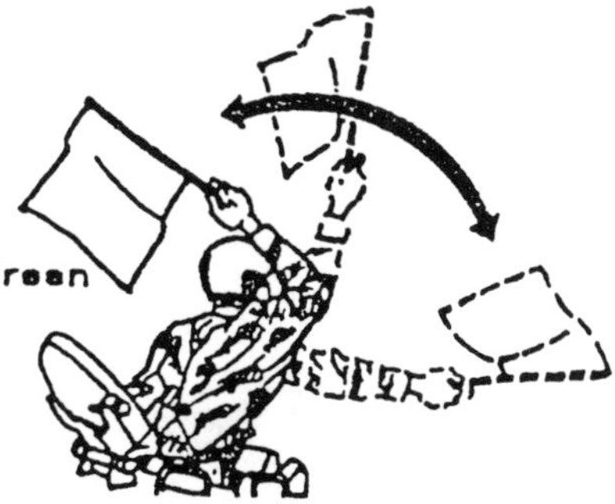

Fig. 31.11. Move out

There are two common types of military pyrotechnics used for signaling: handheld devices and smoke. Handheld pyrotechnics include star clusters, which produce five free-falling pyrotechnic stars, and star parachutes, which produce a single parachute-suspended, illuminated star. Both of these devices are available in green, red, and white.

Smoke may be used for both ground and ground-to-air signaling. It is valuable for marking unit flanks, positions of lead elements, locations of targets, drop zones, tactical landing areas, and medical evacuation landing sites. Smoke grenades are available in white, green, yellow, red, and violet smoke. Smoke may be observed by the enemy; therefore, due regard for secrecy must be considered to try to avoid disclosing positions and/or a unit's intentions.

Fig. 31.12. Star clusters

Fig. 31.13. Single star

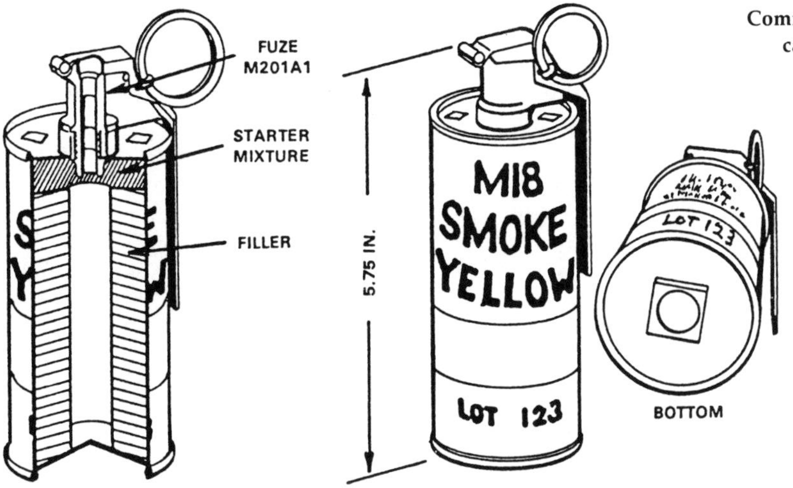

Fig. 31.14. M-18 colored smoke grenade

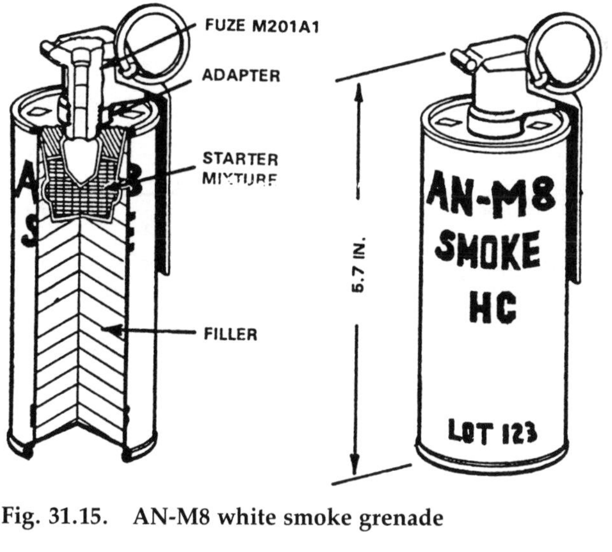

Fig. 31.15. AN-M8 white smoke grenade

Sound Communications

Sound communications consist of both voice and devices such as whistles, horns, gongs, and explosives. Sound signals are used to attract attention, transmit prearranged messages, or spread alarms, but they are good for only short distances. Range and reliability are reduced by battle noise, weather, terrain, and vegetation.

As they may also be heard by the enemy, sound communications may be restricted for security reasons. Sound signals must be simple to avoid misunderstandings. The means for sound signals are usually prescribed by the unit's standard operating procedures (SOP) and CEOI.

Messengers

Messengers are the best way to send long messages and documents; however, they are the slowest means and are vulnerable to enemy action. When using a messenger, messages should be written. The text must be clear, concise, and complete.

Wire Communications

Whenever possible, wire communications should be established within the platoon. Wire is more secure than radio, hard to jam, and allows conversation with break-in capability. Wire equipment normally available within platoons includes the TA-1 telephone (see figure 31.16) and reel equipment CE-11 (see figure 31.17).

Radio Communications

Dangers Radios are used within the platoon only when a message cannot be sent quickly by other means. The enemy can easily intercept radio messages. If he hears the transmission, he can figure out the platoon's mission and location.

The first thing an operator must do when interference disrupts his radio operations is to try to find its cause. The radio operator should not immediately assume that it is due to jamming, as symptoms of enemy jamming are often similar to other types of interference. He can run a simple test: if the interference decreases when the receiver antenna is removed, the interference is due to jamming; if it persists, then it is generated inside the receiver.

If enemy jamming has been identified, the rule is that operators continue operating unless ordered to shut down. All

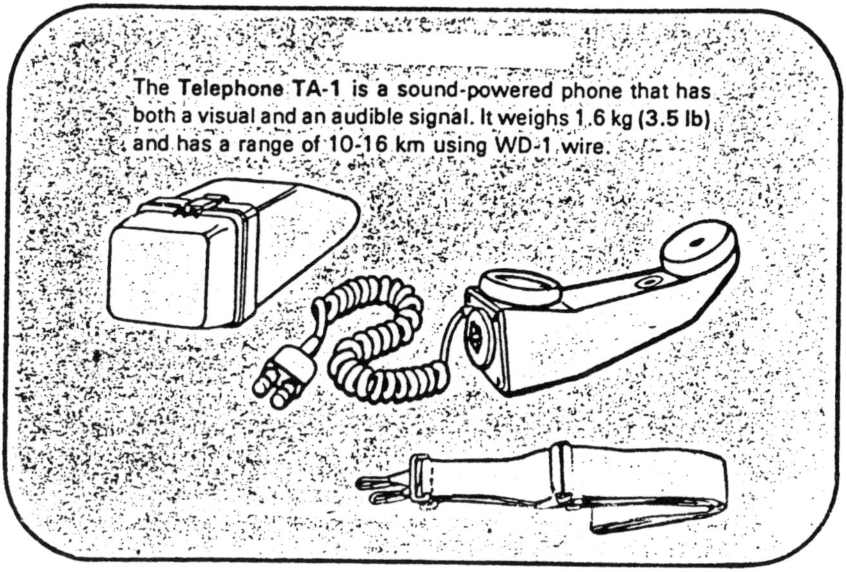

The Telephone TA-1 is a sound-powered phone that has both a visual and an audible signal. It weighs 1.6 kg (3.5 lb) and has a range of 10-16 km using WD-1 wire.

Fig. 31.16. TA-1 telephone

operators must report jamming to their next higher headquarters by wire or messenger.

Prowords, Letters, and Numbers When in contact with the enemy, it may be necessary for a platoon leader to talk to his squad leader on the radio. Transmissions should be short and to the point. Certain procedural words (called prowords) having distinct meanings are used to shorten the time of voice communications and to avoid confusion. All soldiers should use them when talking on the radio. Examples of some of the more common prowords are defined below.

OVER. "This is the end of my transmission to you, and I expect an answer from you."
SAY AGAIN. "Say again all of your last transmission."
CORRECTION. "An error has been made in this transmission (or message indicated). The correct version is ——."
I SAY AGAIN. "I am repeating transmission, or portion indicated."
ROGER. "I have received your last transmission satisfactorily."
WILCO. "I have received your message, understand it, and will comply."

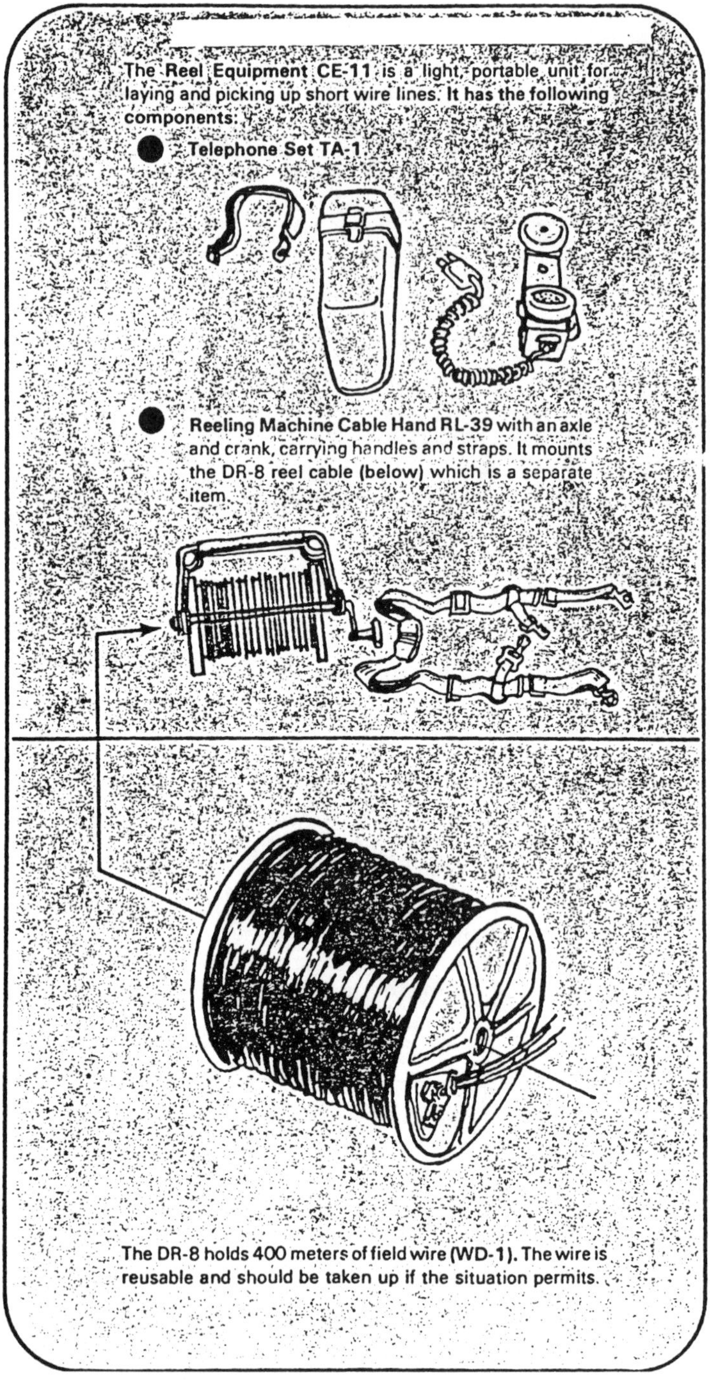

The Reel Equipment CE-11 is a light, portable unit for laying and picking up short wire lines. It has the following components:
● Telephone Set TA-1
● Reeling Machine Cable Hand RL-39 with an axle and crank, carrying handles and straps. It mounts the DR-8 reel cable (below) which is a separate item.
The DR-8 holds 400 meters of field wire (WD-1). The wire is reusable and should be taken up if the situation permits.

Fig. 31.17. Reeling equipment CE-11

A ALPHA (AL FAH)	B BRAVO (BRAH VOH)	C CHARLIE (CHAR LEE)	D DELTA (DELL TAH)
E ECHO (ECK OH)	F FOXTROT (FOKS TROT)	G GOLF (GOLF)	H HOTEL (HOH TELL)
I INDIA (IN DEE AH)	J JULIETT (JEW LEE ETT)	K KILO (KEY LOH)	L LIMA (LEE MAH)
M MIKE (MIKE)	N NOVEMBER (NO VEM BER)	O OSCAR (OSS CAH)	P PAPA (PAH PAH)
Q QUEBEC (KEH BECK)	R ROMEO (ROW ME OH)	S SIERRA (SEE AIR RAH)	T TANGO (TANG GO)
U UNIFORM (YOU NEE FORM)	V VICTOR (VIK TAH)	W WHISKEY (WISS KEY)	X XRAY (ECKS RAY)
Y YANKEE (YANG KEY)	Z ZULU (ZOO LOO)	1 ONE (WUN)	2 TWO (TOO)
3 THREE (TREE)	4 FOUR (FOW ER)	5 FIVE (FIFE)	6 SIX (SIX)
7 SEVEN (SEV EN)	8 EIGHT (AIT)	9 NINE (NIN ER)	Ø ZERO (ZE RO)

Fig. 31.18. Phonetic alphabet

OUT. "This is the end of my transmission to you, and no answer is required."

When necessary to identify any letter of the alphabet, use the standard phonetic alphabet (see figure 31.18). Also, you should take care to distinguish numbers from similarly pronounced words. The numeral 0 is always spoken as "ze-ro," never as "oh." Numbers are always transmitted digit by digit, but multiples of thousands may be spoken as such. For example, 5,000 would be spoken as "five thousand."

Communications Security

Any time you use the radio, you should be sensitive to communications security (COMSEC), which is keeping unauthorized persons from gaining information of value from your radio transmissions. COMSEC includes using authentication to ensure that the other communicating station is a friendly one; using only approved codes; restricting the use of radio transmitters (monitoring radio receivers/listening silence); and enforcing radio-net discipline and radio-telephone procedures.

Appendixes

A. Staff Organizations

The U.S. Army began as the Continental Army, formed by the Continental Congress on 14 June 1775 as a revolutionary force against England. Commanded by Gen. George Washington, the new Army consisted of 10 rifle companies and the militia, which were volunteer, part-time troops lent to Congress by the individual colonies.

Until 1947, the Army was a separate department of the government, as was the Navy. The National Security Act of 1947 created the National Military Establishment (NME), which in 1949 became the Department of Defense (DOD). It is headed by the Secretary of Defense (SECDEF), who is a member of the President's cabinet and a civilian.

Department of Defense

The Department of Defense is the largest government agency in the United States. It spent about 20 percent of the national budget in FY 1992 and employed almost 4 million people, including active-duty service members, civilian employees (about 1 million), and Reserve Component forces. About 1.8 million service members were on active duty with the Army, Navy, Marine Corps, and Air Force. About 1.1 million service members were in the Selected Reserves.

The DOD is composed of the Office of the Secretary of Defense (OSD), Defense Agencies, the Joint Chiefs of Staff (JCS), unified and specified commands, and the Departments of the Army, Navy, and Air Force. (A *unified command* is composed of forces from two or more services, has a broad and continuing mission, and is normally organized on a geographical basis. A *specified command* also has a broad and continuing mission, but it is normally made up of forces from a single service.) The DOD provides for U.S. military security and supports U.S. national policies and interests. The National Security Act of 1947,

Fig. A.1. The Pentagon

as amended, is the controlling military law of the United States.

The DOD Reorganization Act of 1986 made significant changes in the overall DOD organization and functional responsibilities. Major changes were made in the assignment of responsibilities to civilian and military executives of the OSD and the military departments, in the structure and role of the JCS, and in the relationship of unified and specified command officials to other DOD officials and components.

Office of the Secretary

The SECDEF is the principal assistant to the President in all matters relating to the DOD. He exercises direction, authority, and control over the DOD.

The Deputy Secretary of Defense supervises and coordinates the activities of the DOD and takes the place of the SECDEF during an absence or disability.

The Joint Chiefs of Staff

Staff Organization

The JCS consists of the Chairman, the Chiefs of Staff of the Army and Air Force, the Chief of Naval Operations (CNO), and the Commandant of the Marine Corps (CMC). The JCS also includes a Vice Chairman, who is a nonvoting member except when acting as the Chairman in his absence.

The Chairman of the JCS, assisted by other JCS members and supported by the Joint Staff, is responsible for strategic direction of the armed forces; strategic planning; contingency planning and preparedness; advice on department and combatant command requirements, programs, and budgets; doctrine, training, and education for the joint employment of the armed forces; United Nations representational duties; and such other duties as prescribed by law or the President or the SECDEF.

Unified and Specified Commands

Unified and specified commanders operate under the control and direction of the JCS, the President, and the SECDEF. Subject to the authority, direction, and control of the SECDEF, the Chairman of the JCS serves as the spokesman for the commanders of the combatant (unified and specified) commands.

As of 1993, the U.S. unified and specified commands are the European Command, Pacific Command, Atlantic Command, Southern Command, Central Command, Special Operations Command, Transportation Command, Space Command, and Strategic Command.

The Department of the Army

The U.S. Army is a composite of commands, components, branches, and individual members, organized, trained, and equipped for combat in land operations. Today America's Army is organized as a Total Force, that is, an integrated, cohesive melding of the active component (regular Army), Reserve components (Army National Guard and Army Reserve), and civilian employees.

Army Regulation 10-5 sets forth the organization and functions of the Department of the Army (DA). It applies to the active Army, the Army National Guard (ARNG), and the U.S. Army Reserve (USAR). This section will highlight major points that you need to know about the DA. To begin with, let's explain some key terms.

DEPARTMENT OF THE ARMY. The executive department of the Department of Defense charged with supervision of the Army staff and all Army field headquarters, forces, Reserve components, installations, activities, and functions.

HEADQUARTERS, DEPARTMENT OF THE ARMY (HQDA). The highest level headquarters in the DA. It is composed of the Office of the Secretary of the Army (OSA); Office of the Chief of Staff, U.S. Army (OCSA); the Army General, Special and Personal staffs; and specifically designated staff-support agencies (SSAs).

ARMY FIELD COMMANDS. These include all field headquarters, forces, Reserve components (RC), installations, activities, and functions under the control of the Army.

MAJOR ARMY COMMAND (MACOM). This is a command directly subordinate to, established by authority of, and specifically designated by HQDA; Army component commands of unified and specified commands are MACOMs.

FIELD OPERATING AGENCY (FOA). This is an agency under the supervision of HQDA, but not a MACOM or part of a MACOM, that has the primary mission of executing policy.

Office of the Secretary of the Army (OSA)

Congress has provided for a Secretary of the Army, under Title 10 U.S. Code, Sections 3010 and 3012, which state:

Section 3010: "The Department of the Army is separately organized under the Secretary of the Army. It operates under the authority and direction of the Secretary of Defense."

Section 3012: "The Secretary is responsible and has the necessary authority to conduct all affairs of the Department of the Army, including . . .

1) Functions necessary or appropriate for the training, operations, administration, logistical support and maintenance, welfare, preparedness and effectiveness of the Army, including research and development. . . ."

The following chart depicts the organization of the Office of the Secretary of the Army.

ARMY SECRETARIAT ORGANIZATION

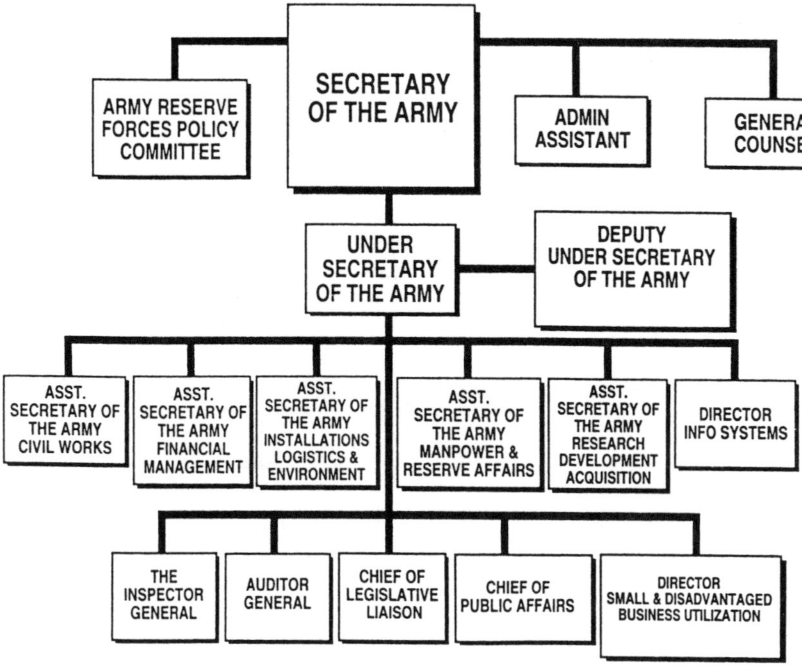

Fig. A.2. Office of the Secretary of the Army

Army Missions and Functions

Congress has also provided the Army with organizational missions in Title 10 U.S. Code, Section 3062. That section states in part:

"[The Army] shall be organized, trained and equipped primarily for prompt and sustained combat incident to operations on land . . . [and] . . . is responsible for the preparation of land forces necessary for the effective prosecution of war, except as assigned and in accordance with integrated mobilization plans, for the expansion of the peacetime components of the Army to meet the needs of war."

The missions of the Army are:

- to deter war or threat to the United States, but if war comes, to fight and win

- to project U.S. power when necessary
- to conduct operations other than war

To do this, the Army must be able to perform the following functions:

- forward presence with units forward deployed
- projection of land forces/contingency operations
- peacetime and wartime reinforcement
- evacuation/protection of U.S. citizens
- support of the nation's war on drugs
- assistance to friendly nations
- support of nation assistance and civil affairs

The following chart depicts how the Army Staff is organized.

Major Commands (MACOM)

To perform the Army's missions and functions, there are sixteen MACOMs:

Name	*Location of Headquarters*
Forces Command	Fort McPherson, GA
Training and Doctrine Command	Fort Monroe, VA
Army Materiel Command	Alexandria, VA
Information Systems Command	Fort Huachuca, AZ
Military Traffic Management Command	Washington, D.C.
Criminal Investigation Command	Falls Church, VA
Medical Command	Fort Sam Houston, VA
Corps of Engineers	Washington, D.C.
Intelligence and Security Command	Fort Belvoir, VA
Military District of Washington	Fort Lesley J. McNair, D.C.
Space and Strategic Defense Command	Arlington, VA
Special Operations Command	Fort Bragg, NC
U.S. Army, Europe	Heidelberg, Germany
Eighth U.S. Army	Seoul, Korea
U.S. Army, Pacific	Fort Shafter, HI
U.S. Army, South	Fort Clayton, Panama

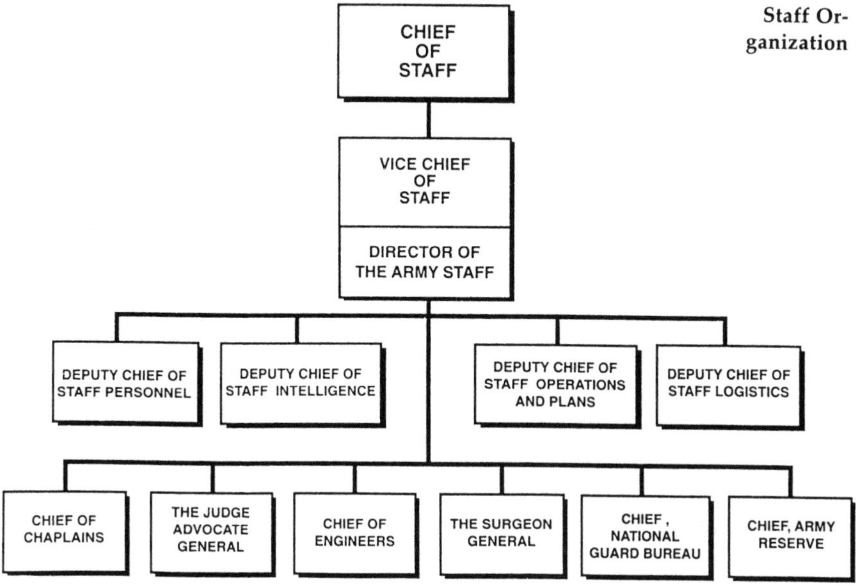

Fig. A.3. The Army staff

B. Army Flags and Streamers

Colors, Standards, and Flags

Tradition and history have left the modern soldier with a confusing terminology for what are today most commonly called "flags" used by the Army. To further complicate matters, terms have been used interchangeably over the years. In reality, however, there are some important distinctions between "flags" depending on the size of the cloth, and the nature of the unit or organization.

Two of the oldest terms used are "color" and "standard." A color was carried by a dismounted unit, and a standard, smaller in size and easier to handle, was carried by a mounted unit. Army units of battalion or regimental size normally carried two colors, one the "national" color or standard that represented the United States. The other color displayed the distinctive battalion or regimental emblem and represented the unit. Designs for both have changed during the life of the Army. Today the national color carried is the "Stars and Stripes." A unit or organizational color is authorized only for battalions and regiments organized under the Army's standard system called the Tables of Organization and Equipment (TO&E). This type of unit is thus referred to as a "color-bearing" unit, and its organizational color bears its official title and coat of arms.

Units above regimental level and non-TO&E elements are not ignored. They carry what are correctly called unit "flags." These flags usually have a set design composed of branch colors and the unit numerical designation. In some cases other design elements may be included.

The Stars and Stripes, when not carried by a unit, such as when it is flown on a pole outdoors, is referred to as the national "flag" or "color." There are several different names for

Fig. B.1. U.S. Army flag with battle streamers

the national flag used by Army posts depending on the size of the flag. These include the garrison flag, the post flag, and the storm flag.

The Army Flags

As a non-TO&E organization, the Army itself is non-color-bearing and is therefore represented by a flag. The United States Army flag is made of white silk with a blue embroidered replica of the official seal of the former War Office, predecessor to the Department of the Army, in the center. The flag is four feet four inches wide by five feet six inches long with a yellow fringe on three edges. Beneath the seal in the center is a scarlet scroll on which are the words "United States Army" in white. Beneath the scroll is the date "1775" referring to the founding of the Army on 14 June 1775. The flag was officially unfurled on 14 June 1956 and flies all the campaign streamers awarded the Army. Prior to that date there had been no Army flag, only colors and flags of individual units and for the nation. See figure B.1.

The Army field flag was authorized in 1962 and is slightly smaller than the United States Army flag. Its color is also different. It has an ultramarine blue background with a white seal and scroll. The words "United States Army" are scarlet, and the numerals "1775" are white. No campaign streamers are flown. This flag is issued to organizations and headquarters not authorized the U.S. Army flag.

Streamers on the U.S. Army Flag

The flag of the U.S. Army proudly carries 172 battle and campaign streamers on its staff. These streamers represent the sacrifice and courage of generations of American soldiers in every corner of this country and around the world. As this guide is being prepared, the Army's 173d campaign is still ongoing in Southwest Asia as American soldiers continue on guard in Kuwait, Saudi Arabia, and northern Iraq. A campaign streamer will be awarded to the Army and its participating units at the conclusion of the campaign. Figure B.2 provides some examples.

Campaign and battle streamers are the only type of streamer displayed on the United States Army flag. These streamers are affixed to an attaching device at the top of the flag staff. The streamers are arrayed in a counterclockwise manner around the top of the staff. LEXINGTON 1775 is the first streamer. When the Army flag is not being carried, the streamers will be arranged in such a way that YORKTOWN 1781 is displayed in the preeminent position, i.e., in the center facing forward. The streamer awarded for the most recent completed campaign, Liberation and Defense of Kuwait 1991, is also placed so as to be visible.

Unit Streamers and Silver Bands

Units of the Army that participated in the officially designated battles and campaigns fly the streamers from their unit colors and flags. Small units of company, troop, battery, or platoon size do not receive a streamer, but instead are given an engraved silver band to display on their guidon staff. Unit colors, flags, and guidons may display other types of streamers and awards also, such as unit awards for heroic action or meritorious service. Such awards, however, are given only to units, not to the Army as a whole, therefore that type of streamer or award is not displayed on the U.S. Army flag.

Figure B.3 gives an illustration of how streamers and silver bands are displayed on unit colors, flags, and guidons. If you look closely at the figure, you will notice that a cordlike device is also shown attached to the top of the flag or guidon staff.

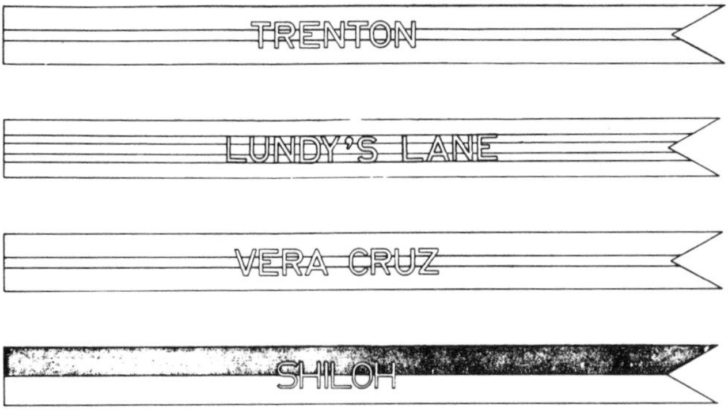

Fig. B.2. Samples of campaign and battle streamers

This cord, called a "fourragère," is a foreign award for heroism. It is designed to be worn around the shoulder of a soldier. When given to a unit it is attached to the top of the unit's color, flag, or guidon staff.

The Army's Campaigns and Battle Honors

Battle and campaign honors were first officially displayed on the colors of Army units in the Civil War. At that time U.S. Army regiments carried both a national (Stars and Stripes) and a regimental color or standard into battle. The designation of a regiment was embroidered on the center stripe of its national

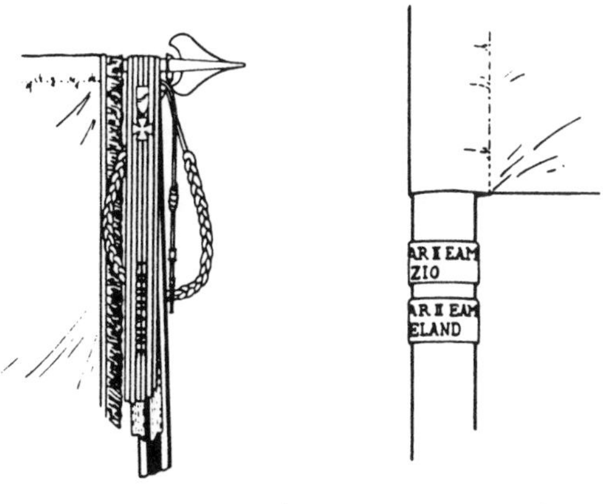

Fig. B.3. Display of streamers on unit flag and of silver bands on guidons

color. In 1861 Union Major General John C. Frémont authorized the units that had participated in the battle of Wilson's Creek, near Springfield, Missouri, to also place the name "Springfield" on their color. Although it was not specified which color, the use of stripes on the national color, and the presence there already of the unit's identity, made it the logical choice.

Within a matter of months the War Department authorized the practice for the whole Union Army. Some Confederate units did likewise. This system continued after the war for a number of years until it became clear there was not enough room on the colors to continue the practice indefinitely. In addition, replacement of the embroidered colors as they wore out was quite expensive. In 1890 it was decided to use silver rings or bands engraved with the name of the battle. One ring was to be placed around the staff of the regimental color for each battle or campaign in which the unit had participated. This continued until World War I.

At the end of World War I the original plan was to have silver rings made in France inscribed with the names of World War I battles. However, the bands could not be prepared before the units returned to the United States. General Pershing directed ribbons with the names of the battles be tied to the tops of the units' colors. This temporary system worked very well and it was officially adopted in 1920. The Army has used it since. The tradition of silver bands did not disappear, however. The Army recognized that small units, which did not have colors, were frequently involved as separate units in a battle and deserved to be recognized. The use of silver bands was retained for them.

There are eight campaigns of World War II for which the Army does not display a streamer because no Army units participated. These are AMERICAN THEATER (Ground Combat and Air Combat), ASIATIC–PACIFIC (Antisubmarine, Ground Combat, and Air Combat), and EUROPEAN–AFRICAN–MIDDLE EASTERN (Antisubmarine, Ground Combat, and Air Combat).

Listed below are all of the 172 campaign and battle streamers the Army has received for its service to the nation since 1775. A description of design of each streamer, which mirrors the design and colors of the ribbon of the campaign medal, is also provided.

Read over the campaign and battles mentioned below in conjunction with the history of the Army in Chapter 1. There will be many names on this list that you recognize, and also many of which you have never heard. It is a roll call of honor for the American soldier. When the campaign is officially concluded, KUWAIT CEASE-FIRE will be the 173rd streamer. History clearly shows that it will not be the last.

Campaign and Battle Streamers

Revolutionary War
Streamer: Scarlet with a white stripe, gold lettering.

LEXINGTON 1775
TICONDEROGA 1775
BOSTON 1775–1776
QUEBEC 1775, 1776
CHARLESTON 1776, 1780
LONG ISLAND 1776
TRENTON 1776
PRINCETON 1777
SARATOGA 1777
BRANDYWINE 1777
GERMANTOWN 1777
MONMOUTH 1778
SAVANNAH 1778, 1779
COWPENS 1781
GUILFORD COURT HOUSE 1781
YORKTOWN 1781

War of 1812
Streamer: Scarlet with two white stripes, gold lettering.

CANADA 1812–1815
CHIPPEWA 1814
LUNDY'S LANE 1814
BLADENSBURG 1814
MCHENRY 1814
NEW ORLEANS 1814–1815

Mexican War
Streamer: Green with one white stripe, gold lettering.

PALO ALTO 1846
RESACA DE LA PALMA 1846
MONTEREY 1846
BUENA VISTA 1847
VERA CRUZ 1847
CERRO GORDO 1847
CONTRERAS 1847
CHURUBUSCO 1947
MOLINA DEL RAY 1847
CHAPULTEPEC 1847

Civil War

Streamer: Blue and gray equally divided, gold lettering.

SUMPTER 1861
BULL RUN 1861
HENRY & DONELSON 1862
MISSISSIPPI RIVER 1862–1863
PENINSULA 1862
SHILOH 1862
VALLEY 1862
MANASSAS 1862
ANTIETAM 1862
FREDERICKSBURG 1862
MURFREESBOROUGH 1862–1863
CHANCELLORSVILLE 1863
GETTYSBURG 1863
VICKSBURG 1863
CHICKAMAUGA 1863
CHATTANOOGA 1863
WILDERNESS 1864
ATLANTA 1864
SPOTSYLVANIA 1864
COLD HARBOR 1864
PETERSBURG 1864–1865
SHENANDOAH 1864
FRANKLIN 1864
NASHVILLE 1864
APPOMATTOX 1865

Indian Campaigns

Streamer: Scarlet with two black stripes, gold lettering.

MIAMI 1790–1795
TIPPECANOE 1811
CREEKS 1813–1814, 1836–1837
SEMINOLES 1817–1818, 1835–1842, 1855–1858
BLACK HAWK 1832
COMANCHES 1867–1875
MODOCS 1872–1873
APACHES 1873, 1885–1886
LITTLE BIG HORN 1876–1877
NEZ PERCES 1877
BANNOCKS 1878
CHEYENNES 1878–1879
UTES 1879–1880
PINE RIDGE 1890–1891

War with Spain
Streamer: Yellow with two blue stripes, scarlet lettering.

SANTIAGO 1898
PUERTO RICO 1898
MANILA 1898

China Relief Expedition
Streamer: Yellow with blue edges, blue lettering.

TIENTSIN 1900
YANG-TSUN 1900
PEKING 1900

Philippine Insurrection
Streamer: Blue with two red stripes, gold lettering.

MANILA 1899
ILOTLO 1899
MALOLOS 1899
LAGUNA DE BAY 1899
SAN ISIDRO 1899
ZAPOTE RIVER 1899
CAVITE 1899–1900
TARLAC 1899
SAN FABIAN 1899
MANDANAO 1902–1905
JOLO 1905, 1906, 1913

Mexican Expedition
Streamer: Yellow with one blue stripe and green borders.

MEXICO 1916–1917

World War I
Streamer: Double rainbow with red center and dark blue on the edges, white lettering.

CAMBRAI 1917
SOMME DEFENSIVE 1918
LYS 1918
AISNE 1918
MONTDIDIER-NOYON 1918
CHAMPAGNE-MARNE 1918
AISNE-MARNE 1918
SOMME OFFENSIVE 1918
OISE-AISME 1918
YPRES-LYS 1918

ST. MIHIEL 1918
MEUSE-ARGONNE 1918
VITTORIO VENETO 1918

World War II (American Theater)
Streamer: Blue with two groups of white, black, red and white stripes, with blue, white, and red in the center.

ANTISUBMARINE 1941–1945

World War II (Asiatic Theater)
Streamer: Orange with stripes and center same as above, black lettering.

PHILIPPINE ISLANDS 1941–1942
BURMA 1941–1942
CENTRAL PACIFIC 1941–1943
EAST INDIES 1942
INDIA–BURMA 1942–1945
AIR OFFENSIVE, JAPAN 1942–1945
ALEUTIAN ISLANDS 1942–1943
CHINA DEFENSIVE 1942–1945
PAPUA 1942–1943
GUADALCANAL 1942–1943
NEW GUINEA 1943–1944
NORTHERN SOLOMONS 1943–1944
EASTERN MANDATES 1944
BISMARCK ARCHIPELAGO 1943–1944
WESTERN PACIFIC 1944–1945
LEYTE 1944–1945
LUZON 1944–1945
CENTRAL BURMA 1945
SOUTHERN PHILIPPINES 1945
RYUKYUS 1945
CHINA OFFENSIVE 1945

World War II (Europe–Africa–Mideast Theater)
Streamer: Green and brown with two stripe groups, one of green, white, red, the other of white, black, and white stripes; with center same as above, gold lettering.

EGYPT–LIBYA 1942–1943
AIR OFFENSIVE, EUROPE 1942–1944
ALGERIA–FRENCH MOROCCO 1942
TUNISIA 1942–1943
SICILY 1943
NAPLES-FOGGIA 1943–1944
ANZIO 1944

ROME-ARNO 1944
NORMANDY 1944
NORTHERN FRANCE 1944
SOUTHERN FRANCE 1944
NORTH APENNINES 1944–1945
RHINELAND 1944–1945
ARDENNES–ALSACE 1944–1945
CENTRAL EUROPE 1945
PO VALLEY 1945

Korean Service

Streamer: Light blue bordered on each side with white, with a white stripe in the center, white lettering.

UN DEFENSIVE 1950
UN OFFENSIVE 1950
CCF INTERVENTION 1950–1951
FIRST UN COUNTEROFFENSIVE 1951
CCF STRING OFFENSIVE 1951
UN SUMMER–FALL OFFENSIVE 1951
SECOND KOREAN WINTER 1951–1952
KOREA, SUMMER–FALL 1952
THIRD KOREAN WINTER 1952–1953
KOREA SUMMER 1953

Vietnam Service

Streamer: Yellow background with three red stripes in the center and one green stripe on each edge, white lettering.

VIETNAM ADVISORY 1962–1965
VIETNAM DEFENSE 1965
VIETNAM COUNTEROFFENSIVE 1965–1966
VIETNAM COUNTEROFFENSIVE, PHASE II 1966, 1967
VIETNAM COUNTEROFFENSIVE PHASE III 1967–1968
TET COUNTEROFFENSIVE 1968
VIETNAM COUNTEROFFENSIVE PHASE IV 1968
VIETNAM COUNTEROFFENSIVE PHASE V 1968
VIETNAM COUNTEROFFENSIVE PHASE VI 1968–1969
TET 69/COUNTEROFFENSIVE 1969
VIETNAM SUMMER–FALL 1969
VIETNAM WINTER–SPRING 1970
SANCTUARY COUNTEROFFENSIVE 1970
VIETNAM COUNTEROFFENSIVE PHASE VII 1970–1971
CONSOLIDATION I 1971
CONSOLIDATION II 1971–1972
VIETNAM CEASEFIRE 1972–1973

Armed Forces Expeditions

Streamer: White stripe in the center with green, yellow, brown, black, and blue stripes on each side, white lettering.

DOMINICAN REPUBLIC 1965–1966
GRENADA 1983
PANAMA 1989–1990

Southwest Asia Service

Streamer: White background with a black and green stripe with yellow edge in the center, a red, white, and blue stripe on each side, narrow black stripe on the edge, white lettering.

DEFENSE OF SAUDI ARABIA 1990–1991
LIBERATION AND DEFENSE OF KUWAIT 1991
KUWAIT CEASE-FIRE 1991–(Named but not yet awarded)

Other Unit Award Streamers

In addition to the campaign and battle streamers, silver bands, and fourragère awards mentioned above, Army units may receive other types of unit awards that are displayed as streamers on the unit color or guidon staff. These include U.S. and foreign awards for unit heroism, meritorious service, and special unit qualification for infantry and medical units. Figure B.4 provides examples of some non-campaign unit award streamers, and figure B.5 illustrates some of the types of special qualification streamers units may win.

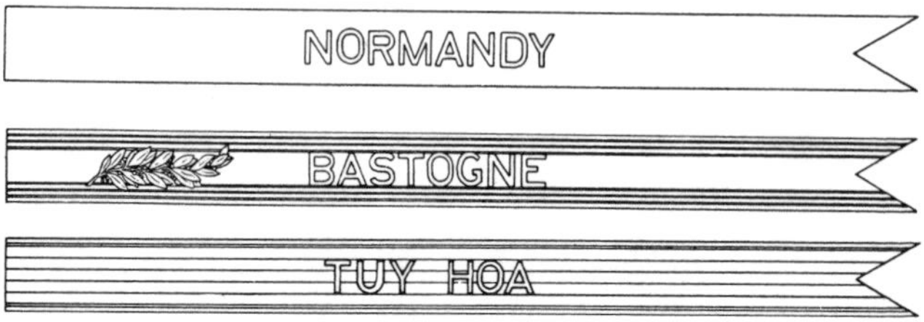

Fig. B.4. Samples of unit award streamers

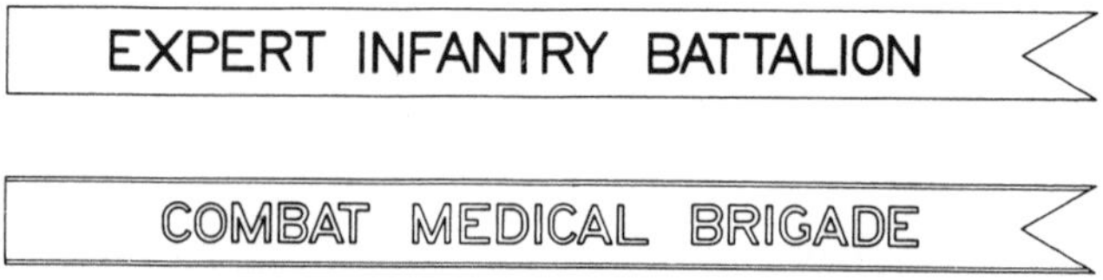

Fig. B.5. Some special qualification streamers

C. Uniform Code of Military Justice

The Uniform Code of Military Justice (UCMS) is a federal law that establishes the U.S. military criminal justice system. It describes what conduct is criminal and the types of military courts and basic procedures used to process military criminal cases (also see chapter 4).

The following is an outline of UCMJ, Articles 1–140:

Outline of UCMJ, Articles 1–140

I. General Provisions	
Definitions	1
Persons subject to this chapter	2
Jurisdiction to try certain personnel	3
Dismissed officer's right to trial by court-martial	4
Territorial applicability to this chapter	5
Judge Advocates and legal officers	6
II. Apprehension and Restraint	
Apprehension	7
Apprehension of deserters	8
Imposition of restraint	9
Restraint of persons charged with offenses	10
Reports and receiving prisoners	11
Confinement and enemy prisoners prohibited	12
Punishment prohibited before trial	13
Delivery of offenders to civil authorities	14
III. Nonjudicial Punishment	
Commanding officer's nonjudicial punishment	15
IV. Courts-Martial Jurisdiction	
Courts-martial classified	16
Jurisdiction of courts-martial in general	17
Jurisdiction of general courts-martial	18

Spies	106
False official statements	107
Military property of the United States—loss, damage destruction, or wrongful disposition	108
Property other than military property of United States—waste, spoilage, or destruction	109
Improper hazarding a vessel	110
Drunken or reckless driving	111
Drunk on duty	112
Drugs—wrongful possession, use, etc., of controlled drugs	112
Misbehavior of sentinel	113
Dueling	114
Malingering	115
Riot or breach of peace	116
Provoking speeches or gestures	117
Murder	118
Manslaughter	119
Rape and carnal knowledge	120
Larceny and wrongful appropriation	121
Robbery	122
Forgery	123
Making, drawing, or uttering check, draft, or order without sufficient funds	123a
Maiming	124
Sodomy	125
Arson	126
Extortion	127
Assault	128
Burglary	129
Housebreaking	130
Perjury	131
Frauds against the United States	132
Conduct unbecoming an officer and gentleman	133
General article	134
XI. Miscellaneous Provisions	135–140

Article 134, properly known as the "general article," is designed to cover all disorders and neglects detrimental to good order and discipline in the armed forces, and crimes and offenses not capital in nature.

D. 1995 Pay Charts

The pay charts in this appendix became effective 1 January 1995. At the time this guide is being written a pay raise is under discussion for 1996. Pay raises are not automatic and must be approved by Congress each year.

TABLE D.1. Monthly Basic Pay, Active Duty

	Years in Service													
Pay Grade	*Under 2*	*Over 2*	*Over 3*	*Over 4*	*Over 6*	*Over 8*	*Over 10*	*Over 12*	*Over 14*	*Over 16*	*Over 18*	*Over 20*	*Over 22*	*Over 24*	*26 & Over*
E-9	0.00	0.00	0.00	0.00	0.00	0.00	2561.70	2619.00	2678.40	2739.90	2801.40	2855.70	3005.40	3122.40	3297.90
E-8	0.00	0.00	0.00	0.00	0.00	2148.00	2209.80	2268.00	2326.80	2388.30	2442.90	2502.90	2649.90	2768.10	2945.10
E-7	1499.70	1619.10	1678.80	1737.90	1797.00	1854.30	1913.70	1973.40	2062.50	2121.00	2179.80	2208.30	2356.50	2473.80	2649.90
E-6	1290.30	1406.40	1464.90	1527.30	1584.60	1641.60	1701.90	1789.50	1845.60	1905.30	1934.10	1934.10	1934.10	1934.10	1934.10
E-5	1132.20	1232.40	1292.40	1348.50	1437.30	1495.80	1554.90	1612.20	1641.60	1641.60	1641.60	1641.60	1641.60	1641.60	1641.60
E-4	1056.00	1115.40	1181.10	1272.00	1322.40	1322.40	1322.40	1322.40	1322.40	1322.40	1322.40	1322.40	1322.40	1322.40	1322.40
E-3	995.10	1049.70	1091.40	1134.60	1134.60	1134.60	1134.60	1134.60	1134.60	1134.60	1134.60	1134.60	1134.60	1134.60	1134.60
E-2	957.60	957.60	957.60	957.60	957.60	957.60	957.60	957.60	957.60	957.60	957.60	957.60	957.60	957.60	957.60
E-1	854.40	854.40	854.40	854.40	854.40	854.40	854.40	854.40	854.40	854.40	854.40	854.40	854.40	854.40	854.40

E-1 with less than 4 months—$790.40

TABLE D.2. Basic Allowance for Subsistence

Conditions	*E-1 with Less Than 4 Months' Service (per day)*	*All Other Enlisted (per day)*
When on leave or authorized to mess separately	$6.44	$6.98
When rations in-kind are not available	$7.26	$7.87
When assigned to duty under emergency conditions where no government messing facilities are available	$9.63	$10.42

TABLE D.3. Basic Allowance for Quarters

Pay Grade	*With Dependents ($)*	*No Dependents ($)*
E-9	599.40	454.80
E-8	552.60	417.60
E-7	513.00	356.40
E-6	474.30	322.80
E-5	426.30	297.60
E-4	370.80	258.90
E-3	345.00	254.10
E-2	328.50	206.40
E-1	328.50	183.90

TABLE D.4. Reserve Drill Pay

	Years in Service														
Pay Grade	*Under 2*	*Over 2*	*Over 3*	*Over 4*	*Over 6*	*Over 8*	*Over 10*	*Over 12*	*Over 14*	*Over 16*	*Over 18*	*Over 20*	*Over 22*	*Over 24*	*26 & Over*
E-9	0.00	0.00	0.00	0.00	0.00	0.00	85.39	87.30	89.28	91.33	93.38	95.19	100.18	104.08	109.93
E-8	0.00	0.00	0.00	0.00	0.00	71.60	73.66	75.60	77.56	79.61	81.43	83.43	88.33	92.27	98.17
E-7	49.99	53.97	55.96	57.93	59.90	61.81	63.79	65.78	68.75	70.70	72.66	73.61	78.55	82.46	88.33
E-6	43.01	46.88	48.83	50.91	52.82	54.72	56.73	59.65	61.52	63.51	64.47	64.47	64.47	64.47	64.47
E-5	37.74	41.08	43.08	44.95	47.91	49.86	51.83	53.74	54.72	54.72	54.72	54.72	54.72	54.72	54.72
E-4	35.20	37.18	39.37	42.40	44.08	44.08	44.08	44.08	44.08	44.08	44.08	44.08	44.08	44.08	44.08
E-3	33.17	34.99	36.38	37.82	37.82	37.82	37.82	37.82	37.82	37.82	37.82	37.82	37.82	37.82	37.82
E-2	31.92	31.92	31.92	31.92	31.92	31.92	31.92	31.92	31.92	31.92	31.92	31.92	31.92	31.92	31.92
E-1	28.48	28.48	28.48	28.48	28.48	28.48	28.48	28.48	28.48	28.48	28.48	28.48	28.48	28.48	28.48

E-1 with less than 4 months—$26.34

E. Career Management Fields and Military Occupational Specialties

Career Management Fields

Listed below are the thirty-five Career Management Fields currently used by the Army.

CMF 11 Infantry
CMF 12 Combat Engineering
CMF 13 Field Artillery
CMF 14 Air Defense Artillery
CMF 18 Special Forces
CMF 19 Armor
CMF 23 Air Defense Systems Maintenance
CMF 25 Visual Information
CMF 27 Land Combat and Air Defense Systems Direct & General Support Maintenance
CMF 29 Signal Maintenance
CMF 31 Signal Operations
CMF 33 EW/Intercept Systems Maintenance
CMF 35 Electronic Maintenance and Calibration
CMF 37 Psychological Operations
CMF 38 Civil Affairs
CMF 46 Public Affairs
CMF 51 General Engineering
CMF 54 Chemical
CMF 55 Ammunition
CMF 63 Mechanical Maintenance
CMF 67 Aircraft Maintenance
CMF 71 Administration
CMF 74 Record Information Operations

CMF 77 Petroleum and Water
CMF 79 Recruitment and Reenlistment
CMF 81 Topographic Engineering
CMF 88 Transportation
CMF 91 Medical
CMF 92 Supply and Service
CMF 93 Aviation Operations
CMF 94 Food Service
CMF 95 Military Police
CMF 96 Military Intelligence
CMF 97 Bands
CMF 98 Signals Intelligence/Electronic Warfare Operations

Military Operational Specialties

Here, in alphabetical order, is a listing of Army Military Occupational Specialties. Those marked with an asterisk are not currently open to female soldiers.

Accounting specialist
Administration specialist
Aerial intelligence specialist
Aeroscout observer*
AH-1 attack helicopter repairer
AH-64 attack helicopter repairer
Aircraft armament/missile systems repairer
Aircraft electrician
Aircraft pneudraulics repairer
Aircraft powerplant repairer
Aircraft powertrain repairer
Aircraft structural repairer
Air defense
Air traffic control operator
Air traffic control systems equipment repairer
Ammunition specialist
Ammunition stock control and accounting specialist
Animal care specialist
AN/TSQ-73 Air Defense Artillery command and control system operator/repairer
Artillery repairer
Automated communications computer systems repairer
Automatic test equipment operator/maintainer
Avenger crew member*
Avenger system repairer
Aviation operations specialist
Avionic communications equipment repairer
Avionic mechanic
Avionic navigation and flight control equipment repairer
Avionic special equipment repairer
Baritone or euphonium player
Bassoon player
Behavioral science specialist
Biological assistant
Bradley fighting vehicle system mechanic*
Bradley fighting vehicle system turret mechanic*
Bridge crew member*
Broadcast journalist

Cannon crew member*
Cannon fire direction specialist*
Cardiac specialist
Cargo specialist
Carpentry and masonry specialist
Cartographer
Cavalry scout*
Chaparral crew member*
Chaparral/Redeye repairer
Chaparral system mechanic*
Chaplain assistant
Chemical operations specialist
Clarinet player
Combat engineer*
Combat signaler
Communications systems circuit controller
Concrete and asphalt equipment operator
Construction equipment repairer
Construction surveyor
Coronet or trumpet player
Counterintelligence assistant
Crane operator
Decentralized automated service support systems computer repairer
Dental laboratory specialist
Dental specialist
Ear, nose, and throat specialist
Electric bass guitar player
Electronic warfare/intercept aerial sensor repairer
Electronic warfare/intercept aviation system repairer
Electronic warfare/intercept strategic processing/ storage subsystem repairer
Electronic warfare/intercept strategic receiving subsystem repairer
Electronic warfare/intercept tactical system repairer
Electronic warfare/signal intelligence analyst
Electronic warfare/signal intelligence specialist (linguist)
Electronic warfare/signal intelligence voice interceptor
Emitter locator/identifier
Engineer tracked vehicle crewman*
Equipment records and parts specialist
Explosive ordnance disposal specialist
Eye specialist
Fabric repair specialist
Field artillery firefinder radar operator*
Field artillery meterological crew member
Field artillery surveyor*
Field artillery tactical fire direction systems repairer
Field communications security equipment repairer
Fighting vehicle infantryman*
Finance specialist
Fire control instrument repairer
Fire control system repairer
Firefighter
Fire support specialist*
Fixed communications security equipment repairer
Flute or piccolo player
Food service specialist
Forward area alerting radar operator*
French horn player
Fuel and electrical systems repairer
General aircraft repairer

General construction equipment operator
Graphics documentation specialist
Graves registration specialist
Ground surveillance systems operator
Guitar player
Hawk continuous-wave radar repairer
Hawk field maintenance equipment/pulse acquisition radar repairer
Hawk fire control crew member
Hawk fire control repairer
Hawk firing section mechanic
Hawk firing control mechanic
Hawk information coordination central mechanic
Hawk missile system crew member
Hawk missile system mechanic
Heavy antiarmor weapons infantryman*
Heavy construction equipment operator
Heavy wheeled vehicle mechanic
Hospital food service specialist
Imagery analyst
Indirect fire infantryman*
Infantryman*
Information systems operators
Integrated family of test equipment operator/maintainer
Intelligence analyst
Interior electrician
Interrogator
Journalist
Land combat support system test specialist
Laundry and bath specialist
Legal specialist
Light wheeled vehicle mechanic
Machinist
MANPADS crew member
Materials quality specialist
Material control and accounting specialist
Material storage and handling specialist
Medical equipment repairer—unit level
Medical laboratory specialist
Medical specialist
Medical supply specialist
Medium helicopter repairer
Metal worker
Military police
Mobile subscriber equipment network switch system operator
Mobile subscriber equipment transmission system operator
Morse interceptor
Motor transport operator
Multichannel communications systems operator
Multiple-Launch Rocket System crew member*
Multiple-Launch Rocket System/Lance fire direction specialist*
Multiple-Launch Rocket System repairer
M-1 Abrams armor crew man*
M-1 Abrams tank system mechanic*
M-1 Abrams tank turret mechanic*
Noncommunications interceptor/analyst

Non-Morse interceptor/analyst
Nuclear weapons specialist
Oboe player
Observation airplane repairer
Observation/Scout helicopter repairer
Occupational therapy specialist
Operating room specialist
Optical laboratory specialist
Orthopedic specialist
Orthotic specialist
Parachute rigger
Patient administration specialist
Patriot missile crew member
Patriot operator/system mechanic
Percussion player
Personnel actions specialist
Personnel administration specialist
Personnel information systems management specialist
Personnel management specialist
Personnel records specialist
Petroleum laboratory specialist
Petroleum supply specialist
Pharmacy specialist
Photo and layout specialist
Physical therapy specialist
Piano player
Plumber
Power generator equipment repairer
Practical nurse
Preventive medicine specialist
Printing and bindery specialist
Psychiatric specialist
Psychological operations specialist
Quarrying specialist
Quartermaster and chemical equipment repairer
Radio repairer
Record telecommunications center operator
Respiratory specialist
Satellite communications systems repairer
Saxophone player
Scout helicopter repairer
Self-propelled field artillery system mechanic
Self-propelled field artillery turret mechanic
Signal security specialist
Signals intelligence analyst
Single-channel radio operator
Small arms repairer
Software analyst
Special electronic devices repairer
Still documentation specialist
Strategic microwave systems repairer
Subsistance supply specialist
Switching systems operator
Tactical fire operations specialist*
Tactical satellite/microwave repairer
Tactical satellite/microwave systems operator
Tactical transport helicopter repairer
Tank turret repairer
Target acquisition/surveillance radar repairer
Technical drafting specialist
Telecommunications terminal device repairer
Telephone central office repairer

Terrain analyst
Test, measurement, and diagnostic equipment
Topographic surveyor
TOW/Dragon repairer
Tracked vehicle mechanic
Tracked vehicle repairer
Traffic management coordinator
Transportable automatic switching system operator/maintainer
Trombone player
Tuba player
Turbine engine driver/generator repairer
Unit level communications maintainer
Unit supply specialist
Utilities equipment repairer
Utility helicopter repairer
Veterinary food inspection specialist
Visual information/audio documentation systems specialist
Visual information/audio equipment repairer
Vulcan crew member*
Vulcan repairer
Vulcan system mechanic*
Water treatment specialist
Watercraft engineer
Watercraft operator
Wheeled vehicle repairer
Wire systems installer
X-ray specialist

List subject to change

F. Branch and Functional Area Insignia

When in dress uniform (and sometimes in work uniforms), every member of the active Army and Army Reserve will wear a collar-lapel insignia identifying his or her branch of service and/or primary MOS, as shown below.

Proper recognition of this insignia by the new soldier will be helpful in locating assistance, becoming knowledgeable about the Army, and establishing contacts with other soldiers.

TABLE F.1 Insignia

	Insignia	
Branch	*Officer*	*Enlisted*
Adjutant General Corps—charged with a variety of administrative duties, including records management, publications, office information systems, and field printing. They also provide unit personnel services.		
Air Defense Artillery—charged with provision of protective air defense over the battlefield		

Armor—responsible for the development and conduct of mobile warfare

Army Medical Specialist Corps—the component of the Army Medical Department that provides dietary, physical therapy, and occupational therapy services

Army Nurse Corps—the component of the Army Medical Department that provides nursing services

Aviation—incorporates all Army aviation assets, except Medical Service Corps aviation

Branch Immaterial—a designation for enlisted personnel serving in a military skill that is not included in any branch

Cavalry—a subcomponent of the Armor Branch that employs less heavily armored vehicles, mainly in screening and reconnaissance roles

Chapel Activities Specialist—a designation for those enlisted personnel who assist Chaplains in the performance of their duties

Chaplain Corps—provides religious services, education, and counseling for the American soldier, the dependent family, and authorized civilians in a military environment

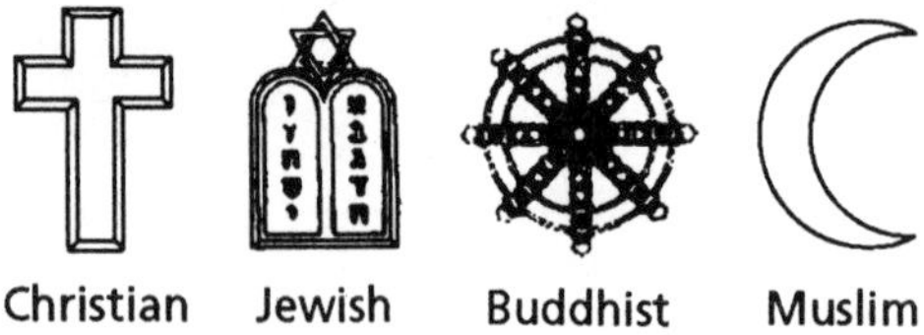

Chemical Corps—concerned with the chemical, radiological, and biological protection of the Army, Navy, Air Force, and Marine Corps. The Chemical Corps also works closely with civil defense authorities and other elements of the U.S. government.

Civil Affairs—a designation for those personnel assigned to provide a liaison between military and civilian authorities in areas of military operations

Corps of Engineers—responsible for the construction, maintenance, and repair of facilities and fortifications, and the breaching of enemy fortifications. The Corps of Engineers is also responsible for navigational and harbor improvements.

Dental Corps—the component of the Army Medical Department that provides dental services

Field Artillery—responsible for employing both cannon and missile fire on the battlefield

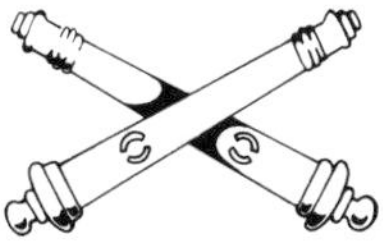

Finance Corps—responsible for accounting, disbursing, administration, and auditing of Army funds

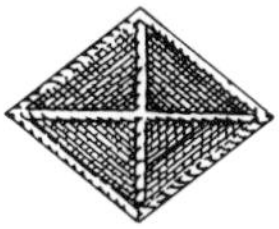

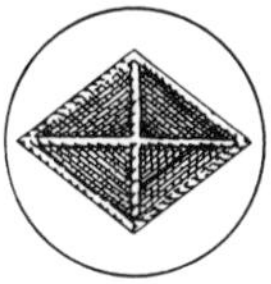

General Staff—a designation for those officers serving on a General's staff

Infantry—employs foot soldiers in both mechanized and dismounted roles

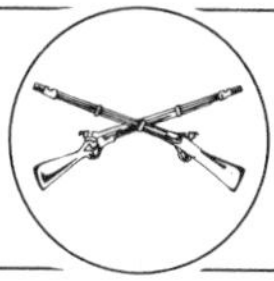

Inspector General—a designation for those personnel assigned responsibility for inquiring into the performance of mission and state of readiness, economy, efficiency, discipline, and morale of a command. The Inspector General Office also administers the IG complaints system.

Judge Advocate General Corps—responsible for the administration of the Uniform Code of Military Justice and the provision of legal advice and assistance within the Army

Medical Corps—the component of the Army Medical Department that sets physical standards and provides physician services for arms personnel and their dependents

Medical Service Corps—the component of the Army Medical Department that provides scientists and specialists in areas allied with medicine, and technicians in the areas of administration, supply, environmental sciences, and engineering related to the provision of medical services

Military Intelligence—responsible for the collection, analysis, production, and dissemination of information on the enemy, and the security of our information

Military Police Corps—charged with police duties and security responsibilities

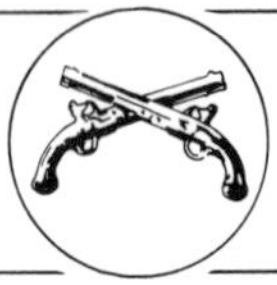

National Guard Bureau—a designation for officers serving on the National Guard Bureau Staff

Ordnance Corps—responsible for logistical management of Army ammunition, weapons, vehicles, and missiles

Psychological Operations—plans and conducts operations to influence foreign opinion and behavior in a theater of operations to support U.S. goals. They are part of special operations community.

Public Affairs—conducts public information and community relations activities in support of the commander's goals.

Quartermaster Corps—concerned with procurement, cataloging, inventory, storage distribution, salvage, and disposal of supplies

Signal Corps—responsible for the overall mission of planning, installing, operating, and maintaining the Army's communications systems

Special Operations/ Special Forces—plans and conducts special operations of all types in support of conventional operations or as independent operations.

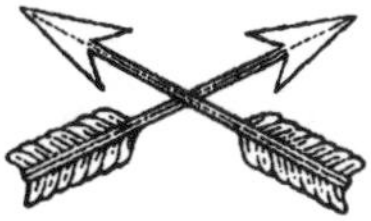

Staff Specialist Corps—a Reserve component designation for personnel serving on a unit staff. These personnel would most likely change their designation to an active component designation upon mobilization.

The Sergeant Major of the United States Army—this individual serves as the senior enlisted adviser and consultant to the Chief of Staff of the Army on matters affecting enlisted personnel

Transportation Corps—responsible for the movement of Army personnel and supplies

Veterinary Corps—the component of the Army Medical Department that provides food hygiene, preventive medicine, and animal medicine

Warrant Officer—a highly skilled technician filling a position above the enlisted level but with too specialized a scope for the position of a more broadly trained, branch-qualified commissioned officer

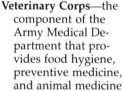

G. Army Songs

The Army Song

"The Army Goes Rolling Along" is the official Army song. When you hear it being played or sung, the appropriate action is to stand at attention. The song was dedicated on Veterans Day, 11 November 1956. (The music was composed in 1908 and was originally known as the "Caisson Song.")

The Army Goes Rolling Along

VERSE:
March along, sing our song
With the Army of the free.
Count the brave, count the true
Who have fought to victory.
We're the Army and proud of our name!
We're the Army and proudly proclaim:

FIRST CHORUS
First to fight for the right
And to build the nation's might,
And the Army goes rolling along.
Proud of all we have done,
Fighting til the battle's won,
And the Army goes rolling along.

REFRAIN:
Then it's hi! hi! hey!
The Army's on it's way,
Count off the cadence loud and strong:
For where'er we go, you will always know
That the Army goes rolling along.

SECOND CHORUS:
Valley Forge, Custer's ranks,
San Juan Hill and Patton's tanks,
And the Army went rolling along.
Minutemen from the start,
Always fighting from the heart,
And the Army keeps rolling along.

REFRAIN: Then it's hi! hi! hey!
The Army's on its way,
Count off the cadence loud and strong:
For where'er we go, you will always know
That the Army goes rolling along.

THIRD CHORUS: Men in rags, men who froze,
Still that Army met its foes,
And the Army went rolling along.
Faith in God, then we're right
And we'll fight with all our might
As the Army keeps rolling along.

REFRAIN: Then it's hi! hi! hey!
The Army's on its way.
Count off the cadence loud and strong:
(two! three!)
For where'er we go, you will always know
That the Army goes rolling along!
(Keep it rolling!)
And the Army goes rolling along!

Running Cadence

Cadence calling is an old Army tradition. Called or sung by the soldier in charge of a moving formation, the calls enhance unit morale and esprit. One verse of one of the more popular cadences is shown below.

Honey Baby

You get a line and I'll get a pole,
Honey, Honey.
You get a line and I'll get a pole,
Baby, Baby.
You get a line and I'll get a pole,
and we'll go down to the fishing hole.
Honey, oh Baby, be mine.
Go with your left, your right, your left.
Go with your left, your right, your left.

Taps

The haunting bugle call of "Taps" has been used by the Army at least since the Civil War. Tradition says Union General Daniel Butterfield composed the tune to replace the firing of muskets at military ceremonies. He supposedly did this to disguise from the Confederates the fact a burial was taking place. The tune became popular throughout the Union Army and replaced "Tattoo" as the last call of the day. Taps was officially adopted in 1891. Played at military funerals, it is the last tribute paid to the soldier.

Taps

Fades the light,
And afar,
Goeth light,
Cometh night,
And a star,
Leadeth all,
Speedeth all,
To their rest.

Fiddler's Green

Each of the Army's branches has its own traditions and music, much of it poking fun at nonmembers. One of the oldest and most colorful tunes is one associated with the horse cavalry. As with many early Army songs it has an Irish feel about it, perhaps reflecting the origins of many American soldiers of the 1800s. Its exact origin, however, has been lost in the dust of the Western plains. While most soldiers today will not recognize its source, the name "Fiddler's Green" is sometimes used for the lounges of NCO and officer clubs. It is a fading Army tradition.

Fiddler's Green

Half way down the trail to Hell,
    In a shady, meadow green,
Are the souls of all dead troopers camped,
    Near a good, old-time canteen.
And in this eternal resting place,
    Marching past, straight through to Hell,
The Infantry are seen,
    Accompanied by the Engineers
Artillery, and Marines,
    For none but shades of Cavalrymen
Dismount at Fiddler's Green.

Though some go curving down the trail
    To seek a warmer scene,
No trooper ever gets to Hell,
    Ere he's emptied his canteen.
And so he rides back to drink again,
    With friends at Fiddler's Green.

And so when horse and man go down
    Beneath a saber keen,

Or in a roaring charge, or fierce malée
You stop a bullet clean,
And the hostiles come to get your scalp,
Just empty your canteen,
And put your pistol to your head,
And go to Fiddler's Green.

Blood on the Risers

The Army's paratroopers have always been known for their spirit and often rather boastful attitude toward the dangers of their chosen method of arriving on the battlefield. Their wry sense of humor can be seen in the traditional songs that they sing. One of the most popular (and gruesome) is this one, usually sung loudly by airborne soldiers when in the company of non-paratroopers. It tells the tragic story of what happened to one luckless soldier on his first jump.

Blood on the Risers
(Tune of "Battle Hymn of the Republic")

"Is everybody happy?" cried the sergeant looking up,
Our hero feebly answered "Yes," and then they stood him up.
He leaped right out into the blast, his static line unhooked,
HE AIN'T GONNA JUMP NO MORE!

(Chorus)
GORY, GORY, WHAT A HELLUVA WAY TO DIE,
GORY, GORY, WHAT A HELLUVA WAY TO DIE,
GORY, GORY, WHAT A HELLUVA WAY TO DIE,
HE AIN'T GONNA JUMP NO MORE!

He counted long, he counted loud, he waited for the shock.
He felt the wind, he felt the clouds, he felt the awful drop.
He jerked his cord, the silk spilled out and wrapped around his legs,
HE AIN'T GONNA JUMP NO MORE!

(Chorus)

The risers wrapped around his neck, connectors cracked his dome.
The lines were snarled and tied in knots, around his skinny bones.
The canopy became his shroud, he hurtled to the ground,
HE AIN'T GONNA JUMP NO MORE!

(Chorus)

The day he's lived and loved and laughed kept running through his mind.

He thought about the girl back home, the one he'd left
behind.
He thought about the medics and wondered what they'd find,
HE AIN'T GONNA JUMP NO MORE!

(Chorus)

The ambulance was on the spot, the jeeps were running wild.
The medics jumped and screamed with glee,
They rolled their sleeves and smiled.
Our hero watched them gather 'round his fatal landing spot,
HE AIN'T GONNA JUMP NO MORE!

(Chorus)

He hit the ground, the sound was "Splatt!" his blood went
spurting high.
His comrades then were heard to say, "A helluva of a way to
die."
He lay there rolling 'round in the welter and the gore.
HE AIN'T GONNA JUMP NO MORE!

(Chorus)

There was blood upon the risers, there were brains upon the
'chute.
Intestines were a'dangling from his paratrooper's boots.
They picked him up still in his 'chute and poured him from
his boots.
HE AIN'T GONNA JUMP NO MORE!

(Chorus)

Dogface Soldier

The origin of the term "dogface" to refer to an infantryman has been long forgotten, but at least dates back to World War II, if not before. In Vietnam the title was replaced by the terms "grunt," and "11-Bush" referring to the infantryman's MOS of "11B." Infantrymen have always taken great pride in their difficult job, and have a keen sense of humor about it. Their nicknames were sometimes said in a derisive manner by others, but the infantrymen adopted them as their own and they wore them as a badge of honor. The song "Dogface Soldier" shows this pride and the disdain the infantryman holds for those unfortunate enough not to be a member of his exclusive brotherhood of riflemen. The song was written by two 3d Division soldiers in 1942 and adopted by the division as its unit song. It is played at all division gatherings.

Dogface Soldier
(3d Infantry Division Song by Gold and Hart)

I wouldn't give a bean to be a fancy pants Marine;
I'd rather be a dogface soldier like I am.
I wouldn't trade my old OD's for all the Navy's dungarees,
For I'm the walking pride of Uncle Sam.
On all the posters that I read
It says the Army builds men,
So they're tearing me down
To build me over again!
I'm just a dogface soldier
With a rifle on my shoulder,
And I eat raw meat for breakfast every day.
So feed me ammunition,
Keep me in the 3d Division.
Your dogface soldier boy's okay.

H. Overseas Tour Locations

TABLE H. Overseas Tour Locations

Country or Area	*Tours in Months* Accompanied	*Tours in Months* Unaccompanied
ALASKA (except as indicated)	36	36
Adak	24	18
Marine Barracks	24	12
Fort Greely	24	12
Clear, Galena, King Salmon, and Shemya	NA	12
AMERICAN SAMOA	NA	12
ARGENTINA	36	24
ASCENSION ISLAND	24	12
AUSTRALIA (except as indicated)	36	24
Alice Springs and Woomera	24	15
Exmouth	24	24
AUSTRIA	36	24
BAHAMAS, THE (as indicated)		
Andros Island	24	24
BAHRAIN	24	12
BELGIUM (except as indicated)	36	24
BELIZE	24	12
BENIN	24	12
BERMUDA	36	24
BOLIVIA	24	18
BOTSWANA	24	12
BRAZIL	36	24
BRITISH INDIAN OCEAN TERRITORY (as indicated)		
Diego Garcia	NA	12
CAMBODIA	NA	12
CANADA (except as indicated)	36	24
Argentia, Newfoundland	24	18
Goose Bay, Labrador	24	12
CHAD	24	12
CHILE	36	24
COLOMBIA	24	18
COSTA RICA	36	24

TABLE H. Overseas Tour Locations *(continued)*

Country or Area	*Tours in Months* Accompanied	*Unaccompanied*
CUBA (as indicated)		
Guantanamo Bay	30	18
Marine Barracks	24	12
CYPRUS (except as indicated)	24	18
Akrotiri	24	12
DENMARK (except as indicated)	36	24
Greenland (Kalaallit Nunaat)	NA	12
DOMINICAN REPUBLIC	36	24
EGYPT (except as indicated)	24	18
Sinai	NA	12
EL SALVADOR	NA	12
FRANCE	36	24
GERMANY (except as indicated)	36	24
Donaueschingen	24	12
GIBRALTER	36	24
GREECE (except as indicated)	36	24
Parnis and Patras	30	18
Crete (except as indicated)	24	18
Souda Bay	NA	12
Thessaloniki	24	15
Araxos, Argyroupolis, Drama, Elefsis, Horiatis, Levkas, Perivolaki, and Yeannitsa	NA	12
GUAM (as indicated)		
Navy personnel	24	24
Army and Air Force personnel	24	15
GUATEMALA	36	24
HAWAII (except as indicated)	36	36
Kauai	30	18
Pohakuloa Training Area	24	18
HONDURAS	24	18
HONG KONG, B.C.C.	36	24
INDIA	24	12
ICELAND (except as indicated)	30	18
Marine Barracks, Air Force and Army	24	12
Hofn	NA	12
INDONESIA	24	12
ISRAEL	24	12
ITALY (except as indicated)	36	24
Ghedi, Martina Franca, Mt. Corna, Mt. Venda, and Rimini	24	18
Mt. Vergine and Crotone	24	15
Mt. Finale Ligure, Mt. Limbara, Mt. Nardelo, Mt. Paganella, and Piano di Cors	NA	12

TABLE H. Overseas Tour Locations *(continued)*

Country or Area	Tours in Months: Accompanied	Tours in Months: Unaccompanied
Sardinia (as indicated)		
La Maddalena	24	24
Decimomannu Air Base	24	15
Sicily (as indicated)		
Sigonella	36	24
Comiso	24	12
JAMAICA	24	12
JAPAN (except as indicated)	36	24
Akizuki Kure	24	12
Ie Shima, Okuma, and Seburiyama	NA	12
Ryukyu Islands (except as indicated)	36	24
MCAS Futema and MCB Butler	36	12
Kuma Shima	NA	12
JOHNSTON ATOLL	NA	12
JORDAN (except as indicated)	24	12
Amman	24	18
KENYA (as indicated)		
Nairobi	36	24
Mombassa	24	12
KOREA (except as indicated)*	NA	12
Camp Carroll, Camp Humphreys, Camp Market, Camp Red Cloud, Camp Walker, Chinhae, Hialeah, K-2 AB, Kimhae, Osan AB, Pusan, Pyongtaek, Seoul, Suwon, Taegu, and Yongsan	24	12
KUWAIT	24	12
LAOS	NA	12
LIBERIA	24	18
MALAYSIA	36	24
MEXICO	24	18
MIDWAY ISLANDS	NA	12
MOROCCO (except as indicated)	24	15
Casablanca	24	12
Errachidia	NA	12
NETHERLANDS (except as indicated)	36	24
Aruba in the Netherlands Antilles	24	18
NEW ZEALAND	36	24
NICARAGUA	24	18
NIGER	24	12
NORWAY	36	24
OMAN	24	12
PAKISTAN	24	18
PANAMA (except as indicated)	36	24
Galeta Island	24	18
PARAGUAY	24	18

TABLE H. **Overseas Tour Locations** *(continued)*

Country or Area	*Tours in Months* Accompanied	*Tours in Months* Unaccompanied
PERU	30	18
PORTUGAL (except as indicated)	36	24
Azores Islands	24	15
PUERTO RICO (except as indicated)	36	24
Caguas, Juana Diaz, Ponce (Ft. Allen), Yauco, and Isabela	36	18
Vieques Island	NA	12
QATAR	24	12
SAIPAN	24	12
SAUDI ARABIA	24	12
SEYCHELLES (Mahe Island)	24	12
SINGAPORE	36	24
SOMALIA	24	12
SPAIN (except as indicated)	36	24
Acoy, Constantina, Elizondo, Rosas, and Villatobos	30	18
El Ferrol	24	24
Sonseca	24	18
Moran AB	24	15
Villatobas	30	18
Santiago	NA	18
Balearic Islands and Gorremandi	NA	15
Adamuz, Ciudal Real, Estaca DeVares	NA	12
SUDAN	24	12
THAILAND (except as indicated)	36	24
Chiang Mai	24	18
TUNISIA	24	18
TURKEY (except as indicated)	24	15
Elmadag, Karatas, and Malatya	24	12
Balikesir, Cakmakli, Corlu, Erhac, Eskisher, Ezururum, Istanbul, Izmit, Murted, Oratakoy, Iskendrum, Pirinclik, Sahihtepe, Sinop, and Yumurtalik	NA	12
UNITED ARAB EMIRATES	24	12
UNITED KINGDOM (except as indicated)	36	24
RAF Machrihanish (Scotland) and RAF Flyingdales	24	18
UPPER VOLTA	24	12
URAGUAY	36	24
U.S. TRUST TERRITORY OF THE PACIFIC ISLANDS (MICRONESIA) (as indicated)		
Northern Marianas (Saipan)	24	12
Marshall Islands		
Enewetak Atoll	NA	12
Kwajalein Atoll	24	18
VENEZUELA	24	18

TABLE H. **Overseas Tour Locations** *(continued)*

Country or Area	*Tours in Months*	
	Accompanied	*Unaccompanied*
VIRGIN ISLANDS	36	24
WAKE ISLAND	NA	12
WEST INDIES (as indicated)		
Antigua and Barbados	36	24
Anguilla	24	18
St. Lucia	NA	12
YUGOSLAVIA	24	18
ZAIRE	24	12

*Not all members are eligible to serve an accompanied tour. Eligibility is controlled by U.S. Forces Korea. Those not eligible to serve an accompanied tour shall be considered to be serving a dependent-restricted tour.

I. Glossary of Army Abbreviations

Here are some of the common Army acronyms and abbreviations. These terms, plus those discussed in the guidebook, should provide you with a basic professional Army vocabulary. You will pick up many more Army terms during your enlistment.

AAFES. Army and Air Force Exchange Service
ABN. Airborne
ACFT. Aircraft
AER. Academic Evaluation Report
AH. Attack helicopter
ALB. AirLand Battle
AP. Armor piercing
APFT. Army Physical Fitness Test
ARTEP. Army Training and Evaluation Program
ASI. Additional skill identifier
AWOL. Absent without leave
BAQ. Basic allowance for quarters
BCT. Basic Combat Training
BDE. Brigade
BDU. Battle dress uniform
BEQ. Bachelor enlisted quarters
BN. Battalion
BTRY. Battery
CA. Civil affairs
CAS. Close air support
CAT. Combined arms team
CEOI. Communication-electronics operations instructions
CEWI. Combat Electronic Warfare Intelligence
C^2. Command and control
C^3I. Command, control, communications, and intelligence
CO. Commanding officer
COIN. Counterinsurgency

CONUS. Continental United States
CPX. Command post exercise
CQ. Charge of quarters
DA. Department of Army
DEERS. Defense Enrollment Eligibility Reporting System
DEROS. Date of estimated return from overseas
DOR. Date of rank
DS. Direct support
EAD. Entry on active duty
E&E. Evasion and escape
ESL. English as a second language
EW. Electronic warfare
FEBA. Forward edge of the battle area
FLOT. Forward line of own troops
FSE. Fire-support element
FTX. Field training exercise
GED. General educational development
GS. General support
HOR. Home of record
IG. Inspector General
IPB. Intelligence preparation of the battlefield
ITT. Intertheater transfer
JTF. Joint Task Force
JTR. Joint Travel Regulations
KIA. Killed in action
KP. Kitchen police
LD. Line of departure
LIC. Low-intensity conflict
LOC. Lines of communication
LOD. Line of duty
LP. Listening post
LRRP. Long-range reconnaissance patrol
MACOM. Major Army command
MBA. Main battle area
MBT. Main battle tank
METT-T. Mission, enemy, terrain, troops, and time available
MILPERCEN. Military personnel center
NATO. North Atlantic Treaty Organization
NBC. Nuclear, biological, and chemical
NCA. National Command Authority
NOK. Next of kin
OJT. On-the-job training
OPLAN. Operation plan
OPORD. Operation order
PCS. Permanent change of station
PMOS. Primary Military Occupational Specialty
POL. Petroleum, oil, and lubricants

POV. Privately owned vehicle
PSYOP. Psychological operations
QMP. Qualitative Management Program
R&R. Rest and recreation
SBP. Survivor Benefit Program
SD. Special duty
SDNCO. Staff Duty Noncommissioned Officer
SGLI. Servicemen's Group Life Insurance
SOF. Special Operations Forces
SQT. Skills Qualification Test
TC. Training circular
TDY. Temporary duty
TOE. Table of Organization and Equipment
USO. United Services Organization
UW. Unconventional warfare
VA. Veterans Administration
VEAP. Veteran's Educational Assistance Program
VGLI. Veteran's Group Life Insurance
WIA. Wounded in action
WO. Warrant officer
XO. Executive officer

The following Army commands also produce material that will affect your Army life. The commands are listed as acronyms since this is the way they are normally identified. Their full title appears in the right-hand column.

Acronym	*Full Title*
AMC	U.S. Army Materiel Command
FORSCOM	U.S. Forces Command
TRADOC	U.S. Training and Doctrine Command
USREC	U.S. Army Recruiting Command

J. Sources and Credits

The material presented in this guide was drawn from many sources. Some were official publications of the Department of Defense, and some were unofficial professional and news sources that covered the continually evolving state of affairs in the Army. The authors are especially grateful to the many people who provided material and pictures, and who maintained their patience while attempting to answer the multitude of questions that came up regarding Army life and policies. It is amazing how much one doesn't know about the Army even after more than thirty years of daily association.

Among those especially helpful were the Army's Office of Public Affairs, the U.S. Army Center of Military History, the Pentagon Library, the Association of the United States Army and its Institute of Land Warfare, and the U.S. Army Sergeant Major Academy. Special thanks also to all the helpful members of Headquarters, Department of the Army, the U.S. Army Recruiting Command (Support), and the U.S. Army Military Personnel Command who provided and validated information.

Several illustrations were made available through the cooperation of Stackpole Books. Pictures are courtesy of the U.S. Army unless indicated otherwise in the caption.

Listed below are the principal printed sources of information used in the preparation of this guide. They shall all be available through the Army library system.

Army Regulations (AR)

AR 10-5, *Department of the Army*
AR 27-10, *Legal Services, Military Justice*
AR 140-1, *Training*
AR 140-10, *Assignments*
AR 320-5, *Dictionary of U.S. Army Terms*
AR 350-30, *Code of Conduct/Survival, Evasion, Resistance, and Escape (SERE) Training*

AR 380-5, *Department of the Army Information Program*
AR 381-12, *Subversion and Espionage Directed Against the U.S. Army*
AR 600-15, *Salutes, Honors, and Visits of Courtesy*
AR 600-3, *The Army Personnel Proponent System*
AR 600-83, *The New Manning System*
AR 600-85, *Alcohol and Drug Abuse Prevention and Control Program*
AR 600-200, *Enlisted Personnel Management System*
AR 614-30, *Overseas Service*
AR 611-201, *Enlisted Career Management Fields and Military Occupational Specialties*
AR 614-200, *Selection of Enlisted Soldiers for Training and Assignment*
AR 623-205, *Enlisted Evaluation Report*
AR 635-205, *Enlisted Evaluation Reporting System*
AR 670-1, *Wear and Appearance of Army Uniforms and Insignia*
AR 672-5-1, *Awards and Decorations*
AR 840-10, *Flags, Description and Use*

Field Manuals (FM)

FM 5-34, *Engineer Field Data*
FM 7-8, *Infantry Rifle Platoon and Squad*
FM 7-10, *Infantry Rifle Company*
FM 7-20, *Infantry Rifle Battalion*
FM 21-10, *Field Hygiene and Sanitation*
FM 21-20, *Physical Fitness Training*
FM 21-75, *Combat Skills of the Soldier*
FM 22-5, *Drill and Ceremony*
FM 22-6, *Guard Duty*
FM 22-100, *Military Leadership*
FM 22-101, *Leadership Counseling*
FM 25-1, *Training*
FM 25-100, *Training the Force*
FM 25-101, *Battle Focused Training*
FM 27-14, *Legal Guide for Soldiers*
FM 100-1, *The Army*
FM 100-5, *Operations (1986, 1993)*
FM 100-10, *Combat Service Support*
FM 101-10-1, *Staff Officers' Field Manual: Organizational, Technical, and Logistical Data*

Miscellaneous Sources

TRADOC Regulation 350-6, *Initial Entry Training (IET) Policies and Administration*, 28 August 1989.
TRADOC Pamphlet 600-4, "IET Soldier's Handbook," 1 January 1991.
Defense Almanac, September/October 1992.
The United States Army Posture Statement, FY 93.
Army Focus, June 1991.
Army Reserve Posture Statement, FY 89.
Reserve Component Programs, *Report of the Reserve Forces Policy Board*, Fiscal Year 1992, January 1993.
Armed Forces Decorations and Awards, Department of Defense, 1992.
Headquarters, Department of the Army, *Soldier's Manual of Common Tasks* (Skill Level 1), October 1990.
The Department of the Army Manual, October 1989.
Manual for Courts-Martial, United States 1984, Appendix 2, Uniform Code of Military Justice.
The NCO Journal
DA Pamphlet 355-27, "Army Heritage"
Army magazine, AUSA (all issues 1992–1994)
The Army Green Book, AUSA, 1991–92, 1992–93, 1993–94
The Army Times, Times Publishing Company (all issues September 1993–March 1994)
Infantry Magazine, Infantry School and Center, (all issues 1992–1994)
Army Career and Alumni Program Transition Guidebook, Dept. of the Army
American Military History, U.S. Army Center of Military History, 1969.
Weapons Systems, United States Army 1992, Dept. of the Army, OASA (RDA)

Index

About the Authors

COLONEL RAYMOND K. BLUHM, JR., USA (Ret.) is a combat veteran, author, historian, and defense-affairs consultant. He served thirty years as an infantry and foreign area officer with tours in Vietnam, South Korea, and Europe. He has broad experience as a trainer of new soldiers and with the introduction of modern concepts of training management into the Army.

COLONEL JAMES B. MOTLEY, USA (Ret.) is a writer, lecturer, and security/intelligence consultant. During his military career, he served as an infantry and Ranger officer and was also assigned to the Office of the Secretary of Defense, to the Department of the Army staff, and to the Joint Chiefs of Staff.